MY ANCESTOR WAS IN THE BRITISH ARMY

HOW CAN I FIND OUT MORE ABOUT HIM?

by Michael J. Watts & Christopher T. Watts

SOCIETY OF GENEALOGISTS ENTERPRISES LTD

Published by
Society of Genealogists Enterprises Limited
14 Charterhouse Buildings, Goswell Road, London EC1M 7BA

© The Society of Genealogists Enterprises and the authors 2009.
1st edition 1992, reprinted with addendum 1995

ISBN 10: 1-903462-99-1
ISBN 13: 978-1-903462-99-7

British Library Cataloguing in Publication Data
A CIP Catalogue record for this book is available from the British Library.

The Society of Genealogists Enterprises Limited is a wholly owned subsidiary of the Society of Genealogists, a registered charity, no 233701.

About the Authors

Michael and Christopher Watts are both amateur family historians, each with almost forty years of experience in that field. They are now retired from their former full-time jobs. Michael worked as a nuclear engineer and later as lecturer in mechanical engineering at the University of Manchester. Chris originally trained as a research chemist, but then worked as an analyst in the defence electronics industry. Since 1997 he has been a part-time Reader-Adviser at the National Archives.

Both have lectured on family history subjects, and given evening classes. Chris has enjoyed travel to give key-note lectures at conferences on many aspects of British genealogy in Canada, USA, Australia and New Zealand. Michael has recently completed two years as a part-time lecturer at the University of Huddersfield, giving courses in family history to beginners and advanced students.

They have also published numerous articles, including several in the *Genealogists' Magazine*, about Merchant Seamen, Army Ancestry, Company Records and Legal Proceedings, as well as the following books.

My Ancestor was a Merchant Seaman - How can I find out more about him? was first published by the Society of Genealogists in 1986, with its second edition plus addendum issued in 2004. It has become the standard work on this topic.

Records of Merchant Shipping and Seamen by Kelvin Smith, Christopher Watts and Michael Watts, Public Record Office Readers' Guide No 20, was published in 1998 and reprinted in 2001.

Tracing Births, Deaths and Marriages at Sea was published by the Society of Genealogists in 2004.

Cover Image - Private Thomas B Watts, Northumberland Fusiliers - with the Imperial Service Badge awarded to Territorials who volunteered for service overseas. Family photograph shows Thomas Banks Watts and the family at home: his parents, Thomas and Isabella Watts, and his sisters Emma and Ethel.

Thumbnail Images - from *The Pictures and Diary of a Wartime Artist* (Len Smith) on www.greatwarartist.com. © Dave Mason/Forgottentitles.com 2008.

Graphic design and layout by Graham Collett

PREFACE

This book is written for the modern family historian who wishes to research the activities of their ancestors or kinsmen who served in the British Army since 1660. It is a practical guide intended to help them find their way into and through the many records now available in archives and on the internet. There is a wealth of such records for the millions of British soldiers who have served their country - many will find surprising and plentiful details of their ancestors while others may struggle to find a one-line mention. In either case, the individual will follow a fascinating thread through British history.

FOREWORD

Of course the authors' own personal research into the army service of father and great-great-grandfather was the starting point for this book. As with many families, it will be found that both near and distant relatives were drawn to the British Army. For those genealogists and family historians who enjoy the scent of a trail, some details are given of our relationship to some of the characters you will meet here. We dedicate this book to their memory.

Father:
Thomas Banks Watts   5 April 1896 South Shields
Private in the Northumberland   16 October 1966 Highcliffe Hants
Fusiliers

Great-great-grandfather:
John Watts   1773 Happisburgh Norfolk
Private   3 November 1846: Happisburgh
6th Regiment of Foot, Royal
Warwickshire Regiment

Mother's cousin:
John Henry Heyman   29 June 1894 Edmonton
                Registration District.
Lieutenant in the Army Service   18 July 1917 Ypres Flanders
Corps

Father's cousin:
Percival John Watts 1895 Charlton Kent
Private in the Royal West Kent 5 November 1915 Flanders
Regiment

Mother's sister
Phyllis Cater Heymann 29 May 1908 Menston Yorkshire
Major 11 November 1990 Kyrenia Cyprus
Queen Alexandra's Royal Army
Nursing Corps

Uncle's brother:
Michael Guthrie 13 April 1893 North Ormesby, Yorks.
Lieutenant 20 June 1977 Dorset
19th (Pioneer) Battalion,
Northumberland Fusiliers

A many-times-great 'uncle':
Emanuel Burton 13 April 1787 Kendal Westmorland
Ensign in 44th Foot (East Essex) 3 April 1865 Brooklyn New York
and 50th Foot (West Kent)

ACKNOWLEDGEMENTS

T he authors wish to express their gratitude to the custodians of all the records described in this book, in particular at The National Archives, formerly the Public Record Office, then at Chancery Lane, but now at Kew.

Besides those mentioned in the previous section, many other soldiers have been followed up. We would like to acknowledge here the help of many individuals - either for providing details from their own research, which we have been glad to incorporate here - or for drawing our attention to categories of records of which we were previously unaware. We trust that those not listed here will excuse our lapse of memory:

The late Jim (James D) Beckett for his enthusiasm and hard work on soldiers' indexes,

Barbara Chambers who continues to index the 1806 Service Returns,

Professor Peter Clark, for information on his project, British Prisoners of Napoleon,

Miss S L Davis for her index to Soldiers' Documents,

Professor Jim (James Playford) Duncan for details of his ancestor, Corporal of Horse Thomas Playford, 2nd Life Guards,

John Ellam for details from the Huddersfield Roll of Honour for World War I,

Major Doug (TJD) Farringdon, for discussion and advice on the holdings of the Queen's Lancashire Museum, Fulwood Barracks, Preston,

Mrs Lesley Frater, Museum Administrator, Northumberland Fusiliers, Alnwick Castle, for discussion and advice on the archives of the Northumberland Fusiliers,

Robin AW Guthrie for information about his uncle, Lieutenant Michael Guthrie,

Pamela Harrison for service records of her father, WO/II Roy Smith, RA,

Austin Hayes and colleagues at the Overseas Section of the General Register Office, for answering endless enquiries about army records in a most helpful manner,

Brian Meringo for information on archives in France,

Nicholas Newington-Irving for details of army holdings in the SoG library,

Marjorie Pollard for information on PoWs in Napoleonic times,

Sheila Powell for an ancestral marriage certificate,

Miss G Rickard for information about the Kent Settlement and Removal indexes,

Graham W Roe for use of his army service papers,

Barbara Rowling and family, for papers and photographs from World War I, kept by her father, Lt G W H (Harry) Potter, RGA

Derek Saunders for his Waterloo Index,

William Spencer for many discussions and much advice at the National Archives,

Michael Stratford for information on his soldier ancestor, John Drought,

Kathleen Threlfall for use of her father's army service papers,

Frank Turner for his 1861 Army Index.

Commonwealth War Graves Commission, for permission to reproduce Casualty Details and the entry from the Roll of Honour for L/Cpl AT Giffin, Dar-es-Salaam Cemetery,

National Army Museum, Dr Peter Boyden, Dr Alistair Massie, for information on their registers of deceased soldiers' effects and permission to use an example and illustration from them,

National Archives of Australia, for permission to use an illustration from the service record of Gunner Joseph Harvey,

The Army Personnel Centre - Beverley Hutchinson, Acting Disclosures Manager, Historical Disclosures Section, Glasgow - for permission to use illustrations from the service records of W/Sgt Graham Roe and Major Phyllis Heymann,

Transcripts and facsimiles of Crown copyright records in The National Archives of the UK appear by permission of the Controller of HM Stationery Office. Permission to reuse illustrations generated while in the employ of TNA, and hence Crown copyright, is acknowledged.

CONTENTS

FIGURES

OTHER RANKS PRIOR TO 1914

WORLD WAR I

WORLD WAR II

CHAPTER ONE
Introduction

A standing army in England and Wales may be said to date from the Restoration of the Monarchy in 1660 with the appointment of a secretary-at-war. There was no regular army in England prior to the outbreak of the Civil War in 1642; individual regiments were raised to meet a specific local or national need, and were usually named after the person who raised them. Until 1707, with the union of the crowns of England and Scotland, Scotland had its own army – see note at the end of this chapter. From 1660 to 1945 (the covering dates of this book), therefore, many of our ancestors were drawn into a centrally organised body, which may be said to be a British Army from 1707 and which has left us many records of its activities.

There have been few periods in history, from the middle ages to the 20th century, when England has not been in conflict either with its neighbours in Europe or overseas in defending trade routes or Empire. The continuing need for men to serve in the army must surely mean that there are few families which have not, at some time, had one of their members serving in it.

Reasons for joining the army were varied. For officers, there was clearly the attraction of an honourable and prestigious career in the service of one's country. Until World War One, they were traditionally drawn from the younger sons of the landed gentry. For other ranks, the rewards were possibly more alluring in anticipation, and the glory more satisfying in retrospect, than the actuality of a common soldier's existence. Our humble ancestor may first have 'gone for a soldier' as a result of the recruiting sergeant's patter, and promise of bounty, regular meals etc; few would resist taking the King's shilling after several free pints of beer, while many 'volunteers' were blatantly kidnapped. At times there was a lack of other employment, and in national emergencies there was conscription.

Once in the army, the common soldier faced the notorious rigours of that service – drill, harsh discipline, low wages after official stoppages, floggings, even execution. However, when required, as noted by Roy Palmer in his 'The Rambling Soldier',

He'd march, fight, left, right,/ Front rank, centre rank,/ Storm the trenches, court the wenches,/ Die with glory, live in story./ He always said a soldier's life, if taken smooth or rough,/ Is a very merry, hey down derry sort of life enough!

The conditions experienced by our soldier ancestor are evocatively echoed by his contemporaries in many writings, of which there is an excellent selection, with an extensive bibliography, in Palmer's 'The Rambling Soldier', and also in Neuburg's 'Gone for a Soldier'.

For the purposes of this book the very general term 'British Army' may be defined to include the following broad categories, consisting of units which existed in some form prior to 1914:

Cavalry: Household Cavalry (Life Guards and Royal Horse Guards), Dragoon Guards, Dragoons, Hussars and Lancers

Artillery: Royal Horse Artillery, Royal Regiment of Artillery

Foot Guards: Grenadier, Coldstream, Scots, Irish, Welsh

Infantry: 1st to 109th Foot, Rifle Brigade

Corps: Engineers, Signals, Chaplains, Service, Medical, Ordnance, Police, Pay, Veterinary, Sandhurst Band, Small Arms School, Provost Staff, Education, Gymnastic, Queen Alexandra's Royal Army Nursing Corps

Indian: East India Company's Forces, Indian Army

Militia: usually by county

Others: Volunteers – Rifle (Infantry), Yeomanry (Cavalry), Fencibles

Clearly there are many types of unit in which an army ancestor may have served and, if one has no initial clues to his service, the choice of places to search is extensive. The majority of soldiers must have been in the infantry or cavalry, although the artillery and Indian forces included large numbers over the years. It is beyond the scope of this book to detail all the units of the British army together with the changes in name and regimental amalgamations. The reader is referred to Brereton's 'Guide to the regiments and corps of the British army' for fuller information. A companion volume by Brereton provides a useful 'social history' of the British soldier. For England, a good guide to their regiments is provided by Ian Beckett's 'Discovering English County Regiments'.

Officer or Other Rank?

The family historian's approach to army records depends completely on whether one is searching for an officer or a soldier (other rank). Regimental historians and genealogists have naturally tended to concentrate on officers, whose personal records are much more readily accessible. However, there were at least eight times as many privates and corporals as sergeants and officers in the army of 1801 – Fortescue quoted the strength of the Regular Army as 23 000 Cavalry, 9 000 Foot Guards and 118 000 Infantry, and recommended adding 1/8th again for sergeants and officers. For the 1914-1918 War, there are 80 volumes of war dead for other ranks, and a further single volume for officers. These approximate proportions indicate that most family historians will be interested in the records of other ranks and hence this book will tend to concentrate on them.

Find the Regiment

A very important initial consideration is to be aware that most army records are arranged by regiment. If this is already known then one can gain ready access to the available material. If the regiment is not known in advance, then there are many possible ways which can lead to the name or number of the regiment, although one cannot guarantee success in every case. Prior to World War One, one should not expect a link between a regiment and a soldier's place of origin, although of course many Scots would have served in Scottish regiments. In this book we give careful attention to the problem of finding the regiment, as this is often the most difficult first task for many researchers.

Extensive records at The National Archives

Fortunately there are very extensive records available for both officers and soldiers, primarily in the War Office (WO) series at The National Archives (TNA). Many records for the period preceding 1914 have been deposited there. Moreover, in recent years, the surviving personnel records for the First World War have been microfilmed, and are now available for consultation at TNA. (They are now also available on-line.) It is sadly a fact that, although these World War I records occupy nearly thirty thousand reels of microfilm, there is only about a forty percent chance that one will find papers for a certain individual.

Personal note

On a personal note, our army research started when we learned of a great-great-grandfather, John Watts (1773-1846), who had fought in the Napoleonic Wars. Also we had known that our father, Thomas Banks Watts (1896-1966), had volunteered for the Northumberland Fusiliers during World War I. It is ironically the case that we can trace the career and movements of John Watts for twenty-three years, while we can find no mention in service records at TNA of Thomas Banks Watts.

Our early soldier ancestor did not actually record his personal reminiscences, but he did leave a clear trail in the many army records which were compiled during his service. Of course, they were not originally assembled for his (or our) benefit. Muster Books and Pay Lists were a check on his attendance and pay, while Description Books were kept in case he deserted. Luckily there are many types of surviving document which can give us a broad outline of a soldier's existence and these can be linked with military and regimental histories to provide as vivid an account of the life of the 'common man' as it is possible to find.

Arrangement of book

This book is divided into four main sections: Officers - prior to 1914, Other Ranks – prior to 1914, World War I (1914-1918), World War II (1939-1945). The reason for this is twofold. Firstly the arrangement of records pre- and post- 1914 is quite different, and thus different research techniques are needed. Secondly, the records of officers are substantially different from those of other ranks, the former being much more readily accessible, especially with limited initial information.

This guide is aimed at genealogists and family historians who seek a way into the maze of records available for an army ancestor. The authors have done just that in their own quest for information, though they do not claim to possess any specialist military or historical expertise.

Soldiers in Scotland before 1707

As Gerald Hamilton-Edwards has noted (In Search of Scottish Ancestry, Phillimore, 1972/1980), 'there was no regular and continuous army in Scotland before the Union – forces were mustered from time to time as situations required them.'

There is very little early printed material, but two volumes were published by the Scottish History Society in 1917. 'Papers relating to the Army of the Solemn League and Covenant, 1643-1647' gives names of officers and some other ranks. Again, Charles Dalton's The Scots Army 1661-1688, gives names of officers and soldiers, together with date and place of muster.

The main manuscript sources relating to individuals in the Scots army before 1707 are to be found in the series of muster rolls, now filed in the Exchequer records at the National Archives of Scotland, Edinburgh. The NAS reference is E 100, and they are arranged by regiment and companies or troops. The earliest date from 1641, most however from 1680. Unless one knows the particular regiment in which an ancestor served, there is a difficult search of up to 4 800 rolls. To date there is no overall name index of soldiers, although a knowledge of their place of origin may narrow the search to one of a few regiments, perhaps commanded by the owner of a local estate.

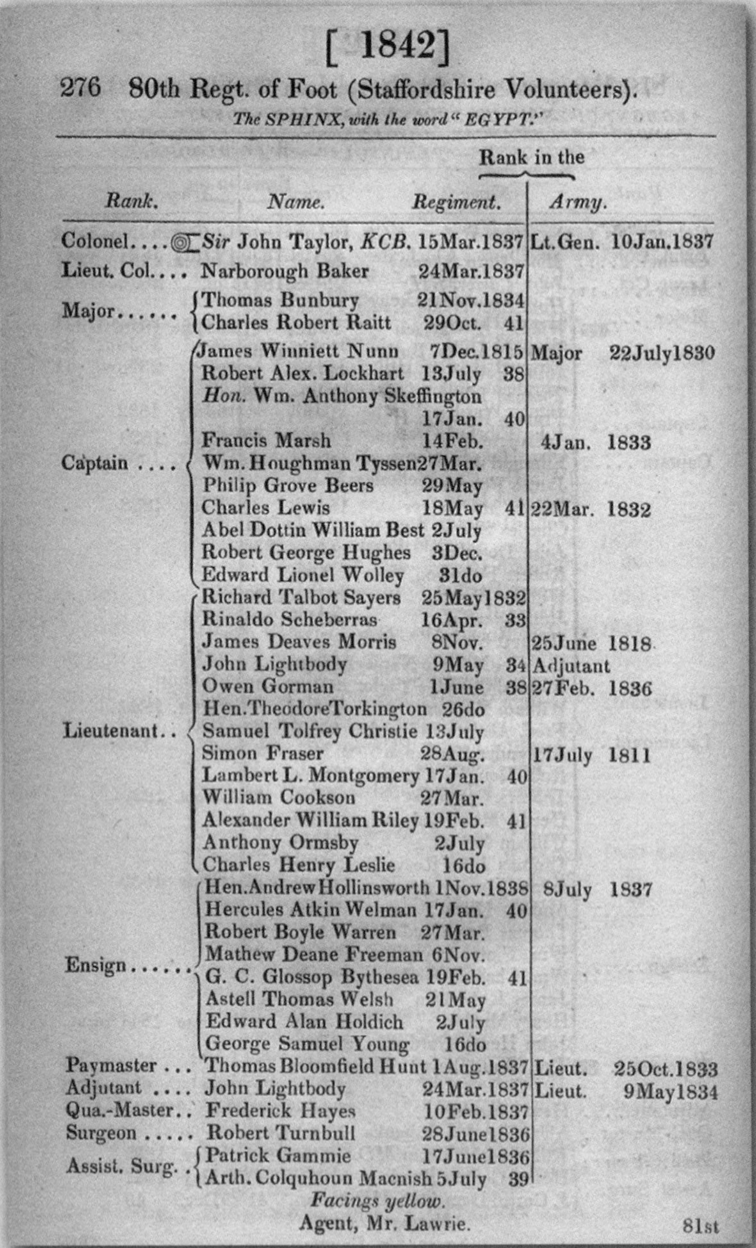

276 80th Regt. of Foot (Staffordshire Volunteers).

The SPHINX, with the word " EGYPT."

Rank.	Name.	Regiment.	Rank in the Army.
Colonel....	◎ *Sir* John Taylor, *KCB*.	15Mar.1837	Lt.Gen. 10Jan.1837
Lieut. Col....	Narborough Baker	24Mar.1837	
Major......	Thomas Bunbury	21Nov.1834	
	Charles Robert Raitt	29Oct. 41	
Captain	James Winniett Nunn	7Dec.1815	Major 22July1830
	Robert Alex. Lockhart	13July 38	
	Hon. Wm. Anthony Skeffington	17Jan. 40	
	Francis Marsh	14Feb.	4Jan. 1833
	Wm. Houghman Tyssen	27Mar.	
	Philip Grove Beers	29May	
	Charles Lewis	18May 41	22Mar. 1832
	Abel Dottin William Best	2July	
	Robert George Hughes	3Dec.	
	Edward Lionel Wolley	31do	
Lieutenant..	Richard Talbot Sayers	25May1832	
	Rinaldo Scheberras	16Apr. 33	
	James Deaves Morris	8Nov.	25June 1818
	John Lightbody	9May 34	Adjutant
	Owen Gorman	1June 38	27Feb. 1836
	Hen.Theodore Torkington	26do	
	Samuel Tolfrey Christie	13July	
	Simon Fraser	28Aug.	17July 1811
	Lambert L. Montgomery	17Jan. 40	
	William Cookson	27Mar.	
	Alexander William Riley	19Feb. 41	
	Anthony Ormsby	2July	
	Charles Henry Leslie	16do	
Ensign......	Hen.Andrew Hollinsworth	1Nov.1838	8July 1837
	Hercules Atkin Welman	17Jan. 40	
	Robert Boyle Warren	27Mar.	
	Mathew Deane Freeman	6Nov.	
	G. C. Glossop Bythesea	19Feb. 41	
	Astell Thomas Welsh	21May	
	Edward Alan Holdich	2July	
	George Samuel Young	16do	
Paymaster ...	Thomas Bloomfield Hunt	1Aug.1837	Lieut. 25Oct.1833
Adjutant	John Lightbody	24Mar.1837	Lieut. 9May1834
Qua.-Master..	Frederick Hayes	10Feb.1837	
Surgeon	Robert Turnbull	28June1836	
Assist. Surg. ..	Patrick Gammie	17June1836	
	Arth. Colquhoun Macnish	5July 39	

Facings yellow.

Agent, Mr. Lawrie.

81st

Figure 1 - Army List page - 80th Regiment of Foot. Staffordshire Volunteers - 1842

CHAPTER TWO
Officers - prior to 1914

Introduction

The tracing of officers in army records is a relatively straight-forward process since there is a variety of sources, both printed and manuscript, which can readily be accessed, even though one has little starting information. The key sources, which will be discussed here, are Army Lists, both printed and manuscript, Returns of Service, Commander-in-Chief's Memoranda Papers, Half Pay Ledgers and Lists and various records relating to Pensions. This sequence is probably one which most researchers would follow in practice.

Army Lists

Army Lists, which cover the period 1702 to the present day, are the starting point for tracing the service of officers, and it is relatively simple to find their regiment(s) from this source. Official Army Lists started in 1740, and regular annual lists commenced in 1754. Many lists are printed, but volumes dating from the early part of the 18th century may be difficult to locate. Even earlier, officers who gained commissions between 1661 and 1727 may be found in Charles Dalton's books.

Those starting their research in London may use the reference sets of Army Lists at TNA; others can locate them in large reference libraries for the period required – there is no need to check every year as information is merely repeated.

The table below summarises the available lists. TNA references are given for material on record there. As mentioned above, large libraries should have good holdings of all sets of lists, except for WO 64 and WO 211.

Army Lists 'on record' at TNA

WO 64	Manuscript Army Lists	1702-1823
WO 65	Printed Annual Army Lists	1754-1879
WO 66	Printed Quarterly Army Lists	1879-1900
WO 211	H G Hart Papers	1838-1875

Printed Army Lists, available in incomplete sets in reference libraries, also in the Reading Rooms at TNA

Annual Army Lists	1754-1879
Quarterly Army Lists	1879-1922
Monthly Army Lists	1798-1940
Half Yearly Army Lists	1923-1950
Quarterly Army Lists	1940-1950
The Army List	1951-date
Hart's New Army List	1839-1915

The extent of information provided in such a wide variety of Army Lists is itself varied; so also is the arrangement. For instance, the printed Annual Army Lists are arranged by regiment and an index is provided from 1766 onwards; the 'record' set at TNA has manuscript corrections. The Monthly Army Lists are also arranged by regiment, but include the location of a unit and the price of commissions; however, they are only indexed from 1867. The earlier series of Quarterly Army Lists included a gradation list of officers in order of seniority, dates of birth and promotions; from 1881, details of service were also given. This continued the pioneering work of Lt Gen H G Hart (1808-1878), whose New Army List contained services of officers, information not included in the official list. Fuller details of precise information available, and interesting career summaries of some officers, are given by Hamilton-Edwards.

It is worth noting the existence of published lists for **medical** officers from 1660 to 1960 (see Peterkin et al), for **artillery** officers from 1716 to 1914 (see Askwith), and for **engineer** officers from 1660 to 1891 (see Conolly and Edwards).

For most researchers, it is sufficient to consult a sample of Army Lists, say at five-yearly intervals, until the main outline of an officer's career is established. The results of such a search are given below for Emanuel Burton who, according to a title deed of 1818 for property in Kendal, Westmorland, was an ensign in the 'King's Fourty Fourth Regiment of Foot'. Army Lists in the period 1819 to 1867 gave the following information. ('Rank in Army' refers to the date officially appointed to that rank; 'Rank in Regiment' refers to the date of arrival in a regiment at that rank.)

1819	Ensign 44th Regt of Foot (East Essex)	Appointed Placed on Half Pay	17 Aug 1815 25 Mar 1816
1826	Ensign 50th Regt of Foot (West Kent)	Rank in Army Rank in Regt	17 Aug 1815 7 Apr 1825
1828	Ensign 50th Regt	Rank in Army Placed on Half Pay	17 Aug 1815 14 Sep 1826
1840	Details as for 1828		
1850	Details as for 1828		
1860	Details as for 1828, but marked as 'Unattached'		
1865	Details as for 1860		
1866	and 1867 – not in Army Lists		

Returns of Service

The War Office first compiled returns of officers' service in the early 19th century, based evidently on information supplied by the officers themselves. Prior to then, regimental record offices had kept some details of officers' service, now transferred to WO 76.

These returns of service, listed below, may be used following a check in the Army lists, or they may be referred to directly if one has easy access to TNA. Additionally, the Reading Rooms at TNA contain a series of card indexes of names of officers; many of the returns of service listed below in WO 25 and WO 76 are covered.

WO 25/744-748	Returns of Officers' Services	1809-1810
WO 25/749-779	Services of Officers (retired) on Full and Half Pay	1828
WO 25/780-805	Services of Officers on Full Pay	1829
WO 25/808-823	Services of Retired Officers	1847

WO 25/824-870	Officers' Services	1870-1872
WO 25/3913-3919	Records of Service of Engineer Officers	1796-1922
WO 54/248-259	Returns of Engineer Officers	1786-1850
WO 54/684	Records of Service of Artillery Officers	1727-1751
WO 76/1-551	Records of Officers' Services (originally in regimental record offices, including records for Artillery Officers 1777-1870)	1764-1954

The content of the War Office returns of service is again varied. The first (1809-1810) merely gives service details. The second and third series (1828 and 1829) also include information about the officers' families, with dates of marriage and children's births; their place of baptism may well be given, as may date and place of birth of the officer, in the full pay return of 1829. Similar service and family details are given in the fourth (1847) and fifth (1870-1872) series.

A typical entry in the **Returns of Officers on Full and Half Pay, October 1828**, is that for Ensign Emanuel Burton (WO 25/751):

Emanuel Burton

Age on first appointment to HM Service: 26

Date of Appointment	*Full Pay*	*Half Pay*
Aug 17 1815 44th Regt	*Ensign Purchase*	*Ensign Reduction of 2nd Bttn*
Apr 7 1825 50th Regt	*Ensign Restoration without paying the difference*	*Ensign By exchange receiving the difference*

Sep 14 1826   Unattached

Desirous of Service?:   Not at present

Service: Full pay 2 years
*   Half Pay 11 years*
*   Total 13*

Served upwards of Three years in the Royal Westmorland Militia previous to purchasing into the 44th Regt.

Marriage: August 11th 1826 at Drogheda
Children: Margaret Rose born 27th July 1827
Not wounded. Never held Civil Situation.

Christian and Surnames of the Officer	Age on first Appointment, and to His Majesty's Service	Dates of first Appointment, and of each subsequent Promotion, Removal, or Exchange, whether to Full-Pay or Half-Pay	Regiments in which the several Commissions have been obtained, or upon the Half-Pay of which the Officer may have retired	FULL-PAY		HALF-PAY		The Officer is here required to state, whether he be desirous of Service
				Each successive Rank held by the Officer while upon Full-Pay, is to be stated underneath	How obtained; whether by purchase or without purchase; and if by restoration, whether by paying the difference, or without	Each successive Rank held by the Officer while upon Half-Pay, is to be stated underneath	Whether placed thereon by reduction; by the purchase of a Half-Pay Commission; by Exchange, receiving the difference; by Exchange, without the difference; or at the request of the Officer from private motives, or from ill-health	
Emanuel Burton	26	August 10th 1815 June 9th 1825 September 14th 1826	44th Regiment 50th Regiment Unattached	Ensign Ensign	Purchase. Restoration without paying the difference	Ensign Ensign	Reduction 2 batt. By Exchange, receiving the difference.	Not at Present

MARRIED OFFICERS

If the Officer is Married, he is required to state, underneath, when and where the Marriage took place	Place of Marriage	Date of Marriage	If the Officer has any Children, their Names and Dates of Birth are to be stated underneath	Names of Children	Dates of their Birth
	Donghadee	August 11th 1826		Margaret Ann	July 27th 1827

WOUNDED OFFICERS

If the Officer is in the Receipt of a Pension for Wounds, the Amount of that Pension; the Station where the Officer was serving when Wounded; and the Date of the Commencement of the Grant is to be stated	Amount of Pension	Where serving when wounded	Date of the commencement of the Grant
	None		

OFFICERS HOLDING CIVIL SITUATIONS

If the Officer is employed in any Civil Office under His Majesty, or in the Service of any other Government, the Title and Nature of the Employment, and the Annual Amount of Emoluments and Salary attached thereto, are to be stated	Title and Nature of the Employment	Annual Amount of Salary and Emoluments	The Officer is here required to state where he has been generally resident during the last Five Years
	None held any Office of Arms		In Ireland in Tipperary 44th Regt 50th Regt in England in Donghadee now going on half pay if unattached

Figure 2 – Returns of Officers on Full and Half Pay – 1828. Ensign Emanuel Burton, unattached, formerly 44th and 50th Foot, WO 25/751

11

Residence last 5 years: In Kendal on half pay, 44th Regt
Depot, 50th Regt & in Drogheda since going on half pay of
unattached.
Signed: Emanuel Burton

The **Returns of Service of Retired Officers, 1847** contain similar information, as this further example relating to Emanuel Burton shows (WO 25/809):

Name, Rank and Regiment: *Emanuel Burton, Ensign, Unattached*
Present Age: *56*
Age on entering the Army: *23*

Dates of the several   *Rank: Regimental Ensign by Purchase*
Commissions in succession,   *Date: August 17th 1815, 44th Regt*
specifying whether   *Rank: Regimental Ensign*
Regimental or Brevet: *Date: April 7th 1825, 50th Regt*

Date of last retirement on   *Sept 14th 1826. Own request on account of*
Half Pay and cause of retirement: family considerations

State whether liable to refund   *Liable, having received the Difference, but perfectly*
the difference before returning   *incompetent to refund*
to Full Pay in consequence of
having received it on retirement
to Half Pay

If under 60 years of age, state if   *Perfectly active and fit for service, and free from all*
you consider yourself fit to serve   *bodily and mental disability*
again, or if you are labouring
under any disability which you
conceive renders you unfit, state
the nature of it, and how it originated

If under 60 years of age, state   *No Employment*
whether you have any   *I have, in vain, long sought it, either Civil or*
employment which would   *Military having literally no means except my*
interfere with your serving   *half-pay*
permanently or temporarily
on Full Pay

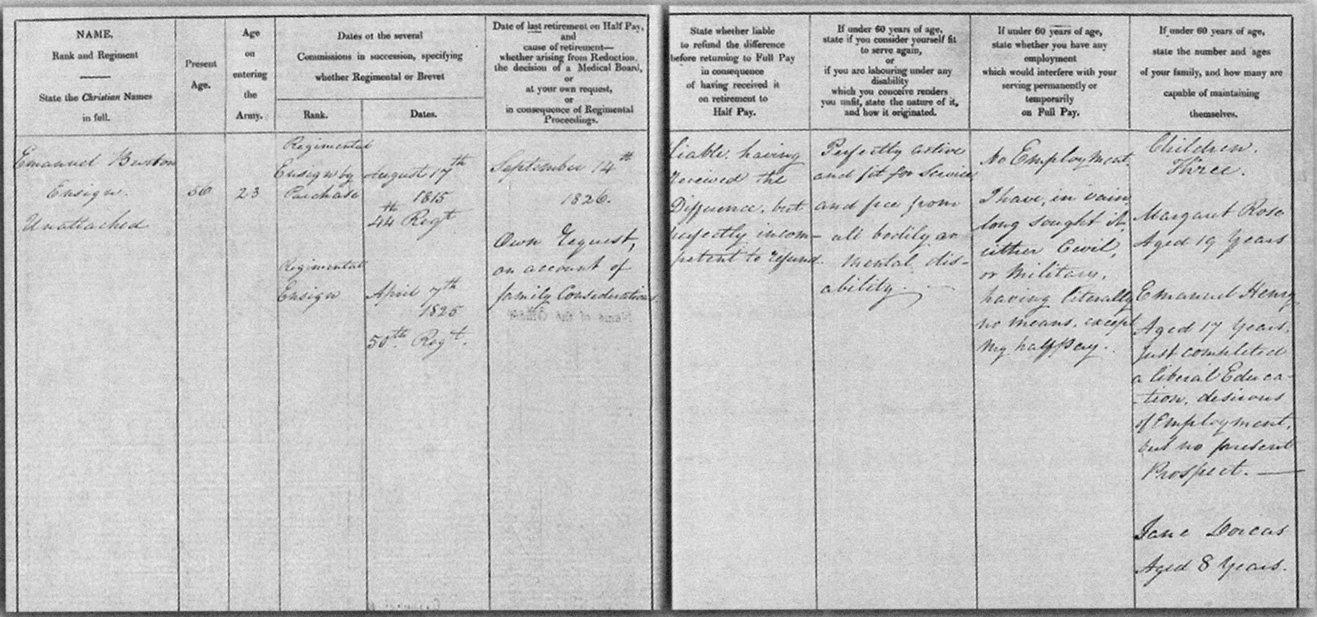

NAME, Rank and Regiment — State the Christian Names in full.	Present Age.	Age on entering the Army.	Dates at the several Commissions in succession, specifying whether Regimental or Brevet.		Date of last retirement on Half Pay; and cause of retirement—whether arising from Reduction, the decision of a Medical Board, or at your own request, in consequence of Regimental Proceedings.	State whether liable to refund the difference before returning to Full Pay in consequence of having received it on retirement to Half Pay.	If under 60 years of age, state if you consider yourself fit to serve again, or if you are labouring under any disability which you conceive renders you unfit, state the nature of it, and how it originated.	If under 60 years of age, state whether you have any employment which would interfere with your serving permanently or temporarily on Full Pay.	If under 60 years of age, state the number and ages of your family, and how many are capable of maintaining themselves.
			Rank.	Dates.					
Emanuel Burton, Ensign, Unattached	50	23	Regimental Ensign in Royal York Rangers the 44th Regt. Regimental Ensign	the 1815 44th Regt June 7th 1826 50th Regt	September 14th 1826. Own Request on account of Family Considerations …	Not liable, having received the Difference, but … not fit for Service …	Perfectly active and fit for Service. … lost part of an ability …	No Employment. Have in every way sought … either Civil or Military.	Children Three. … Margaret … Aged 19 years. … Edward, Aged 17 years … Isaac Emanuel Aged 8 years.

Figure 3 - Returns of Service of Retired Officers - 1847 Ensign Emanuel Burton, unattached, formerly 44th and 50th Foot, WO 25/809

If under 60 years of age, state the number and ages of your family and how many are capable of maintaining themselves	Children Three Margaret Rose aged 19 years, Emanuel Henry aged 17 years, just completed a liberal Education, desirous of Employment but no present Prospect, Jane Dorcas aged 8 years

In the Royal Westmorland Militia upwards of 3 years, previous to Purchasing into the 44th regiment.

Dated at Wicklow this 21st day of September 1847

Signature of the Officer:	Emanuel Burton

As mentioned earlier **Lt Gen H G Hart's papers**, though not official War Office returns, can add supplementary information. They include correspondence from officers, and questionnaires completed in response to Hart's enquiries for details to be included in a biographical dictionary (sadly never published) of Army Officers. For instance, the career of Lt Colonel William Balfour may be traced in the usual Services of Officers on Full Pay (WO 25/801), or else in Hart's papers, as the following example shows (WO 211/8):

STATEMENT of the Services of Lt Colonel Wm Balfour of the 82nd Regiment of Foot with a Record of such Particulars as may be useful in the case of his Death

Where Born; Edinburgh   Date of Birth: 16th July 1784

Age on his first Entrance into the Service: 15 years

Ranks	Regiments		Full Pay	Half Pay
	Full Pay	Half Pay	Dates	
Ensign	40th Regt		Jun 1799	With Purchase
Lieut.	do		Jul 1799	Without Purchase
Captain	do		2 Sep 1802	With Purchase
Major	do		2 Feb 1808	Without Purchase
Lt Colonel	do		2 Apr 1814	
Major		40th Regt	14 Nov 1814	Placed on Half Pay in consequence of ill health without receiving the difference
Do	3rd Regt of Foot		Jul 1819	Paying the difference
Do	40th Foot		Aug 1820	Removed to the 40th Foot

80th Regt. of Foot (Staffordshire Volunteers).

The *Sphinx*, with the word "EGYPT."

Years' Serv.		
Full Pay.	Half Pay.	

Colonel.

48		✠ Sir John Taylor,[1] KCB. *Ens.* Nov. 1794; *Lieut.* 6 Dec. 94; *Capt.* 9 Sept. 95; *Major,* 2 Sept. 1801; *Lieut.-Col.* 28 Feb. 05; *Col.* 4 June, 13; *Major-Gen.* 12 Aug. 19; *Lieut.-Gen.* 10 Jan. 37; *Col.* 80th Regiment, 15 March, 37.

Lieut.-Colonel.

36	0	Narborough Baker,[2] *Ens.* 17 April, 06; *Lieut.* ᴾ 10 March, 08; *Capt.* ᴾ 18 Nov. 19; *Major,* ᴾ 25 May, 32; *Lieut.-Col.* ᴾ 24 March, 37.

Majors.

29	6	✠ Thomas Bunbury,[3] *Ens.* 7 May, 07; *Lieut.* 17 Aug. 09; *Capt.* 25 Oct. 14; *Major,* ᴾ 21 Nov. 34.
12	0	Charles Robert Raitt, *Ens.* 13 June 30; *Lieut.* ᴾ 4 Oct. 33; *Capt.* ᴾ 22 June 38; *Major,* ᴾ 29 Oct. 41.

			ENSIGN.	LIEUT.	CAPTAIN.	BREVET-MAJOR.
		CAPTAINS.				
38	0	Jas. Winniett Nunn[4]	7 Apr. 04	6 May 05	13 Dec. 10	22 July 30
12	0	Rob. Alex. Lockhart	ᴾ 11 June 30	ᴾ 5 Oct. 32	ᴾ 13 July 38	
8	0	Hon. Wm. A. Skeffington	ᴾ 9 May 34	ᴾ 22 June 38	ᴾ 17 Jan. 40	
30	0	Francis Marsh	5 Mar. 12	30 Dec. 19	4 Jan. 33	
7	0	Wm. Houghan Tyssen ..	ᴾ 30 Jan. 35	ᴾ 23 June 38	ᴾ 27 Mar. 40	
16	0	Philip Grove Beers	ᴾ 11 July 26	ᴾ 15 June 30	ᴾ 29 May 40	
23	0	Ronald Macdonald......	ᴾ 11 Feb. 19	25 Jan. 25	26 Jan. 41	
26	3⅟₁₂	✠ Charles Lewis[7]	9 June 13	30 Dec. 19	22 Mar. 32	
5	0	Abel Dottin Wm. Best..	ᴾ 21 Apr. 37	ᴾ 4 Oct. 39	ᴾ 2 July 41	
12	0	Robert George Hughes ..	ᴾ 29 June 30	ᴾ 6 July 32	ᴾ 3 Dec. 41	
		LIEUTENANTS.				
15	0	Rich. Talbot Sayers	ᴾ 19 Apr. 27	ᴾ 25 May 32		
16	0	Rinaldo Scheberras	ᴾ 16 Mar. 26	16 Apr. 33		
13	15⅟₁₂	Jas. Deaves Morris......	14 Apr. 14	25 June 18		
10	0	John Lightbody	ᴾ 25 May 32	ᴾ 9 May 34		
15	0	Owen Gorman[6]	26 Oct. 30	27 Feb. 36		
7	0	Hen. Theodore Torkington	ᴾ 14 Aug. 35	ᴾ 26 June 38		
6	0	Sam. Tolfrey Christie ..	ᴾ 22 Jan. 36	ᴾ 13 July 38		
12	20⅝	Simon Fraser	7 Mar. 10	17 July, 11		
4	0	Lambert L. Montgomery	ᴾ 22 June 38	ᴾ 17 Jan. 40		
4	0	Wm. Cookson..........	ᴾ 23 June 38	ᴾ 27 Mar. 40		
4	0	Alex. Wm. Riley	ᴾ 26 June 38	ᴾ 19 Feb. 41		
4	0	Anthony Ormsby	ᴾ 13 July 38	ᴾ 2 July 41		
4	0	Cha. Henry Leslie	ᴾ 20 July 38	16 July 41		
		ENSIGNS.				
5	0	H. A. Hollinsworth	8 July 37			
2	0	Hercules Atkin Welman	ᴾ 17 Jan. 40			
2	0	Rob. Boyle Warren	ᴾ 27 Mar. 40			
2	0	Mathew Deane Freeman	ᴾ 6 Nov. 40			
1	0	Geo. Cha. Glossop Bythesea	ᴾ 19 Feb. 41			
1	0	Astell Thomas Welsh ..	ᴾ 21 May 41			
1	0	Edward Alan Holdich ..	ᴾ 2 July 41			
1	0	George Samuel Young ..	16 July 41			

2 Lieut.-Col. Baker was at the capture of the Isle of France in 1810.

3 Major Bunbury served in the Peninsula from 1808 to the end of the war, including capture of Oporto, battles of Talavera and Barrosa, defence of Tarifa 1812, capture of Seville, defence of the Bridge of Puente Largo near Aranjuez, battles of Nivelle and Nive (severely wounded), investment of Bayonne, and battle of Toulouse.

4 Major Nunn served the Egyptian campaign of 1807; present at the capture of Genoa in 1814.

6 Quarter-Master, 15 Nov. 1827, from which date the period of service has been computed.

7 Capt. Lewis served in the Peninsula from Aug. 1813 to the end of that war in 1814. Served also the campaigns of 1825 and 26 in Burmah, as Brigade-Major.

16	0	*Paymaster.*—Tho. Bloomfield Hunt, 1 Aug. 37; *Ens.* ᴾ 19 Jan. 26; *Lieut.* 25 Oct. 33.
10	0	*Adjutant.*—John Lightbody, (*Lieut.*) 24 March, 37.
5	0	*Quarter-Master.*—Frederick Hayes, 10 Feb. 37.
24	4⅜	*Surgeon.*—Robt. Turnbull, 28 June, 36; *Assist.-Surg.* 14 May, 15; *Hosp.-Assist.* 3 Oct. 13.
6	0	*Assistant-Surgeons.*—Patrick Gammie, 17 June, 36.
3	0	Arthur Colquhoun Macnish, 5 July, 39.

Facings Yellow.—*Agent,* Mr. John Lawrie.

1 Sir John Taylor served the campaign of 1799 in Holland, as Aid-de-Camp to Major-Gen. Hutchinson, with whom he went to Egypt, and was present in the different battles of that campaign. Sir John has received a medal and two clasps for Nivelle, Orthes, and Toulouse, and was severely wounded in France, Feb. 1814.

232

Figure 4 - Hart's Army List page - 80th Regiment of Foot - Staffordshire Volunteers - 1842 Serving at New South Wales

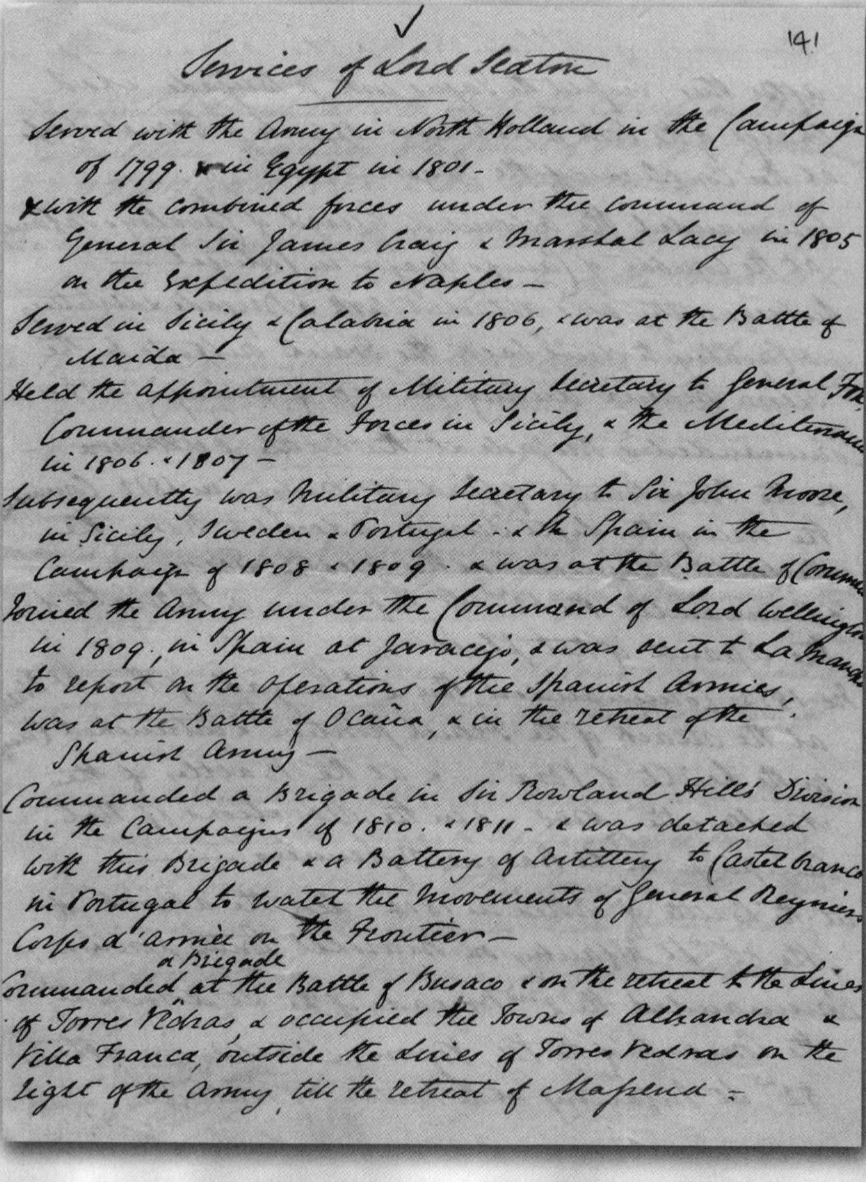

Services of Lord Seaton

Served with the Army in North Holland in the Campaign
of 1799, & in Egypt in 1801 –

& with the combined forces under the command of
General Sir James Craig & Marshal Lacy in 1805
on the Expedition to Naples –

Served in Sicily & Calabria in 1806, & was at the Battle of
Maida –

Held the appointment of Military Secretary to General ﬀ
Commander of the Forces in Sicily, & the Mediterranean
in 1806 & 1807 –

Subsequently was Military Secretary to Sir John Moore,
in Sicily, Sweden & Portugal – & in Spain in the
Campaign of 1808 & 1809 – & was at the Battle of Corunna

Joined the Army under the Command of Lord Wellington
in 1809, in Spain at Jaracejo, & was sent to La Mancha
to report on the operations of the Spanish Armies,
was at the Battle of Ocaña, & in the retreat of the
Spanish Army –

Commanded a Brigade in Sir Rowland Hill's Division
in the Campaigns of 1810 & 1811 – & was detached
with this Brigade & a Battery of Artillery to Castel Branco
in Portugal to watch the movements of General Reynier's
Corps d'armée on the Frontier –

Commanded a Brigade at the Battle of Busaco & on the retreat to the Lines
of Torres Vedras, & occupied the Towns of Alhandra &
Villa Franca, outside the Lines of Torres Vedras on the
right of the army, till the retreat of Massena –

*Figure 5 - Hart's Papers - Service Summary for Lord Seaton in Holland, Egypt, Sicily,
Spain and Portugal - 1799-1812, WO 211/28*

Lt Colonel	*40th Foot*	*1827*
Appointed to	*82nd Foot*	*1828*
Lt Colonel	*do*	*27 Jun 1833*

Retired from the Service by the Sale of his Commission on the 27th June 1833

Lists, and Dates of any Battles, Sieges and Campaigns, in which the Officer was present: specifying the Regimental or Staff Situation he held on each occasion, and the name of the Officer in the chief command.

Campaign in N Holland in 1799. As Lieutenant.
General Sir Ralph Abercromby and Field Marshal the Duke of York, Chiefs in Command. Helder 27 Aug 1799, St Martins 10 Sep 1799, Onds Carrpel 19 Sep 1799, Bergen 2 Oct 1799

Siege of Copenhagen. As Captain.
Aide-de-Camp to Major Gen Spencer, General Lord Cathcart Chief in Command

Battle of the Nivelle, Nive, Orthes, Toulouse. As Major. Duke of Wellington in Command. Medal for Commanding 40th Regt at the Battle of the Nivelle, South of France.

Service Abroad

From	*To*	*Station*
Aug 1799	*Nov 1799*	*Holland*
Jan 1800	*1802*	*Minorca and Malta*
Aug 1807	*Nov 1807*	*Zealand*
Sep 1813	*Jul 1814*	*Peninsula and France*
Sep 1823	*Jun 1827*	*N S Wales and Van Diemens Land*
Jun 1828	*Dec 1829*	*Mauritius*
Jan 1830	*Mar 1832*	*do*

True extract from the regimental records X Y M............ Lt Col............

The above particulars from Hart's Papers are virtually the same as the entry in the Services of Officers on Full Pay (WO 25/801), but the latter includes details of Lt Colonel Balfour's family, as given below. (Of course it is always prudent to check all contemporary records.)

If the Officer be Married, specify

When	Where	To whom		The wife living at the date of
1810	Dublin	Miss Charlotte Stanley Clarke		Dead 22nd August 1825
				Launceston Van Diemen's Land

If the Officer has any legitimate Children, specify

Names	Dates of Birth	Where Baptised
David William	23 Jun 1811	Dublin
Charlotte	31 Aug 1813	(Genava) Barracks, Waterford
John	15 Jul 1815	Belfast
William	18 Oct 1816	do
Charles Anthony	28 Nov 1817	do
Marion	31 Jul 1819	do
George Macintosh	19 Dec 1821	Newcastle, Cty Limerick
Catherine	Jun 1824	Sydney, N S Wales

Purchase and Issue of Commissions

The references in the above examples to purchase of a commission, to half pay and to receiving the difference remind us of the system by which commissions in the army could be obtained, until the abolition of this method in 1871. The origins of the purchase system can be traced to medieval times – see Anthony Bruce for a definitive account. In 1159, Henry II introduced scutage, by which a knight could avoid obligation of military service, by payment of an agreed sum. The king could then use this money to finance mercenaries to fight in his campaigns. Mercenary companies were primarily commercial and aimed at maximization of profit. Any individual or group with sufficient capital could raise a body of soldiers and offer their services to a client. Appointments to commissions in the company and division of profits were related to initial investment. Hence wealthy men could more easily raise a company and the largest shareholders would become the senior officers. Professional expertise as a soldier was naturally a requirement for success, and hence skilled but less wealthy individuals might still progress.

Each rank, therefore, had a financial value, which could be bought and sold like shares in a commercial venture. Kings later reconciled this mercenary role to national needs. However, antipathy to the purchase system was first recorded in 1641 and continued strongly after 1714, with the Hanoverians. Despite dissatisfaction with the basic system, the authorities found it difficult to end it, as this would have disadvantaged those in office at the time. The alternative was the introduction of regulations to control the purchase system.

By the time of the Peninsular War, as pointed out by Michael Glover, there was strictly no need to buy a commission. At that time, purchase accounted for only about one in five first commissions; the main reason for purchase was to ensure that one could gain entry to a regiment of one's choice. Thus purchase accounted for about half the first commissions in the cavalry and foot guards.

Prior to 1821, the regulation price for purchase of an ensigncy in the infantry was £400; promotion to the next rank of lieutenant was by seniority, provided that the candidate was adjudged suitable – by examination after 1821 – and was willing to pay the purchase price, in this case, £550. Of course, the newly promoted lieutenant would expect to 'sell' his original rank to his successor for £400, so that he would merely have to find the difference of £150. In this way a successful officer could rise to captain, major or lieutenant-colonel for (total) sums of £1500, £2600 and £3500 respectively (prior to 1821). Considerably higher figures applied in the cavalry or foot guards regiments.

The issue of commissions is fully described in TNA's Research Guide: British Army: Officers' Commissions. Of particular note are:

WO 4/513	Indexed Letter Books: correspondence about the purchase and sale of commissions	1704-1858
WO 25/1	Commission Books, Series 1	1660-1873
WO 25/89	Commission Books, Series 2	1728-1818
WO 25/122	Notification Books of the Secretary at War	1708-1848
WO 25/209	Succession Books, Series 1, Secretary at War arranged by regiments	1754-1808
WO 25/221	Succession Books, Series 2, Secretary at War arranged by date	1773-1808
WO 74/1	Original applications from officers of the British and Indian establishment, with certificates of service attached, indexed by regiment	c1871-1891
WO 74/177-183	Registers of service of every officer holding a commission on 1st November 1871, with later additions	(1871)

Commander in Chief's Memoranda Papers

These papers were concerned with appointments, promotions and resignations of officers; they are preserved at TNA in WO 31 for the years 1793-1870. The original applications have been retained together with any letters of recommendation or covering letters from commanding officers (COs) and agents. They are arranged chronologically, so that the date of appointment, promotion or resignation must first be found from the Army Lists, Returns of Service or the London Gazette.

A brief example relating to Emanuel Burton is contained in the Commander-in-Chief's Memoranda Papers for the 17th August 1815 (WO 31/426):

> *Purchased Ensigncy in 44th Regt vice Peacock promoted. Paid £400.*
> *Recommendation from (illegible) concerning Emanuel Burton's good military conduct in His Majesty's Regt of Royal Westmorland Militia.*
> *Purchase agreed by General the Earl of Suffolk.*

Ensign Burton appears to have been one of many caught up in the euphoria following Waterloo (18th June 1815). As noted above, under 'Returns of Service', he was active on full pay for only eight months, until the second battalion was reduced and he was then placed on half pay. Nine years later he managed to obtain a full pay commission again by transferring to another regiment (WO 31/552):

> *April 7th 1825 50th Foot*
> *Ensign Emanuel Burton from the half-pay 44th Regt.*

Even this change of regiment did not result in much active service and Ensign Burton returned to half pay after a further one year and five months. His 1847 Return of Service (see above) gave the reason for this retirement as 'family considerations' following his marriage in August 1826. The Commander-in-Chief's Memoranda papers contain a reference to an Ensign Reynolds, who paid £150 to Ensign Burton for the transfer (WO 31/561):

> *September 14th 1826 50th Foot*
> *Ensign Henry Reynolds from the half pay to be Ensign vice Emanuel Burton who exchanges receiving the difference*

These papers also include a letter written personally by Emanuel Burton (WO 31/561):

Drogheda Sept 5th 1826 (To the Military Secretary)

Sir,

Being desirous to go on Half Pay, as soon as it can be accomplished, and receiving the difference; may I request the favor of expediting the necessary arrangements; and if necessary beg a reference to Major Anderson Commanding, now in Belfast.

I have the honor to be, Sir,

Your most obedient Humble servant

Emanuel Burton

Ensign 50th Regt

These brief examples show how the Memoranda Papers can expand the outline available from Army Lists or Returns of Service. Extensive family biographies were derived from these papers by Hamilton-Edwards, who quoted other letters, e.g. 'memorials and prayers' for advancement or promotion. Glowing references or good connections could be indispensable to progress in the army.

Half Pay Ledgers and Lists

Until 1871 officers were not entitled to a pension as of right; when they wished to retire, they either sold their commissions or went on to half pay. Responsibility for payment of half pay and pensions rested with the Paymaster-General, amongst whose records are many which may be of use.

PMG 4	Army Establishment Half Pay	1737-1921
PMG 5	Commissariat Half Pay, Pensions, etc (from 1840 includes widows' pensions)	1834-1855
PMG 6	Army Establishment Foreign Half Pay, Pensions, etc (for foreign corps)	1822-1885
PMG 7	Army Establishment, Hanover, Foreign Half Pay (mainly to King's German Legion)	1843-1862
PMG 8	Army Establishment, Hanover, Chelsea Out-Pensions	1844-1877
PMG 9	Army Establishment, Pensions for Wounds	1814-1921
PMG 10	Army Establishment, Compassionate List and Royal Bounty	1812-1916
PMG 11	Army Establishment, Widows' Pensions	1810-1920
PMG 12	Ordnance Half Pay, Pensions etc	1836-1875
PMG 13	Militia, Yeomanry and Volunteers Allowances	1793-1927
PMG 14	Army Establishment, Miscellaneous Books	1720-1861

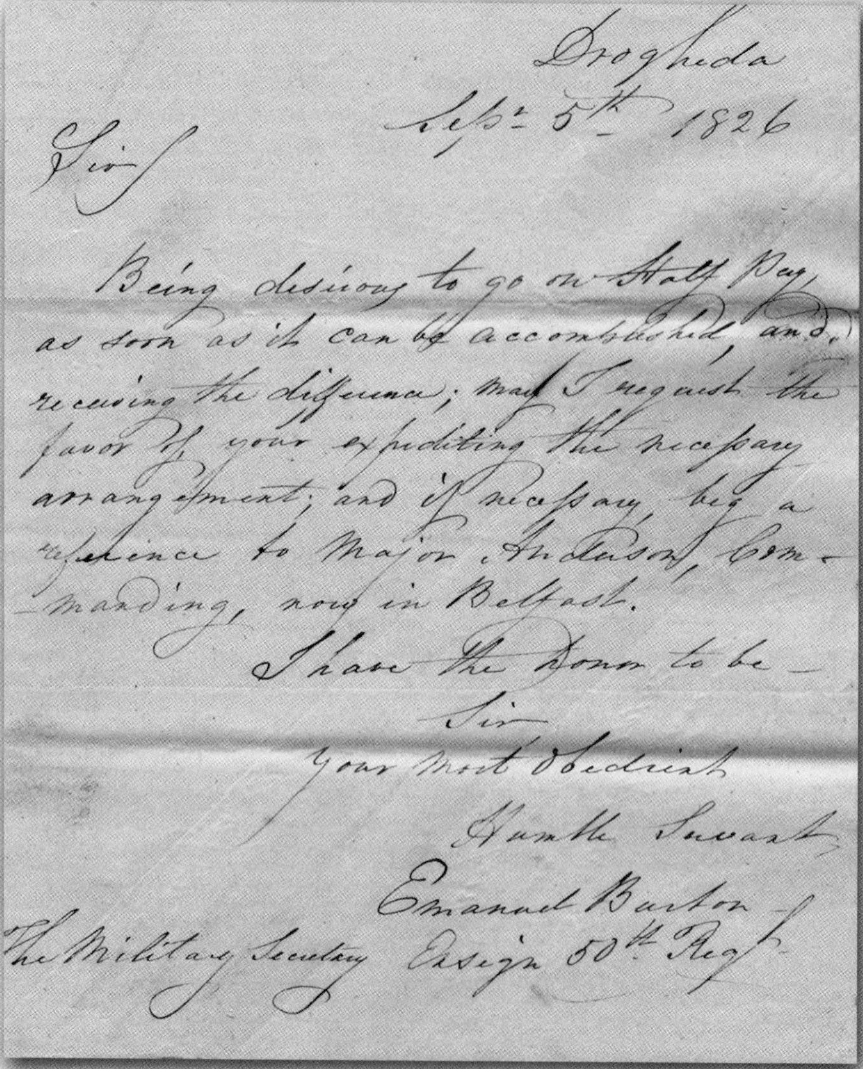

Drogheda
Sep. 5th 1826

Sir,

Being desirous to go on Half Pay, as soon as it can be accomplished, and receiving the difference; may I request the favor of your expediting the necessary arrangement; and if necessary, beg a reference to Major Anderson, Commanding, now in Belfast.

I have the honor to be –
Sir
Your Most Obedient
Humble Servant,
Emanuel Burton
Ensign 50th Regt.

The Military Secretary

Figure 6 - Commander-in-Chief's Memoranda Papers -1826 Letter from Ensign Emanuel Burton of the 50th Regiment requesting permission to go on Half-Pay, WO 31/561

As may be seen from the 'retirement' of Emanuel Burton in 1826, he managed to obtain the 'difference' of £150 from Ensign Reynolds and was also placed on half pay of 3/- per day. He continued to hold a commission so that he was in theory available for future service, indicating that half pay could be regarded either as a retainer or as a pension. It is clear from Emanuel Burton's Return of Service for 1847 (see above) that he hoped to be able to return to full pay without refunding the difference; one may therefore conclude that half pay was treated as a legitimate emolument for an officer while not in service, whatever the reason. In this respect he was clearly in a much better position than the average soldier, even though he might not be very well off by the standards of officers and gentlemen of the time.

Much interesting information may be obtained from Half Pay Ledgers and Lists. For Emanuel Burton, they gave his whereabouts from 1829 until his death in 1865; clearly such details can save much unrewarding searching, particularly when the subject decided to emigrate! Some extracts from Half Pay ledgers concerning Ensign Emanuel Burton are given below. He received 3/- per diem; as he was paid quarterly in arrears, he obtained typically £13 10s.

PMG 4/	Year	At	Agent
176	1829	Drogheda	Greenwood & Co
205	1838	Dublin	Greenwood & Co
216	1853 (to 31 March)	17 Capel St Dublin	R.H.Cox
218	1853 (from 1 April)	119 Leonard St New York	Cox and Hammersley
	to1856	240 Fulton St Brooklyn	Cox and Hammersley
	then	163 Sands St Brooklyn	Cox and Hammersley
224	1862 to 1865 (31 March)	81 Sands St Brooklyn	Cox & Co
226	1865 (1 Apr-30 Jun)	No address, amount or agent entered	

Emanuel Burton died on the 3rd April 1865 in the New York District of Brooklyn. His death was not recorded in the Half Pay ledgers, which are however often annotated with such information.

It is worth noting that the monies were often collected on the officer's behalf by agents, and that some authority was needed for this. Such authorisation was recorded in **Enrolment Books of letters of attorney and probate (AO 15)**; a

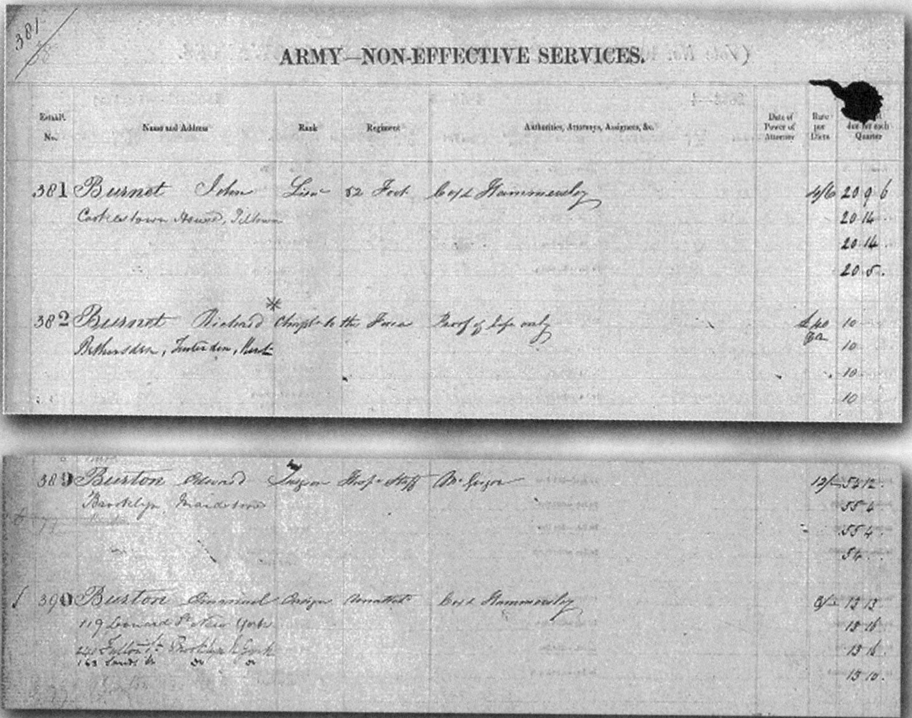

Half-pay payments to officers
Lowest entry:
Emanuel Burton, Ensign, Unattached
Authority: Cox & Hammersley, Rate per diem: 3/-
Quarterly payments of £13.13s, £13.16s, £13.16s and £13.10s
Addresses: Leonard St New York, Fulton St Brooklyn N York and Sands St
Brooklyn N York

Figure 7 - Half Pay Ledger - 1853-1856 Emanuel Burton in New York and Brooklyn,
PMG 4/218

search in the 1826-27 volume revealed the following for Emanuel Burton. (AO 15/151, fo 338)

27 Jan 1827
A like Letter from Ensign Emanuel Burton upon Half Pay unattached
Dated the 4th Jany 1827.
Empowering Messrs Greenwood, Cox & Hammersley as aforsd jointly and severally.
E Burton   Witness Thomas Henry

Further registers and **lists of half pay officers** are contained in classes WO 23 (Royal Hospital Chelsea, Chelsea Registers, etc), WO 24 (Establishments) and WO 25 (Registers, Various). A selection of material available is listed below.

WO 23/66-78	Registers of Half Pay Officers (arranged alphabetically)	1858-1894
WO 23/79-81	ditto for Officers of Foreign Regiments	1858-1876
WO 23/82	ditto for Artillery and Engineers	1815-1874
WO 24/660-747	Lists of those entitled to half pay (arranged by regiment)	1713-1809
WO 24/748-762	ditto for British-American forces	1783-1813
WO 25/2979-2989	Half pay and retired pay lists	1712-1763
WO 25/2990-3004	Registers of warrants for half pay and retired pay	1763-1859
WO 25/3005-3008	Half Pay - miscellaneous	
WO 25/3013-3019	lists and registers	1811-1858

It was possible to commute pensions to a lump sum, although few did this. Records may be found at TNA in NDO 7/49 (1871-1897) and NDO 14 (1869 onwards).

Widows' Pensions and Pensions to Wounded Officers

There was some provision for the widows and dependents of officers killed on active service. For officers' widows with an income of less than £30 per annum, there were, from 1818, fifteen annuities available under the will of Col John Drouly. Pensions to widows, children or dependent relatives might also be paid out of the Royal Bounty and the Compassionate Fund. A table of some material available at TNA (Kew) is given below. Material for commissariat, foreign and ordnance officers or their widows may be found in other PMG classes (see table above).

PMG 9	Army Establishment, Pensions for Wounds	1814-1921
PMG 10	Army Establishment, Compassionate List and Bounty - includes Drouly Annuities for	1812-1916 1870-1882
PMG 11	Army Establishment, Widows Pensions - includes Drouly Annuities for and	1810-1920 1827-1870 1883-1920
WO 23/83-87	Registers, Pensions for Wounds	1815-1892
WO 23/88-92	Registers, Widows' Pensions and Drouly Annuities	1815-1892
WO 23/105-113	ditto continued	
WO 23/114-123	Registers, Compassionate List and Bounty	1858-1894
WO 24/804-883	Ledgers, Widows' Pensions and Drouly Annuities	1713-1829
WO 25/3020-3045	Pensions to Widows of Full Pay Officers	1735-1811
WO 25/3046-3057	Pensions to Widows of Half Pay Officers	1755-1778
WO 25/3069-3107	Registers of Warrants and Application Papers for Widows' Pensions and Bounty	1807-1856
WO 25/3108-3125	Widows' Pensions, Compassionate Papers, Miscellaneous Papers, Registers and Indexes	1748-1851

It is worth noting that lists of names of those receiving Royal Bounty or Compassionate Allowance, during the period 1812 to 1820, are contained in the House of Commons Journals. The 1818 list included reference to many killed at Waterloo. For example, Anne Maria Currie was to receive £150 per annum, from 19th June 1815, being the 'widow of Lt Col Edward Currie of the 90th Foot, who was killed at Waterloo; she being left with three children unprovided for'. (Other ranks rarely featured in these lists. An exception, in 1814, was Alexander Hopkins, 'Private Soldier in the 52nd Regt of Foot, for his good conduct at the Battle of Busaco, wherein he took the French General Simon, Prisoner'. He received £20 per annum from 13th October 1813.)

Other Record Sources for Officers

Sandhurst is popularly associated with the training of officers. However, the Royal Military Academy there was formed in 1947 by the merger of the Royal Military College (formed in 1800 at Great Marlow but moved to Sandhurst in 1812) and the Royal Military Academy, Woolwich, which had been founded in 1741. The latter institution had been formed so that the Royal Engineers and Royal Artillery could train their officers before they were granted commissions. (There was no purchase system in these corps and promotion was by seniority.) The following classes of records of the cadets who trained at these establishments are held at the Royal Military Academy, Sandhurst.

| WO 149 | Royal Military Academy, Woolwich, Registers of Cadets | 1760-1939 |
| WO 151 | Royal Military Academy, Sandhurst, Registers of Cadets | 1806-1946 |

Militia are discussed more fully below (at the end of Chapter Four), but the main sources for Militia Officers' records are summarised here.

HO 50	Military Correspondence – including lists of commissions in Militia and Volunteers	1782-1840
HO 51	Military Entry Books – including commissions, appointments and warrants relating to Militia, Volunteers, Yeomanry and Ordnance	1758-1855
WO 68	Militia Records – including Officers' services	1759-1925

Printed Militia lists are available in the library at TNA for various dates in the 18th and 19th centuries.

For those commencing their search for officers at TNA (Kew), it is worth repeating that there is a series of **card indexes of names of officers**. The cards themselves may include some family details and dates of marriage. They cover material from the following:

WO 25/744-748	Returns of Officers' Services	1809-1810
WO 25/749-779	Services of Officers (retired) on Full and Half Pay	1828
WO 25/780-805	Services of Officers on Full Pay	1829
WO 25/808-823	Services of Retired Officers	1847
WO 25/824-870	Officers' Services	1870-1872
WO 25/3090-3107	Application Papers for Widows' Pensions and Bounty	1807-1856
WO 25/3913-3919	Records of Service of Engineer Officers	1796-1922
WO 43/1-1059	Secretary at War: Correspondence: Selected 'Very Old Series' and 'Old Series' Papers	1809-1857
WO 76/1-554	Records of Officers' Services (originally in regimental record offices)	1764-1954
WO 76/399-417	Forester Brigade Group	
WO 76/420-460	Highland Brigade Group	

There are many sources for further information on officers which may be followed up in individual cases. Among these are:

WO 25/3239-3245	Reports of Officers' Marriages	1830-1882
WO 32/8903-8920	Registered Files; General Series Certificates, as for WO42, below	1777-1892
WO 42/1-73	Certificates of Births, Baptisms, Marriages, Deaths and Burials	1755-1908
WO 138	Selected Personal Files (Closed for 75 years after closure of file)	1830-1963

There are partial card indexes and typescript volumes at TNA to some of the pieces listed above in WO 25, WO 32 and WO 42.

Records of **courts martial** for officers and for other ranks are described together in Chapter Four.

CHAPTER THREE

Other Ranks - prior to 1914
Finding the Regiment

Introduction

The first major objective in the search for an ancestor soldier's career is to discover in which regiment he served, since the available documents are mostly arranged by regiment. Unfortunately there is no single overall name index for soldiers who served in the ranks, unlike officers, for whom there are Army lists. Here, we concentrate on the problem of finding the regiment, since this is a common hurdle for many researchers.

The possibility of discovering the regiment before visiting the National Archives (TNA) at Kew is first explored. That is, by making use of other information available, before consulting the main army records themselves. For example, one thinks immediately of civil registration and census returns, which may give a good clue to a man's regiment.

Also, nowadays, there are several indexes available to the main army sources, some 'on-line'. For example there is on-line access to a nominal index to Soldiers' Documents (WO 97), for the period 1760 to 1854.

If this does not succeed, then one must visit Kew and search directly in the various 'Army Sources' preserved in the War Office (WO) department records at TNA. This technique is described next.

Finally, the major army sources are examined in detail, in Chapter Four. Let us assume that the searcher does find the right regiment, possibly after many trials and tribulations. The extensive range of army documents now beckons to the eager genealogist and it is almost certain that these will yield more details for the 'common man' than could be found for many other occupations.

A. FINDING THE REGIMENT BEFORE GOING TO THE NATIONAL ARCHIVES

There are many sources, any of which may lead to the desired information regarding the regiment. None of these sources is guaranteed to lead to success, but it is worth trying all the relevant ones before turning to the army sources at TNA.

Civil Registration

After 1837, in England and Wales, (or 1855 in Scotland and 1864 in Ireland), it is quite possible to find a reference to a soldier's regiment on a birth, marriage or death certificate. For instance, the death certificate for James Sells included the following information:

Where and when died	*2nd June 1843*	*Britten Street Chelsea*
Name and Surname	*James Sells*	
Age	*48 years*	
Occupation	*Beer retailer*	*Pensioner of Chelsea Hospital 7th Regiment of Foot*
Cause of death	*Consumption*	

In this case it was a simple matter to proceed to the Soldiers' Documents (WO 97). These showed that he had been born at Eastchurch in Kent, had enlisted at Dover aged 18 on 8th December 1815, and had served with the Royal Fusiliers (or City of London Regiment, the 7th Regiment of Foot) until his discharge, still as a Private, to a pension of 9d a day on 7th May 1826 at Dover (WO 97/292). The searcher was very fortunate to obtain a birthplace from his army records – James Sells was one of those inconsiderate ancestors who died before the 1851 census, leaving a major problem finding his birthplace.

The death record of our own soldier ancestor, a great-great-grandfather, left us only this tantalising clue:

Where and when died	*3rd November 1846*	*Hasbro (Norfolk)*
Name and Surname	*John Watts*	
Age	*73 years*	
Occupation	*Soldier*	
Cause of death	*Diseased stomach certified*	

Marriage certificates may also contain the required information about the regiment. Here are some extracts from an example which gives evidence of two generations of soldiers. It refers to a ceremony at the parish church in Liverpool; the address column is omitted below - both parties lived in Clifford Street.

When married	*12th August 1851*	
	Groom	*Bride*
Name and surname	*James White*	*Mary Ann Honey*
Age	*minor*	*minor*
Condition	*bachelor*	*spinster*
Rank or profession	*Drummer in HM 46 Regt of Foot*	
Father's name and surname	*Thomas White*	*Joseph H Honey*
Rank or profession of father	*soldier*	*mariner*

Census Returns

It is quite possible to find a reference to an Army career in the census returns, every ten years from 1841, and currently available to 1901. For instance, in the 1861 census for Ludham in Norfolk, we found the family of Samuel Goodens. (RG 9/1197)

Name and surname	*Samuel Goodens*	*Joana Goodens*	*Catherine Goodens*
Relation to Head of family	*head*	*wife*	*daughter*
Age	*47*	*47*	*13*
Rank/Profession/ Occupation	*Chelsea Pensioner and Agr Labourer*		
Where Born	*Ludham Norfolk*	*Cork Ireland*	*Poona East Indies*

It is clear that Samuel Goodens must have served at least in Ireland and India, but there is no indication as to his regiment. However, since he had a daughter born abroad, it would be sensible to check in the Indexes to Regimental Registers of Birth. (See next section for details of Goodens births recorded in the indexes there.)

A further example of some census entries that give a probable indication of a military career was found in the 1851, 1861 and 1871 census returns for Happisburgh, Norfolk. In these extracts, one can also note the variations that can occur in recorded name and birthplace.

1851 census for Happisburgh (HO 107/1808)

Name and surname	Edward Smith	Elizabeth Smith	Henry Hasplink	James Smith
Relation to Head of family	head	wife	son	son
Age	37	36	8	7 months
Rank/ Profession/ Occupation	Farm Labourer			
Where Born	Lessingham Nfk	Prescot	W Indies	Hasbro

1861 census for Happisburgh (RG 9/1199)

Name and surname	Edward Smith	Elizabeth Smith	Henry Smith	
Relation to Head of family	head	wife	son	(also sons James Smith 10 and John Smith 8 both born Hasbro)
Age	47	46	18	
Rank/ Profession/ Occupation	Pauper			
Where Born	Lessingham Nfk	Ireland	Jamaica	

1871 census for Happisburgh (RG 10/1795)

Name and surname		Henry Geo Hasplink	Elizabeth Smith (widow)
Relation to Head of family		head	mother (now living nearby with married son James Smith)
Age		29	56

Rank/ Profession/ Occupation	Labourer on a farm	
Where Born	Hill New Castle Jamaica India (sic)	Prescott

Following the discovery of such a census entry – involving the birth of children abroad – there are two methods of proceeding. Firstly, as discussed above, one may go to the Indexes to Regimental Registers of Birth. (This was successful for the Hasplink family and the results are quoted in the next section.) However, it may be that no relevant entries are found there for children of that family. In this case, the location referred to in the birthplace column of the census entry can be used.

As Henry Hasplink's place of birth would seem to be Jamaica, the Monthly Returns (either WO 17 or WO 73) for that Depot may be consulted at TNA to find the regiments there in his year of birth, about 1843. These were found to be the Royal Artillery, the Royal Engineers, and the 48th, 60th, 77th and 82nd Regiments of Foot. (WO 17/2033). One can then search for the father, either in the Muster Books (WO 10, 11 or 12) or in the Soldiers' Documents (WO 97), for the six units stationed in Jamaica. The father was actually found to be another Henry Hasplink, serving in the 60th foot, having enlisted aged 15 at Dublin in the 81st foot in September 1820. (WO 97/731). Kitzmuller's 'In search of the forlorn hope' may also help in identifying the regiments at a particular location.

It is difficult to state what proportion of soldiers or pensioners would have had their regiment quoted in a census return. A check on the 1851 census for Kendal, Westmorland, which had a population of 11 829 revealed 14 pensioners and soldiers, but in only four cases was the regiment given. Extracts from some of these census entries are given below. (HO 107/2442)

Address	Name	Age	Rank Profession or Occupation	Where Born
Peartree Cottages	John Cropper and family	53	Army Pensioner and Sergeant-Major of Yeomanry Cavalry	Lancs Manchester
Highgate	Charles Gaze	29	Sergeant of 55th regiment	Norfolk Burgh
Fellside Pond	William Rigg	75	Chelsea Pensioner & Woollen Handloom Weaver	Westmorland Kendal

Stricklandgate	*William Carradus*	*67*	*Chelsea Pensioner*	*Lancs Liverpool*
			25th foot regiment
Stricklandgate	*Patrick Flood*	*68*	*Tailor and Chelsea*	*Ireland*
			Pensioner
Stricklandgate	*James M*	*65*	*Late Paymaster in*	*East Indies*
	Pennington		*the army (48th*
			regiment)

If one has information about a barracks where an ancestor soldier was stationed, then clearly the relevant census returns should be sought.

Regimental Registers, Chaplains' Returns and Army Returns

Apart from the familiar indexes to births, marriages and deaths held by the General Register Office , there are also indexes to 'overseas' registers. Some of these relate to births/baptisms, marriages and deaths/burials of soldiers and their families, and they may well be used as a starting point for a search for a soldier ancestor. These miscellaneous indexes – as well as the regular ones - are now available on microfiche at many locations worldwide, and on-line.

The registers originated with the army, and relate primarily to overseas service of the various regiments, but they are now preserved by the Overseas Section of the General Register Office (of England and Wales) at Smedley Hydro, near Southport. They form an extremely important record of military family life, and are quite separate from the main army collections at TNA. Microfiche versions of the indexes are for sale, from the GRO, Smedley Hydro, Trafalgar Road, Birkdale, Southport, Merseyside PR8 2HH. This data may also be searched on-line with a subscription to www.findmypast.com

There are broadly speaking three major series of records, Regimental Registers (1761-1924), Chaplains' Returns (1796-1880) and, from 1881 onwards, Army Returns for those serving outside the UK.

1. Regimental Registers (1761-1924)

These are registers of births, baptisms and marriages of soldiers or members of their families and were compiled by regiments serving overseas. The regiments and the covering dates for each one are quoted in 'A List of Regiments, Corps and Depots from which Records of Marriages, Births and Baptisms and Deaths have been received'. It is also to be found at the end of the microfiche version of these indexes

(Fiche numbers F 1190 and F 1191). A brief summary of the covering dates of these regimental registers is given in Appendix 2 - Lists of Regiments and their Records. It can be seen that the covering dates for the available registers are by no means comprehensive, although there is generally quite a lot of material for the 19th century.

Indexes to all births and baptisms in these registers, for the period 1761 to 1924, are now accessible on microfiche at many centres worldwide, and online.

An example of the entries found in the index is given below for the Hasplink family. In the section on 'Census Returns', it was noted that Henry Hasplink had been born in Jamaica about 1843. The index to regimental births and baptisms confirmed this as well as providing data on other members of the family. Most importantly, the regiment of the father is given, so that army records at TNA can now be used.

Surname & Name of Child	Station	Year	Regiment or Register	Vol	Page
HASPLINK Chas.W	Quebec	1835	60th	1076	7
Chas.W	Quebec	1845	60th	149	148
Harriett	Templemore	1833	60th	1077	24
Harriett	Corfu	-	Ion. Is.	2	50
Harriett	Corfu	-	Ion. Is.	11	122
Henry G	Jamaica	1842	60th	1076	3
John H	Corfu	-	Ion. Is.	2	45

A second example relates to births in the Goodens family, also mentioned above under 'Census Returns'. Again, the required regimental information is given. A full certificate of any required event will provide more details and may be ordered in the usual way from the General Register Office.

Surname & Name of Child	Station	Year	Regiment or Register	Vol	Page
GOODENS Sarah	Dublin	1840	22nd Foot	915	54
Samuel	Poona	1843	do	915	61
Mary E	Poona	1844	do	915	64
Joseph	Coloba	1845	do	915	69
John	Coloba	1845	do	915	69
Catherine	Poona	1847	do	915	74

As in the previous example, one can now go directly to the Soldiers' Documents (WO 97) to find the dates of Samuel Goodens' enlistment and discharge, before proceeding to Muster Books and other documents.

Unfortunately no public index exists in relation to marriages and burials in the Regimental Registers. However, if a researcher has found a baptism of a soldier's child in a particular regiment, then they would be well advised to apply to the General Register Office, to see if the child's parents' marriage was recorded by that regiment. The staff there will then check the relevant marriage register, and advise whether it took place under the auspices of that regiment and, if so, a full certificate can be purchased in the usual way.

An example of an entry in a marriage register was obtained in the described way, for the parents of the character who features in our earlier examples, Henry Hasplink. His father (also Henry) had clearly served in the 60th regiment of foot, later to become the Royal Rifle Corps. A search was conducted in the marriage register of this regiment, revealing the marriage of Private Henry Hasplink, a bachelor, and Elizabeth Wilson, a spinster, at St Paul's, Dublin, on 16th June 1832. (Volume 1076 of Regimental Registers.)

Chaplains' Returns (1796-1880)

In 1796 the Army Chaplains' Department was officially formed under a Chaplain General and their records of baptisms, marriages and burials at stations abroad also commence in that year. A separate series of indexes relating to these registers is therefore available, for the whole period from 1796 to 1880, for each of the three major events: births, marriages and deaths. The regiment name or number is sometimes given in these indexes.

For example:

Index	Surname & Name of Child	Station	Year	Reference (page no)
Birth	Watts Elizabeth	Gibraltar	1840-3	91
Marriage	Watts John	Trinidad	1834	515
Death	Watts Jane	Madeira	1814	270

Army Returns (1881-1955)

The Registration of Births, Marriages and Deaths (Army) Act of 1879 established formally the provision for keeping registers of such events. It was also under this act that the registers described above were transferred to the General Register Office. From 1881 onwards returns were made annually to the GRO, covering births, marriages and deaths connected with army personnel serving overseas. There are several series of indexes available, also in microfiche form and online.

Indexes to the GRO Overseas Registers may be obtained on a set of about 1190 microfiche, or found on-line but in a different arrangement, for example on www.familyrelatives.com. They include the following which relate to army research.

Index to	Covering Dates	GRO fiche number
Army Chaplains - Deaths	1796-1880	001
Army - Deaths	1881-1955	002-018
Service Depts - Deaths	1955-1960	019
War Deaths - Army Other Ranks	1914-1921	113-222
War Deaths - Army Officers	1914-1921	223-234
War Deaths - Army Other Ranks	1939-1948	247-275
War Deaths - Army Officers	1939-1948	276-278
War Deaths - Indian Services	1939-1948	310-311
Natal and S African Forces - Deaths	1899-1902	533-539
Army Chaplains - Births	1796-1880	540-542
Regimental Births	1761-1924	908-1002
Regimental Births - Supplement	1761-1924	1003-1010
Ionian Islands - Military Births	1818-1864	1011-1013
Ionian Islands - Military Deaths	1818-1864	1014
Ionian Islands - Military Marriages	1818-1864	1015
Ionian Islands - Chaplains Births	1818-1864	1019-1020
Ionian Islands - Chaplains Deaths	1818-1864	1021
Ionian Islands - Chaplains Marriages	1818-1864	1022
Army Chaplains - Marriages	1796-1880	1023-1024
Army Marriages	1881-1955	1025-1063
Service Dept Marriages	1956-1965	1064-1073
Marriages Abroad	1966-1994	1134-1185
Army Marriages within British Lines	1914-1925	1186
Lists of Army Registers		1190-1191

If successful in searching the indexes, a certificate may be obtained in the usual way from the Overseas Section of the General Register Office. However, it should be pointed out that very little extra information is given on a war death certificate; cause of death would usually be 'killed in action', location may be very general, such as 'France or Flanders', and the burial place is not given. (The latter may be obtained, from 1914 onwards, from the Commonwealth War Graves Commission – see Chapter 6 - World War I)

From 1956-1965, registration of army events overseas is contained in Service Department Registers, while from 1966 to date, they are to be found in the omnibus Registers of Births Abroad and Registers of Deaths Abroad.

If a soldier ancestor was of Scottish or Irish origin, it is quite possible that a return was additionally made to the GRO Scotland or the GRO Ireland. Further details may be sought in their indexes.

If the event occurred in India, a record may also be found in the Ecclesiastical Returns in the India Office collection now at the British Library.

Medals, Names of Battles and Overseas Service

Many people start their search for an army ancestor with some family tradition such as:'Your grandfather received a medal for his services at Kandahar in 1880', but the medal is now lost. 'One of our ancestors fought in a Norfolk regiment at Waterloo' was the vague clue which started the authors on their delving into army documents and thence to the writing of this book. Similarly, oral tradition may recall service at some particular place overseas.

Where references to medals are concerned, there are published lists of some of the more famous awards, eg the VC, DSO, DCM, the Army of India Medal 1799-1826, the Military General Service Medal 1793-1814. However, for most medals, one would have to visit TNA to consult the various Medal Rolls, WO 100 to WO 102.

If one wishes to identify a regiment from some family tradition about a medal, one may start by consulting Norman's 'Battle Honours of the British Army', which has a comprehensive index. To continue with the example of Kandahar, the chapter on the Second Afghan War shows that the honour for the battle of Kandahar on the 1st September 1880 is borne by no less than 27 units. These include the 9th Lancers, Foot Regiments Nos 7, 60, 66, 72, 92 and numerous forces of the Indian Army, so the search for the regiment has been narrowed down quite a lot. The next step would be to use the army records at TNA, either looking in the medal rolls (WO 100 to WO 102) or in the Muster Books and Pay Lists (WO 12 etc) for these particular regiments.

A similar situation prevails for references to names of battles or campaigns. Norman's book contains a place index from which one may discover which regiments gained battle honours. However, not all regiments which fought or served at a particular location received honours, and a more complete list of regiments must be sought. Again this requires research at TNA, using either Monthly Returns (WO 17), or Monthly Returns, Distribution of the Army (WO 73). Both sets of returns show regiments in numerical order, but WO 73 also includes the distribution of the army by station.

Precise details of honours with dates, full regimental names and Army Order information are contained in Leslie's 'Battle Honours of the British and Indian Armies'. A useful listing of places of service abroad is contained in Kitzmuller's 'In search of the forlorn hope, a guide to locating British regiments and their records'. A brief summary of campaigns and honours is given in Appendix 1. Those interested in medals themselves may seek information from many publications by collectors and dealers, for instance Joslin's compilation for Spink & Son, or William Spencer's book 'Medals: The Researcher's Companion'.

In our own search we had started only with the reference to a 'Norfolk regiment at Waterloo'. Let us see how this might be followed up. The list of regiments which fought at Waterloo was found in Dalton's 'Waterloo Roll Call' which includes a list of all officers who fought at Waterloo. In fact, there is also Dwelly's published list of all the men and NCOs in the cavalry at Waterloo, but regrettably the same author was unable to complete and publish a corresponding list of infantry before his death.

We soon discovered that no Norfolk regiment had actually fought at Waterloo, although the 54th (West Norfolk) had been in reserve and the 9th (East Norfolk) had arrived after the battle to form part of the army of occupation in France. Here were two possibilities to follow up in the army records at TNA. Of course, we did not neglect to look in the published cavalry lists, where we found a Sergeant John Watts in the 11th Light Dragoons and a John Watts in the 7th (Queen's Own) Light

Dragoons. Neither of these regiments had any strong affiliations with Norfolk, but soldiers at this time could actually be recruited almost anywhere, so it was prudent to check the service of both these John Watts at TNA to see if either fitted any of the known facts about our ancestor.

Army indexes now available outside TNA

1760-1854 - Index to Soldiers' Documents (WO 97/1-1271)

There is an extremely useful index to the discharge papers of those soldiers discharged to pension during the period 1760 –1854. This is available on-line through the website www.nationalarchives.gov.uk – all the entries are incorporated in the Catalogue. The records themselves, which extend to 1913, are currently (2008) being digitized and should be on-line by 2010.

A search was made for two soldiers, Edward Smith and Henry Hasplink, both mentioned above in the census section. (On the Search Catalogue page, a full name is placed in the first search box, and WO in the third one.) This results in the following information:

> *WO 97/731/54 HENRY HASPLINK born BANDON Cork, served in the 60th Foot Regiment, 81st Foot Regiment. Discharged aged 40. Covering dates 1820-1846*

Among only 58 Edward Smiths, it was a simple matter to locate:

> *WO 97/884/19 EDWARD SMITH born INGHAM Norfolk, Served in the 77th Foot Regiment. Discharged aged 32. Covering Dates 1834-1849*

(The curious reader, maybe wondering how Henry Hasplink, junior, ended up in 1851 with the family of Edward Smith in Norfolk, will be interested to learn that, according to the IGI, Edward Smith married the widowed Elizabeth Wilson Hasplink at St Thomas Portsmouth on 21st December 1848.)

1787-1813 Index to Chelsea Discharge Documents of Pensioners (WO 121/1-136)

As for the early set of Soldiers' Documents described in the paragraph on WO 97, the soldiers listed in these papers have been indexed into TNA's Catalogue which is also available on-line.

1806-1838 The Beckett Index to Chelsea Pensioners (WO 120/20-30)

This is an index to eleven pieces of the Regimental Registers of Chelsea Pensioners,

Results:

You ran a search on "**john AND watts**" restricted to reference(s): "**WO 97**"

There are **41** results within The Catalogue. Hits 1 to 20 are shown below sorted by date range.

Catalogue:

page 1 2 3 ⊙ ⊗

(Refine search ›)

Sort by: Catalogue reference ❯ | Former reference ❯ | Date range ❯ | Relevance ranking ❯

Catalogue Reference	Title/Scope and Content	Covering Dates
WO 97/628/99	ⓘ JOHN WATT [Not Known] Served in 48th Foot Regiment; other regiment(s) unspecified Discharged aged [Not Known] Covering date gives year of discharge.	1764
WO 97/1120/157	ⓘ JOHN WATTS Born BROMAR, Wiltshire Served in 2nd Royal Veteran Battalion; 31st Foot Regiment; 62nd Foot Regiment; 1st Dragoons Discharged aged 53	1782-1815
WO 97/1202/247	ⓘ JOHN WATT Born [Not Known] Served in 48th Foot Regiment; 4th Invalid Company Discharged aged [Not Known] Covering date gives year of discharge.	1785
WO 97/1111/139	ⓘ JOHN WATTS Born LITTLE NEWCASTLE, Pembroke Served in Pembroke Militia Discharged aged 60	1789-1829
WO 97/806/132	ⓘ JOHN WATT Born MCGUIRES BRIDGE, Fermanagh Served in 67th Foot Regiment; 4th Royal Veteran Battalion; 18th Foot Regiment; 12th Royal Veteran Battalion Discharged aged 48	1792-1813
WO 97/286/82	ⓘ JOHN WATTS Born HASBURY, Norfolk Served in 6th Foot Regiment; 99th Foot Regiment Discharged aged 46	1793-1816
WO 97/1014/61	ⓘ JOHN WATT Born DUSKFORD, Banffshire Served in 92nd Foot Regiment Discharged aged 42	1794-1814
WO 97/417/76	ⓘ JOHN WATT Born KILMADOCK, Lanarkshire Served in 21st Foot Regiment Discharged aged 39	1800-1816

Figure 8 - Index (1760-1854) to Soldiers' Documents, TNA Catalogue Search for John Watts, born 'Hasbury', Norfolk, served 1793-1816, 99th and 6th Regiments of Foot, WO 97/286

WO 120/20-30, and it covers the period 1806-1838. All infantry regiments, Guards and cavalry, but not artillery, have been incorporated into an index of about 82,000 names. Microfiche versions are generally available in record offices, or may be bought from the Manchester and Lancashire Family History Society.

The format of the index is illustrated by the following entries for John and Robert Watts:

Year	Name	Age	Regiment	Birthplace	County
1818	Watts Jn	34	3FG	Wantage	Brk
1826	Watts Jn	40	1FG	Blakesley	Nth
1814	Watts Jn	25	94	Chippenham	Wil
1816	Watts Jn	46	6	Hasbury	Nfk
1808	Watts Jn	49	7	Cawley	Gls
1820	Watts Jn	37	22	Paisley	Rfw
1811	Watts Jn	22	14	Hardington	Nth
1816	Watts Jn	38	7DR	Berkeley	Gls
1820	Watts Jn	27	7DR	Pentonville	Mdx
1817	Watts Robt	42	80	Tyrone	
1812	Watts Robt	36	2FG	Trowbridge	Wil
1806	Watts Robt	92			
1817	Watts Robt	37	1DG	Holstead	Lei

1793-1854 The Beckett Soldiers Index

This index of about 300 000 soldiers, with service between 1793 and 1854, was compiled over a period of forty years by JD Beckett. It includes soldiers from a wide range of sources, as it became apparent to Jim Beckett that many men were not recorded in the usual army pension sources.

The soldiers mentioned above in WO 120/20-30 were firstly brought in. Then more were added from parish registers and census returns. Lists of soldiers were donated by medal collectors who had transcribed the names of thousands of Napoleonic War veterans. Indexes were acquired from military historians with specialist interests. Army deserters for the period 1828-1841 are included, as are British Pensioners Abroad, from the book by Norman Crowder.

The index is appearing in book-form, with its first section, for soldiers beginning with letters A to C, published in 2003. Typical, single-line entries, for five James

Bowens, are as follows:

BOWEN JAS	*HEIC*	*Artillery B. Limerick-IRE 1809. Deserted 1829*
BOWEN JAS	*22Ft*	*B. Dublin-IRE 1817. Pens 1847*
BOWEN JAS	*2FG*	*B. Horstead-Nfk 1795. Waterloo. Pens 1836*
BOWEN JAS	*46Ft*	*Marr Susan Green at St James Poole Dorset Aug 1799*
BOWEN JAS	*55Ft*	*China War 1841-2. Pensioned Madras INDIA May 1843*

1861 Frank Turner's Index of Other Ranks

The Turner Index covers all soldiers from the rank of sergeant-major downwards, for the April-June quarter of 1861, corresponding to the 1861 census. (Of course, the only soldiers who would feature in the 1861 Census would be those located in barracks or elsewhere in the UK.) The index gives number, rank and regiment for every name listed in the Muster Rolls and Pay Lists, that is, in the general pay lists (WO 12), Royal Engineer pay lists (WO 11), and the Royal Artillery pay lists (WO 10). Officers are adequately covered by printed Army lists. An appendix gives where the regiment was stationed and its depot. The July 1862 lists for men of the 19th-21st Dragoons and of the 101st-109th Foot have also been included as the first pay lists of these regiments do not start, excluding their early 19th century lists, until July 1862. These regiments were formed from men who were serving with the East India Company's European regiments, before the British Government took over direct control of India following the mutiny.

The compiler of the 'Army, Other Ranks, April-June 1861' index is Mr FB Turner, 27 Kings Barn Lane, Steyning, West Sussex BN44 3YR, who welcomes enquiries. (email on fanda.turner@tesco.net). It is best to contact him first for a quotation as the number of names supplied can be variable – a total of about 200 000 men are included in this index.

In our own searches, it seemed interesting to see if either of John Watts' sons, Robert and John, had followed him into the army. The list provided by Frank Turner was as follows.

Name		*Regiment*	*Number*	*Rank*	
Watts	*Jno*	*4th Light Dragoons*	*92*		
	John	*3rd Light Dragoons*	*175*		
	John	*4th Light Dragoons*	*1506*	*Orderly Room Clerk*	
	John	*Scots Guards*	*365*		
	John	*3rd Ft 1st Bn*	*3409*	*Cpl John*	*4th Ft*

2nd Bn	1106		
John	7th Ft 1st Bn (Depot)	2428	C/Serg
John	21st Ft 1st Bn (Depot)	327	
John	23rd Ft 1st Bn	4397	
John	23rd Ft 1st Bn	5369	
John	41st Ft	4094	
Jno	86th ft	287	
John	87th Ft	3399/712	
John	96th Ft (Depot)	477	Drummer/Fifer
John	101st Ft	1130	
John	York Recruiting Depot	–	Recruit (for RA)
Robert	6th Ft 1st Bn	1569	C/Serg
Robert	57th Ft (Depot)	2212	

1806 Barbara Chambers' Regimental Indexes (WO 25/871-1120 in progress)

A series of booklets is being produced by Barbara Chambers, who has extracted information on soldiers from what was in effect a census of the whole army in 1806. It can be very difficult to trace a man's army service in the early 19th century, if he was not discharged to pension. In this case, he would not appear in the Soldiers' Documents (WO 97) described above.

The records are to be found in WO 25/871-1120, often termed Service Returns No 1, and are a 'Statement of the periods of service of all the non-Commissioned Officers, Drummers, Fifers and Privates of the ….. Regiment of …… who were liable to serve Abroad on the 24th June 1806'. However, it is clear from the dates of enlistment quoted that the list was extended to cover recruits to the regiment at later dates.

In the original papers, the following column headings are given: rank, surname and forename, trade and place of birth where more than one of the same name, date of enlistment in the present corps, former service if any in this or other corps – or whole period on out pension, deductions made – eg if enlisted under 18 years or absent by desertion, total service, additional period of service, rates of pay, remarks.

In the indexes, only the following extracts are given, from which it is then possible to check the original papers for the further details. surname, forename, enlistment date, rank, regiment and reference number for the required piece of WO 25.

Some examples are given below from the index to the men serving in the 1st (Royal) Regiment of Foot, 1st, 3rd and 4th Battalions (WO 25/909-911), the first volume to be published of this series. Recruits continued to be added to this list up to 1808.

PEARSON John 1793 6 Nov Corporal 1st Foot WO 25/909
PFINGSTON Alex C 1807 13 Jan Boy 1st Foot WO 25/911
SLEADEN Thomas 1799 25 Dec Private 1st Foot WO 25/909

At the time of writing, Barbara Chambers has published year 1806 indexes for the following regiments, in either booklet or fiche form. CD compilation versions are also appearing.

	Unit (see Appendix 2 for further details)	Battalion	WO 25/
Volume 1	1st Foot (Royal)	1,3,4	909-911
Volume 2	2nd Foot (Queen's)	1	912-916
	3rd Foot (Buffs)	1,2	
	4th Foot (King's Own)	1,2	
Volume 3	1st & 2nd Life Guards;		871-873
	Royal Horse Guards (Blues);		
	Dragoon Guards 1st (King's)		877-879
	2nd (Queen's Bays)		
	3rd (Prince of Wales)		
Volume 4	5th Foot (Northumberland)	1,2	917-922
	6th Foot (Warwickshire)	1,2	
	7th Foot (Royal Fusiliers)	1,2	
Volume 5	8th Foot (The King's)	1,2	923-928
	9th Foot (Norfolk)	1,2	
	10th Foot (North Lincolnshire)	1,2	
Volume 6	11th Foot (North Devon)	1	929-933
	12th Foot (East Suffolk)	2	
	13th Foot (1st Somerset)	1	
	14th Foot (Bedfordshire)	1,2	
Volume 7	Dragoon Guards: 4th (Royal Irish)		880-884
	5th (Princess Charlotte of Wales)		
	6th (Carabiniers)		
	7th (Princess Royal's)		
	Dragoons: 1st (Royal)		

Volume 8	15th Foot (Yorkshire East Riding)	1,2	934-939
	16th Foot (Bedfordshire)	1	
	17th Foot (Leicestershire)	1	
	18th Foot (Royal Irish)	1,2	
Volume 9	19th (Princes of Wales' Own Yorks)	1	940-944
	20th Foot (East Devonshire)	1	
	21st Foot (Royal North British)	1,2	
	22nd Foot (Cheshire) 1		
Volume 10	23rd Foot (Royal Welch Fusiliers)	1,2	945-950
	24th Foot (2nd Warwickshire)	1,2	
	25th Foot (King's Own Borderers)	1,2	
Volume 11	Dragoons: 2nd (Royal North British)		885-889
	3rd (King's Own)		
	4th (Queen's Own)		
	5th (Royal Irish - not here - disbanded		
	from 1799-1855), 6th (Inniskilling)		
	7th Light Dragoons (Queen's Own)		
Volume 12	26th (Cameronians)	1,2	951-956
	27th (Inniskilling)	1,2	
	28th (North Gloucestershire)	1,2	
Volume 13	29th (Worcestershire)	1	957-962
	30th (Cambridgeshire)	1,2	
	31st (Huntingdonshire)	1	
	32nd (Duke of Cornwall's Light Infantry)	1,2	
Volume 14	33rd (Yorkshire West Riding)	1	963-967
	34th (Cumberland)	1,2	
	35th (Sussex from 1805)	1,2	
Volume 15	8th (King's Royal Irish),		890-895
	9th (Queen's Royal),		
	10th (Prince of Wales' Own), 11th,		
	12th (Prince of Wales' Royal, &13th Light Dragoons		
Volume 16	36th (Herefordshire)	1,2	968-974
	37th (North Hampshire)	1	
	38th (1st Staffordshire)	1,2	
	39th (East Middlesex from	1,2	
	1807 Dorsetshire)		
Volume 17	14th(Duke of York's) Light Dragoons;		896-901
	15th(King's) Light		
	Dragoons, 16th, 17th 18th &		
	19th Light Dragoons		

Volume 18	40th (2nd Somerset)		1,2	975-980
	41st (The Welsh)	1		
	42nd (Royal Highland)	1,2		
	43rd (Monmouthshire)	1,2		

A CD is now available for the 1st to 25th Regiments of Foot, as listed above. The information for cavalry regiments, volumes 3, 7 and 11, is not on this CD, as it is planned to produce a separate cavalry CD when all their returns have been indexed.

Up to date information on the above volumes and on other publications by Barbara Chambers may be obtained from her at 9, Hunter Steading, Innerwick, Dunbar, East Lothian EH42 1SR, or by email bj.chambers@mypostoffice.co.uk .Her website is http://webspace.mypostoffice.co.uk/~bj.chambers/homepage.html

1775-1817 - 1st or Grenadier Foot Guards - Barbara Chambers' Index

Records for the Grenadier Guards are held at their headquarters. Barbara Chambers has produced a database to surviving attestations and other documents for the period 1775-1817. This index is now available on CD - see previous section for contact details.

1803 - Army of Reserve - Barbara Chambers' Index

With the renewal of war with France in 1803, the threat of invasion of Britain was also resumed. Acts of Parliament were passed to raise or augment County Militia regiments and Volunteer forces. Ballots were also organized to make up numbers if volunteers were insufficient. There were many categories of exemption, while balloted persons were permitted to find substitutes. In theory at any rate, men who had enlisted in the Army of Reserve were not to be compelled to serve outside Great Britain, Ireland or the Channel Islands, unless they freely and voluntarily chose to transfer to a regiment for general service. The system was complicated and difficult to maintain. The sixteen Reserve battalions were merged in 1805, and many men were transferred to Garrison battalions by the end of 1806.

Currently, Barbara Chambers' index features all counties of England and Wales, with over 26 000 names. It is hoped to cover records for Scotland and Ireland. The indexes give surname, forename, parish (usually), county, whether balloted or substitute, regiment or reserve battalion. Most of the information has been gleaned from E 182, some from WO 12. The eleven booklets or fiche sets are being replaced by a composite CD, which is already available.

1855-1872 Miss Davis's Index to Soldiers' Documents (WO 97/1272-1721)

Miss SL Davis has personally indexed the papers of soldiers discharged to pension over the period 1855 to 1872. These are from WO 97/1272-1721. This is a very useful index, as it covers the time when many soldiers were discharged after the Crimean campaign, some having served a relatively short time. Also it bridges the gap between the index for 1760-1854 (see above) and the later pieces of WO 97, from 1873 to 1882, which are more conveniently arranged - actually in seven alphabetical sequences.

The index provides the WO 97 reference, regiment, age at enlistment (quoting year and place thereof) and gives the stated birthplace. This index also includes items from a 'Supplementary Series' of miscellaneous papers which must have been filed separately or at a later date. These are from WO 97/6355-6383 and relate to the period 1843-1899. A total of about 97 000 soldiers are contained in the index, of whom about a third were born in Ireland.

Application should be made to Miss SL Davis, 18 Manor Road, East Molesey, Surrey KT8 9JX, initially enclosing an SAE and requesting the fee involved, or email postmaster@ArchivesResearch.co.uk

1781-1782 Militia Musters by Family History Indexes (WO 13)
These indexes have been made from the militia muster and pay lists in WO 13. The lists provide details of each man at the three or four musters during the two year period, 1781-1782. County regiments, although recruited locally, often served away from home and these indexes tell precisely where, under whom and on what dates the men were mustered. The indexes are available on either fiche, 3 ½ inch disks or CD. An index is published for each county, though some larger counties feature on two or three disks eg Devon East, Devon North and Devon South. Further details are on the website www.fhindexes.co.uk

Indexes to Militia Attestation Papers (WO 96) and other indexes by Jenifer Edmonds

Indexes to Attestation Papers for Militia Regiments, from WO 96, are available from Jenifer Edmonds. Postal enquiries to 51 Horns Lane, Norwich, Norfolk NR1 3ER. These indexes are on fiche, diskette and CD.

The documents themselves show soldier's name, birthplace, residence and employer, together with a personal description, service record, next of kin and whether they transferred to the Regular Army. The indexes published listed below, part of a very large ongoing project, give an idea of the range of material covered.

Index to Militia unit	Years
Antrim, Ulster & Waterford RGA	1886-1910
Carmarthen Royal Garrison Artillery	1882-1912
Cheshire Regiment (Militia)	1892-1907
Clare RGA	1884-1910
Cornwall & Devon Miners RGA	1885-1912
Cork RGA	1886-1911
Devon RGA	1882-1911
Donegal RGA	1886-1910
Dorset Regiment (Militia)	1862-1901
Dublin RGA	1884-1915
Duke of Cornwall's Light Infantry	1880-1909
Edinburgh & SE Scotland RGA	1882-1913
Essex Regiment (Militia)	1886-1910
Fife RGA	1882-1911
Forfar & Kincardine RGA	1881-1915
Hants and Isle of Wight RGA	1875-1912
Kent RGA	1872-1913
East Kent 3rd Foot Regiment, The Buffs (Militia)	1874-1895
Limerick RGA	1874-1912
Lincolnshire 10th Foot Regiment (Militia)	1870-1903
Londonderry RGA	1872-1910
Middlesex Regiment (Militia)	1860-1901
Norfolk Regiment (Militia)	1882-1906
Norfolk RGA	1874-1912
Northumberland RGA	1874-1912
South East Scotland Regiment (Militia)	1877-1913
Sligo RGA	1872-1911
Suffolk Regiment (Militia)	1887-1908
Suffolk RGA	1872-1912
Surrey – 2nd Foot Queen's Royal West Surrey (Militia)	1881-1895
Sussex RGA	1877-1913
Tipperary RGA	1886-1912
Wicklow RGA	1874-1912
York and Lancaster Regiment (Militia)	1882-1902

Details of the latest militia indexes and of other publications by Jenifer Edmonds may be found on her website www.jenlibrary.u-net.com.

A partial index to these militia papers, based on the work done by Jenifer Edmonds, is also available on-line via British Origins where it is described as a Militia Attestations Index 1860-1915. Website: www.britishorigins.com

The whole series of papers, WO 96, is currently (2008) in the process of digitization and should be available on-line by 2010.

Miscellaneous

Needless to say, there are many sources that could lead one to discover the regiment of a soldier ancestor other than the major ones, or the newly available indexes described above. Foremost among these must be family papers, or recollections, which are always first sought by any serious genealogist, however remote the relative or family friend may be.

Local newspapers may be searched near a relevant date, possibly of enlistment, to see which regiments had been recruiting in a particular area. However, there is no guarantee, especially around the start of the 19th century, that a regiment associated with a particular county was the only one to recruit soldiers in that county.

To conclude this section, we will summarise the full extent of the information with which we started our own search. There was the oral tradition of an ancestor fighting in a Norfolk regiment at Waterloo. When great-great-grandfather John Watts died at Happisburgh, Norfolk, in 1846, the occupation on his death certificate was given as soldier. None of the methods described above had led us to the number or name of his regiment. Sadly for us, the Beckett Index of Chelsea Pensioners was not published until 1990. We had to seek John Watts' regiment using the army sources available at the Public Record Office, now The National Archives. This is the procedure which will be outlined in the next section.

B. FINDING THE REGIMENT USING SOURCES AT THE NATIONAL ARCHIVES

If all the sources suggested above in Section A have failed to reveal an ancestor's regiment, then the next step must be to visit the National Archives at Kew and consult the original army records preserved there. An alternative is to use, where they are available, microform copies of these records, eg at LDS libraries.

The following table lists some possible starting points, roughly in chronological order, except that medals and awards have been placed at the head of the list. A commentary and further information follow the table.

WO 100/1-397	Campaign Medals	1793-1912
WO 101/1-7	Meritorious Service Awards	1846-1919
WO 102/1-16	Long Service & Good Conduct Awards	1831-1902
WO 146/1-155	Distinguished Conduct Medal	1855-1909

WO 25/1121-1131	Service Returns No 3, Discharges	1783-1810
WO 25/871-1120	Service Returns No 1	24th June 1806
WO 25/1196-1358	Muster Master Generals' Index of Casualties	1797-1817
WO 25/1359-2410	Casualty Returns	ca 1810-1840
WO 25/2411-2755	Index to Casualty Returns	ca 1810-1840
WO 22/1-300	Royal Hospital Chelsea Pension Returns	1842-1862
WO 23/26-65	Chelsea Registers of Out-Pensioners	ca 1820-1875

If discharged to pension:

WO 97/1722-2170	Soldiers' Documents Alphabetical for each of	1873-1882
WO 97/1722-1762	Cavalry	
WO 97/1763-1848	Royal Artillery	
WO 97/1849-1857	Royal Engineers	
WO 97/1858-1870	Foot Guards	
WO 97/1871-2147	Infantry	
WO 97/2148-2170	Corps and Miscellaneous Units	

If not killed in service:

WO 97/2171-6322	Soldiers' Documents Alphabetical for whole of Army	1883-1913

NB If a man went on to serve during World War I then his records would normally have been removed from WO 97 and placed with his WWI service records.

The table above comprises the 'Army Sources' which one could use on a first visit to TNA if the regiment of a soldier ancestor was still not known. Some words of guidance and warning may be helpful. There is no general index to other ranks prior to 1914. However, some sources are maybe more accessible than others as a starting point, and this section is intended to be an initial guide to their use for this purpose.

Medals

The first four sources relate to medals. Taking the Kandahar example further one can now refer to the series of Campaign Medals in WO 100 to see if the soldier sought was a recipient of the 'Kabul to Kandahar Star 1880'. Reference to the Series List will show that piece numbers 51 to 53 relate to the Afghan campaign from 1878 to 1880. (See also a brief list of Campaigns and Medals in Appendix 1.) The lists of recipients are arranged by regiment, but a complete search should not be a lengthy task. If the required soldier was not found in the medal rolls, then it would be worth searching the Muster Books and Pay Lists (WO 16 etc) of the regiments present at Kandahar.

The use of the remainder of the table depends very much on the approximate dates when a soldier may have served and on any other clues one may have accumulated. For the period from about 1783 until 1817, there are three complementary returns under **Registers, Various in WO 25**, which should cover all soldiers during the 'Napoleonic period', a time when the British army underwent first a dramatic expansion, then contraction.

These are:

Service Returns No 3 - Discharges 1783-1810   These twelve volumes (WO 25/1121-1131) contain lists of all soldiers discharged, other than by death or for a casualty, during this period. In the words of the time, they list soldiers who were 'discharged between 25 Dec 1783 and 24 June 1806, but were not known to be dead or disqualified from service' ie they were possibly available for recall. The attraction of these volumes is that each one contains data for several (ten to twenty) regiments, so that the whole army is covered by only twelve pieces. For example, WO 25/1125 covers the 1st to 17th Foot. If it is suspected that your soldier came into this category, it would be a practical proposition to search the whole army in these lists for soldiers of the required name.

Service Returns No 1 - 24th June 1806   These have been introduced already, under the Index section, as Barbara Chambers is progressively publishing indexes to what is effectively a census of the army on this date in 1806 (WO 25/871-1120). If one has some hint of possible regiments in which a soldier may have served, then these returns would be well worth looking at. There are some 250 volumes, so a complete search would not be merited. There is one piece per battalion, with the soldiers listed alphabetically giving their full name, rank and details of service. For example, from WO 25/919 for the 1st Battalion of the 6th Foot:

Rank	*Corporal*
Surname	*Watts*
Christian Name	*John*
Trades and Places of Birth where	
more than one of the same name	
Date of Enlistment in the present Corps	*14th April 1796*
Former Service in this or other Corps	
or whole period on the Out-Pension	
Corps or Out-Pension	*99th Foot*
From	*6th March 1793*
To	*13th April 1796*

In each Corps when in more than one, to the	*99th*	*3 years 39 days*
24th June 1806, or half the period on	*6th*	*10 years 72 days*
the Out-Pension		
	Total	*13 years 111 days*

Entitled to pay for Corporal; served more than 7 but less than 14 years.

Muster Master Generals' Index of Casualties - 1797-1817 These contain lists of all soldiers rendered ineffective due to casualty during this period; there is usually one piece per battalion within which soldiers are arranged alphabetically giving the date and place of casualty (WO 25/1196-1358). Of course, in the army the term 'casualty' referred to anyone who had ceased to be actively present for whatever reason. Death, going missing or being invalided were obvious reasons, but being transferred to another battalion or regiment, being promoted or demoted were also reasons for inclusion in these lists.

An example taken from the index for the 6th Foot (1st Battalion to 1817, 2nd Battalion to 1815) in WO 25/1227 contains:

Names		*Casualties*	
Watts, Hugh	*(Pte)*	*Dischd*	*24 Nov (1800)*
Watts, Willm	*(Pte)*	*Struck off*	*24 Sept 1802*
Watts, Jno (Corp)		*Fm 1o*	*31 July (1805)*
		To 1o	*1 Sept 1807*
Watts, John	*(Pte)*	*To 2 Battn*	*25 July 1813*
Watts, John	*(Pte)*	*To Out Pension*	*16 Aug (1816)*

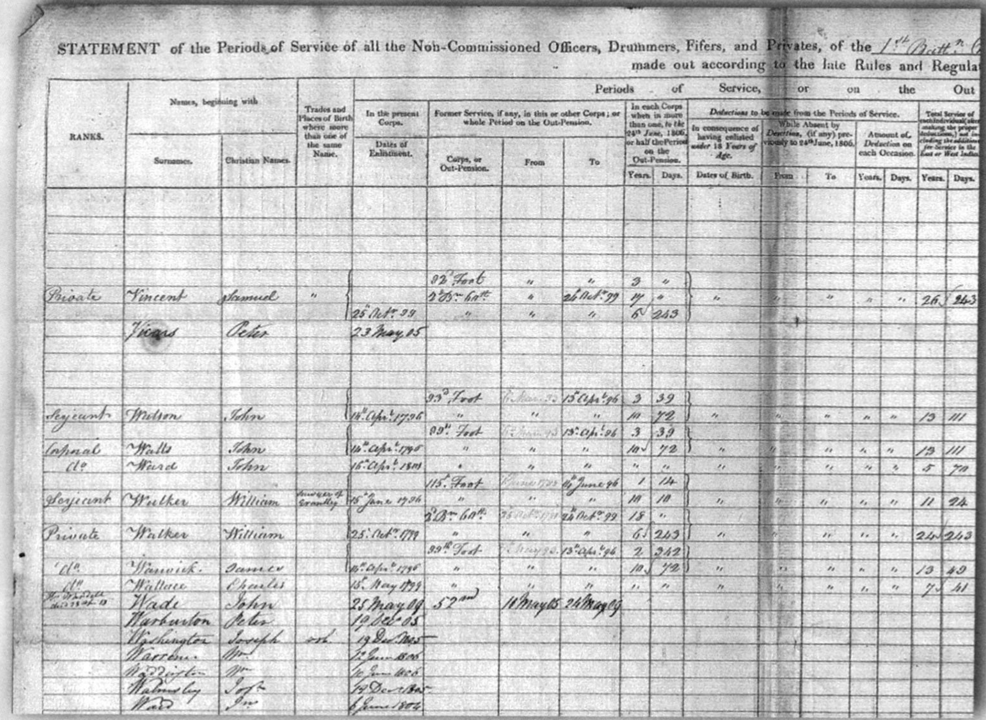

STATEMENT of the Periods of Service of all the Non-Commissioned Officers, Drummers, Fifers, and Privates, of the 1st Batt.n 6[illegible] made out according to the late Rules and Regula[tions]

Ranks	Surnames	Christian Names	Trades and Places of Birth where more than one of the same Name	In the present Corps: Dates of Enlistment	Former Service: Corps, or Out-Pension	From	To	In each Corps: Years	Days	Deductions, in consequence of having enlisted under 18 Years of Age: Dates of Birth	While Absent by Desertion: From	To	Amount of Deduction: Years	Days	Total Service: Years	Days
					92d Foot	"	"	3	"							
Private	Vincent	Samuel	"		2d Bn 60th	"	26 Oct 99	17	"	"	"	"	"	"	26	243
				25 Oct 99	"	"	"	6	243							
	Vicars	Peter		23 May 05												
					93d Foot	[illegible]	15 Apr 96	3	39							
Serjeant	Wilson	John		14 Apr 1796	"	"	"	10	72	"	"	"	"	"	13	111
					99th Foot	[illegible]	13 Apr 96	3	39							
Corporal	Watts	John		14 Apr 1796	"	"	"	10	72	"	"	"	"	"	13	111
Do	Ward	John		16 Apr 1801	.	"	"	"	"	"	"	"	"	"	5	70
					115 Foot	[illegible]	14 June 96	1	14							
Serjeant	Walker	William	[illegible]	15 June 1796	"	"	"	10	10	"	"	"	"	"	11	24
					2d Bn 60th	[illegible]	24 Oct 99	18	"							
Private	Walker	William		25 Oct 1799	"	"	"	6	243	"	"	"	"	"	24	243
					99th Foot	[illegible] May 93	13 Apr 96	2	342							
Do	Warwick	James		14 Apr 1796	"	"	"	10	72	"	"	"	"	"	13	49
Do	Wallace	Charles		15 May 1799	"	"	"	"	"	"	"	"	"	"	7	41
[illegible]	Wade	John		25 May 09	52nd	11 May 05	24 May 09									
	Warburton	Peter		19 Dec 05												
	Washington	Joseph	[illegible]	19 Dec 1805												
	Warren	Wm		1 June 1806												
	Waddington	Wm		4 June 1806												
	Walmsley	Jos		14 Dec 1805												
	Ward	Jn		6 June 1806												

See Line 4: Corporal John Watts, served in 99th Foot, 6 March 1793 to 13 April 1796, in present Corps (6th Foot), 14 April 1796 to 24 June 1806; Total 13 years 111 days

Figure 9 - Service Returns Number One, 24th June 1806, 6th Foot 1st Battalion, WO 25/919

Following these three indexes, which apply predominantly for the duration of the Napoleonic conflicts, a series of **Casualty Returns** is available for the period ca 1810 to ca 1840 (WO 25/1359-2410). Again the task of searching the Returns is made easier by the provision of an index (WO 25/2411-2755), but even the latter contains 345 pieces and it would only be worth a lengthy search if one was quite certain that a soldier had served during this time and had not been discharged to pension.

If a soldier was **discharged to pension** during the nineteenth century then any of the three remaining sets of documents listed at the end of the above table may be utilised in an attempt to find the regiment in which he served. These are the Pension Returns (for the Royal Hospital Chelsea) (WO 22), Chelsea Registers of Out-Pensioners (contained in WO 23) and Soldiers' Documents (WO 97).

Pension Returns (WO 22) primarily for 1842-1862

These exist for the whole of the British Isles in WO 22. At first sight this may not appear to be a promising period for investigation, but the arrangement of these Pension Returns makes them particularly useful. They were the means by which we found the regiment of our soldier ancestor John Watts.

The key to their use is that they are arranged by Pension District. Prior to 1842 it would appear that soldiers' pensions were distributed by local officials; 1842 saw the institution of the army's own system of payment in 59 districts in England, 2 in Wales, 12 in Scotland and 33 in Ireland. Thus, if one knows the part of the country in which a soldier ancestor lived, then reference to that area's Pension Returns may well be worthwhile.

The Returns are not records of regular payments to pensioners. A soldier will be found in these so-called Pension Returns – broadly speaking – if he transferred to or from a District, if he was a new out-pensioner, if the pension rate was changed in any way, or if pensions ceased due to death or felony, during the stated period.

It can be seen therefore that these returns could include Peninsula and Waterloo veterans, many of whom would survive to – and then die during – that period, as well as the Crimea pensioners who were discharged to pension in the 1850s.

An example is given below of the Pension Returns, that for the Norwich District, 1842-1852 (WO 22/76). This was the appropriate district for the village of Happisburgh, on the north-east coast of Norfolk, where our suspected soldier ancestor John Watts lived. After much searching we had finally confirmed that he had been a soldier and we had now discovered which regiment he had served in.

Quarterly Return for Outpensioners of Chelsea Hospital for
1 October to 31 December 1846

VI Pensions ceased by death

Regt	Rate of pension	Rate of poundage	Rank and Name of pensioner	Pension Permt. or Tempy.	Date of Decease	Age at Decease
6	1/1	5	*John Watts*	*Permt.*	*1 Novr.*	76

These Pension Returns must be considered a major potential source for the determination of a soldier's regiment and it is therefore worthwhile listing the centres at which pensions were paid. There are usually two volumes, each covering a ten-year period for each district.

Returns are available for all centres for both periods 1842-1852 and 1852-1862, unless indicated here by
(1) = Returns for 1842-1852 only, or by
(2) = Returns for 1852-1862 only.

England

Bath; Birmingham; Bolton; Brighton; Cambridge; Canterbury; Carlisle; Chatham; Chester; Coventry; Deptford; Derby; Durham (1); Exeter; Falmouth; Gloucester; Halifax; Hull; Ipswich; Leeds; Leicester; Lincoln; Liverpool 1st ; Liverpool 2nd (2); London 1st East; London 2nd East; London 3rd East (2); London 1st West; London 2nd West; London 1st North; London 2nd North; London South; London Woolwich; Lynn; Manchester 1st; Manchester 2nd; Newcastle; Northampton; Norwich; Nottingham; Oxford; Plymouth 1st ; Plymouth 2nd ; Plymouth 3rd (2); Portsmouth 1st ; Portsmouth 2nd ; Preston; Salisbury; Salop; Sheffield; Southampton; Stafford; Stockport; Taunton; Trowbridge; Wolverhampton; Worcester; York (2).

Wales
West; East

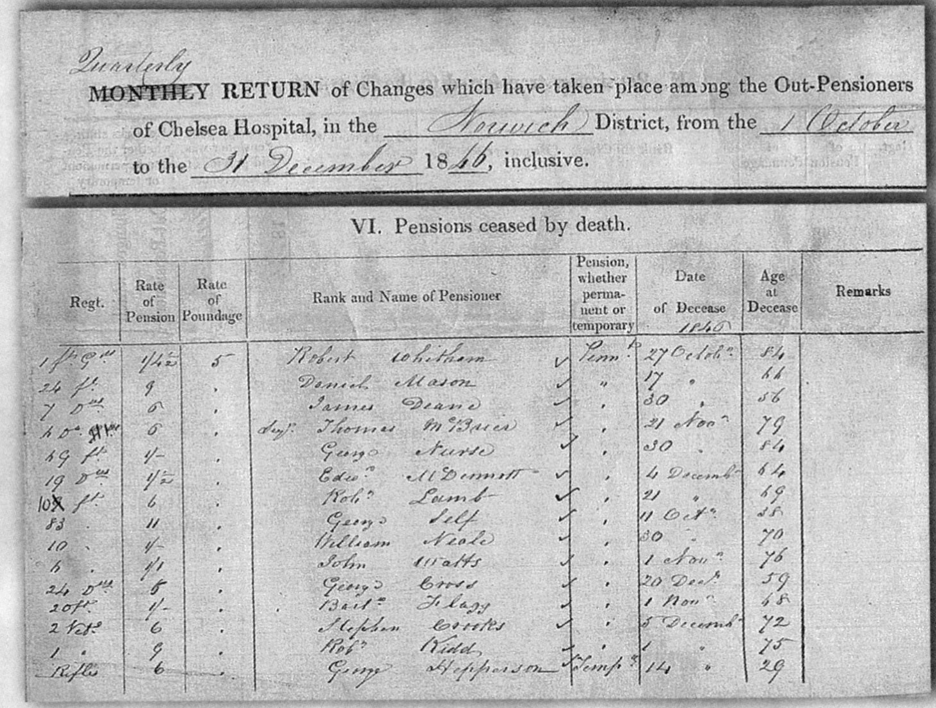

VI. Pensions ceased by death.

Regt.	Rate of Pension Poundage	Rank and Name of Pensioner	Pension, whether permanent or temporary	Date of Decease	Age at Decease	Remarks
1st G.G.	1/1½	5	Robert Whitham	Tem	27 Octobr 1846	84	
24 f.t.	2		David Mason		17	64	
7 D.R	5		James Dean		do	58	
10 L.D	½		Serj.t Thomas McGuire		24 Novr	79	
19 f.t	1/.		Geo.o Leete		do	64	
19 D.R	1/2		Geo.o McDermot		4 Decembr	64	
10 f.t	6		Robt Lunt		21	69	
83	11		Geo.o Self		11 Octr	35	
10	11/.		William Lind		do	70	
6	1/1		John Watts		1 Novr	76	
24 D.R	6		George Orr		22 Decr	59	
20 f.t	1/.		Ralph Athay		1 Novr	65	
2 f.t	6		Stephen Evans		9 Decembr	72	
1	8		Robt Webb		1	75	
Rifle	6		Geo.o Stephenson	Perm	14	29	

See Line 10: 6th Foot, Pension 1/1, John Watts, Date of Decease 1 November, Age 76

Figure 10 - Pension Returns for Norwich District (1842-1852), Quarterly Changes which have taken place among the Out-pensioners of Chelsea Hospital, WO 22/76

Scotland

Aberdeen; Ayr (2); Dundee; Edinburgh 1st ; Edinburgh 2nd ; Glasgow 1st ; Glasgow 2nd ; Inverness; Paisley; Perth; Stirling: Thurso

Ireland

Armagh; Athlone; Ballymena; Belfast 1st ; Belfast 2nd (2); Birr; Boyle (1); Carlow (1); Cavan; Charlemont; Clonmel (1); Cork 1st ; Cork 2nd ; Drogheda; Dublin 1st; Dublin 2nd; Ennis; Enniskillen; Fermoy; Galway; Kilkenny; Limerick; Londonderry; Longford; Maryborough (1); Monaghan; Newry; Omagh; Roscommon; Sligo; Tralee; Tullamore; Waterford

Overseas

Canada West (2); Channel Islands (1); Isle of Man (2); Jersey (2); Miscellaneous (2)

There are a few further returns for some Irish centres in 1882-1883 and some returns for pensioners on convict ships in 1862-1867. For descendants of soldiers who emigrated, there is also a series of returns covering the period 1845 to 1880 for Australia, Bengal, Black Pensions, Bombay, Canada, Cape of Good Hope, Ceylon, Colonies, Consuls, Hanoverian, India office, Madras, Malta, New South Wales, New Zealand, Nova Scotia, Queensland, Tasmania and Victoria. Rosemary Oliver has pointed out that it may not be sufficient to search the volumes for the obvious county town and that pensioners sometimes went to a more convenient place, eg to Carlisle from Annan, or to Sheffield from Worksop.

Admissions Registers of Chelsea Out-Pensioners (WO 23/26-65) for 1820-1875

If one has not been successful in locating a soldier using the District Pension Returns for the period 1842 to 1862 , it may well be that he commenced his pension before 1842 and died after 1862. In this case, there is a further series of pension registers which should be searched. These are the Admissions Registers of Chelsea Out-Pensioners (WO 23/26-65), which cover the period from about 1820 to 1875. They are arranged by regiment, but each volume contains a list of pensioners for about ten to fifteen regiments. If all else had failed, it might be practicable to search all forty pieces of this class. Typically the following information, taken from the Chelsea Hospital Admissions Register, ca 1821-1854, 1st-9th Foot (WO 23/36), would be given:

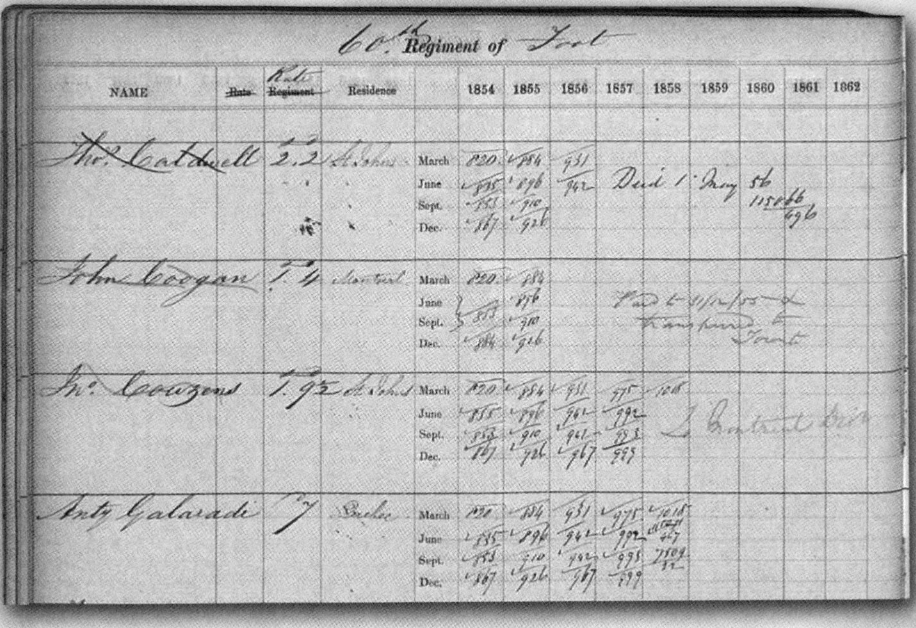

60th Regiment of Foot

NAME	~~Rate~~ Rate	~~Regiment~~	Residence		1854	1855	1856	1857	1858	1859	1860	1861	1862
Thos Caldwell	2.2		St Johns	March	820	884	931						
				June	835	896	942	Died 1 May 56					
				Sept.	853	910					1150 66 / 496		
				Dec.	867	926							
John Coogan	1.4		Montreal	March	820	884							
				June		896		Paid to 31/12/55 & transferred to Toront					
				Sept.	853	910							
				Dec.	884	926							
Jno Couzens	1.9½		St Johns	March	820	884	931	975	1018				
				June	855	896	961	992	to Montreal Dist				
				Sept.	853	910	961	983					
				Dec.	867	926	967	995					
Anty Galaradi	7		Quebec	March	820	884	931	975	1018				
				June	835	896	942	992					
				Sept.	853	910	942	993					
				Dec.	867	926	967	999					

Thom Caldwell	2/2	St John's	died 1 May 1856
John Coogan	1/4	Montreal	paid to 31/12/55 & transferred to Toronto
Jno Couzens	1/9½	St John's	to Montreal District
Anty Galaradi	7d	Quebec	

Figure 11 - Pension Returns for discharges in the Colonies from the 60th Regiment of Foot, Canada, 1854-1861, WO 22/242

6th Foot	Rate	Date of Admission	Residence	Died
Jno Watts	1/1	16th August 1816	Walsham Norfolk Norwich	1st Nov 1846
Saml Whitcomb	1/1 16th August 1816		London 2nd West	-

Although this Admissions Register is nominally for 1821 to 1854, it can be seen that earlier admissions had been copied in, presumably to make a current register of surviving pensioners. This feature may be regarded as typical of pension records, in that there are many overlaps and duplications; all possible registers should be searched.

The whole range of Chelsea Registers is described in the next chapter, on Sources for Other Ranks prior to 1914. It will be shown that the above entry, from WO 23/36, is virtually duplicated in the Chelsea Hospital Regimental Registers, under WO 120/55. Therefore, as an alternative to WO 23/26-65, it would be equally valid to search WO 120/20-30, for 1806-1838, or WO 120/52-64, which records pensions paid between 1845 and 1854 with additions to 1857, and deaths noted to 1877. Details of the Beckett Index to Chelsea Pensioners are given above, under 'Army Indexes now available outside TNA'.

Soldiers' Documents (WO 97) for 1873-1913

Finally we reach the period from 1873 to 1913. The table shows that for the first ten years, from 1873 to 1882, the Soldiers' Documents (WO 97) of all pensioners are arranged alphabetically for each of the main sections of the army ie for cavalry, foot guards, infantry, artillery, engineers and other corps. Hence one can proceed directly to these papers and discover which regiment or unit a soldier belonged to. If a soldier was not discharged to pension in this period, 1873-1882, then there is no easy way to find which regiment he served in, in order to gain access to the muster books and pay lists.

For the remaining thirty years, from 1883 to 1913, the outlook for finding evidence of any soldier who was not killed in service rises to a near certainty. The Soldiers' Documents for the whole army are arranged alphabetically in over 4 000 boxes. Sadly the corresponding papers have not survived for those killed in service.

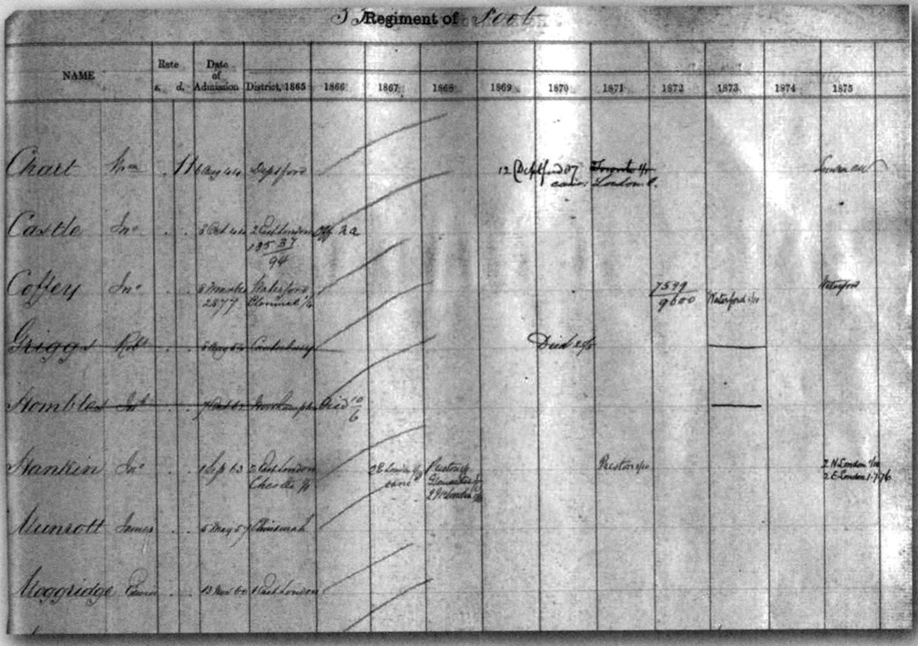

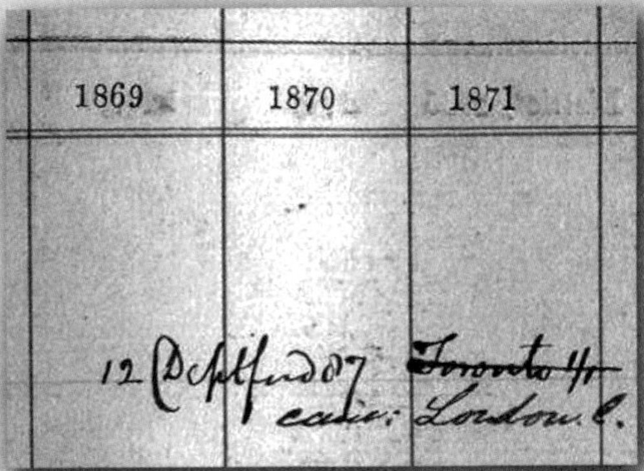

NAME	Rate s. d.	Date of Admission	District 1865	1866	1867	1868	1869	1870	1871	1872	1873	1874	1875
Chart	Wm	1 May 44	Deptford				12 Deptford D07 can London	Toronto Un London C					London
Castle	Jno	5 Oct 44	2 E.London 1853 37/94	22									
Coffey	Jno	4 March 1877	Halifax Clonmel 76							1599 9600	Waterford 80		Waterford
Griggs	Rt	1 May 60	Canterbury				Died 69						
Hombles	Jas	9 June	London Enfield 10/6										
Hankin	Jno	1 Sep 63	2 E.London Chorlton 76		CE.London 1 came	Restored Somerset E.Wilmslow 73			Restored 72		N London Un 2 E.London 1776		
Munrott	James	6 May 5	Portsmouth										
Moggridge		10 Nov 60	Wellington										

Figure 12 - Admissions Register of Chelsea Out-pensioners showing changes of payment district, WO 23/59

CHAPTER FOUR

Other Ranks - prior to 1914
Major Sources

Introduction

In this section the major sources of information about other ranks during the period prior to 1914 are described. It is now assumed that the soldier's regiment is known. The main sources include Soldiers' Documents, Muster Books and Pay Lists, Description Books and Hospital Records for Chelsea and Kilmainham. Some guidance is also given on Deserters and Courts Martial. The emphasis for these sources will be in relation to the cavalry, foot guards and infantry. A final section summarises the material available for the artillery, engineers, other corps, militia and volunteers.

Soldiers' Documents

Soldiers' Documents for Royal Hospital, Chelsea (WO 97)

The so-called Soldiers' Documents (WO 97) for the Royal Hospital at Chelsea are the best starting point for details of a soldier's career. They are believed to have survived, however, only for soldiers who were discharged to pension between 1760 and 1882 – or, for the later period from 1883 to 1913, only for those who were not killed in service. The survival rate of

discharge papers appears to be low for men discharged overseas. As mentioned earlier, these Soldiers' Documents are currently (2008) being digitized and should be available on-line in 2010. Similar documents for those discharged via the Royal Hospital, Kilmainham, near Dublin in Ireland, are referred to below.

The broad arrangement of the Chelsea Soldiers' Documents is given in the following table.

	Arrangement	Year of Discharge
Soldiers Discharged to Pension		
WO 97/1-1271	By regiment number, then soldiers' names alphabetically	1760-1854
WO 97/1272-1721	By regiment in numerical order, then soldiers'names alphabetically	1855-1872
WO 97/1722-2170	Alphabetical for each of	1873-1882
WO 97/1722-1762	Cavalry	
WO 97/1763-1848	Royal Artillery	
WO 97/1849-1857	Royal Engineers	
WO 97/1858-1870	Foot Guards	
WO 97/1871-2147	Infantry	
WO 97/2148-2170	Corps and Miscellaneous Units	

Soldiers Not Killed in Service

WO 97/2171-6322	Alphabetical for whole of army	1883-1913

Supplementary Series from Misfiled Documents

WO 97/6355-6383	Alphabetical	1843-1899
WO 97/6323-6354	Alphabetical	1900-1913

(NB If a man went on to serve during World War I then his records would normally have been removed from WO 97 and placed with his WWI service records. This feature, together with the fact that records for soldiers killed in service overseas do not survive, probably accounts for the difficulty in finding papers for those who served in the South African wars.)

Soldiers' Documents comprise discharge and, very often, attestation papers. They usually include details of age, birthplace, trade or occupation on enlistment, physical description, statement of service and reason for discharge to pension. From the 1860s a medical history may well be included and from 1883 the papers usually refer to next-of-kin, wife and children. The amount of information included depends very much on the date. A typical example of a relatively early document is afforded by that for John Watts, consisting of a single folded sheet (from WO 97/286).

6th Foot	P John Watts	31st May (18)16	(Cover)
Aged 46	Served 20 4/12		
	99th 3 1/12	23 5/12 (years)	
Worn Out	Hasbury Norfolk	A Gardiner	

I, John Watts, do acknowledge that I have received all my Clothing, Pay, Arrears of Pay and all Just Demands whatsoever from the time of my enlisting in the Regiment mentioned on the other Side, to this Day of my Discharge in Witness my hand this 24 th Day of April 1816.

J Hayes
Sergt Major   *his*
6th Regt   *Jno*   *X*   *Watts*
         mark

I do hereby Certify that the cause which has rendered it Necessary to Discharge the within Mentioned John Watts as stated on the opposite Side has not been from Vice or Misconduct and that he is not to my Knowledge incapacitated by the Sentence of a General Court Martial from receiving his Pension.

John Fisher   *A Campbell*
Surgeon 6th Regt   *Lt Colonel Com.*

                      (Inside of sheet)
His Majestys 6th (or 1st Warwickshire) Regiment of Foot whereof General Sir George Nugent Bt VGCB is Colonel

These are to Certify that John Watts Private in Capt Jas Thomson's Company in the Regiment aforesaid born in the Parish of Hasbury in or near the Town of Hasbury in the County of Norfolk hath served in this Regiment for the Space of Ten [sic] years and One Hundred and Fourteen Days, as likewise in other Corps according to the following Statement but in consequence of being Worn Out, is considered unfit for further Service abroad and is proposed to be Discharged and has been ordered by John Fisher, Surgeon to the 6th Reg Depot that his case may be finally determined on having first received all Just Demands of Pay, Clothin &c from his Entry into the said Regiment to the Date of this Discharge as appears by the Receipt on the back hereof.

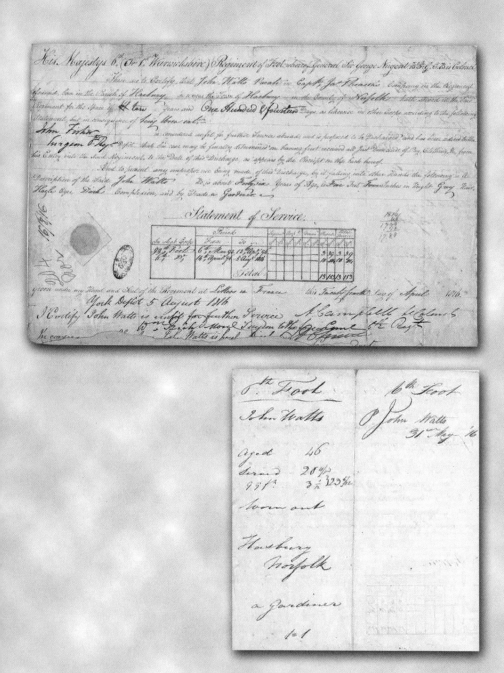

Figure 13 - Soldiers' Document, Discharge Paper for John Watts, from 6th Foot, 1816, Discharge Details, WO 97/286

And to prevent any improper use being made of this Discharge, by it falling into other
Hands, the following is a Description of the said John Watts. He is about Fortysix
Years of Age, is Five Feet Four Inches in Height Grey Hair Hazle Eyes Dark
Complexion and by Trade a Gardiner

Statement of Service

	Period		Total Service (all as Private)	
In What Corps	*From*	*To*	*Years*	*Days*
99th Foot	*6th Mar 93*	*13th Apr 96*	*3*	*39*
6th Foot	*14th Apr 96*	*5th Aug 1816*	*10[sic]*	*114*
		Total	*13[sic]*	*153*

Given under my Hand and Seal of the Regiment at Lillers in France this Twenty fourth
day of April 1816

        A Campbell Lt Colonel 6th Regt

York Depot 5 August 1816

I certify John Watts is unfit for further Service   Wm Richs Mo.... Surgeon to the .....

Later, documents were set out on a variety of printed forms. The Soldiers'
Document for Thomas Playford, discharged in 1834, is a seven page printed paper
with many more details than given for John Watts. Some extracts are given below
(WO 97/8).

HIS MAJESTY'S SECOND REGIMENT OF LIFE-GUARDS, WHEREOF
THE KING IS COLONEL IN CHIEF
and General the Rt Honbl The Earl Cathcart is Colonel

No. 7 Thomas Playford, Corporal of Horse, BORN in the Parish of Barnbydun in or
near the Town of Doncaster in the County of York by trade a Farmer

ATTESTED for the Second Regiment of Life Guards at London in the County of
Middlesex on the 18 Sept 1810 at the age of 18 years

1st SERVICE

			Years	Days
Enlisted 2nd Life Guards	*16 Sept 1810*			
2nd Life Guards Private	*25 June 1810*	*8 Augt 1816*	*6*	*45*
Promoted Corporal of Horse		*9 Augt 1816*	*17*	*269*
		Waterloo	*2*	
Total Service up to 5 May 1834			*25*	*314*

Served in the Peninsula and on the Continent from November 1812 to July 1814, at the Battle of Vittoria 21 June 1813, on the Continent from May 1815 to February 1816, at the Battle of Waterloo 18 June 1815

2nd DISABILITY

According to the surgeon's report it appears that this is a case of disease or disability contracted in and by the service without being attributable to neglect vice or intemperance and the board concurs in the opinion of the surgeon.

Corporal Playford of the 7th Troop has been frequently in the Regimental Hospital since his period of foreign service for various attacks of rheumatism and rheumatic gout in the joints apparently contracted by service and from no intemperance of his own. In consequence he has long been unfit for the active duties of a dragoon and I consider him to be unfit for further service of the kind. His conduct in hospital has been uniformly good.

> J D Broughton, Surgeon, 2nd Life Guards, Windsor Cavalry Barracks.

3rd CHARACTER

The Regimental Board is of the opinion that his conduct has been very good.

4th PAY and CLOTHING

He has received all just Demands from his Entry into the Service, up to the 5th May 1834

DESCRIPTION of Thomas Playford at the time of his Discharge

He is 42 years of age, 6 feet 2 inches in Height, Dark Hair, Dark Grey Eyes, Dark Complexion, By Trade a Farmer

MARCHING ALLOWANCE

None paid

The Board have verified that his Soldier's Book is correctly balanced and signed by the Officer commanding his troop, and they further declare, that have impartially inquired into, and faithfully reported their opinion on all the matters brought before them...

George Greenwood	Lt Col	2nd Life Guards	President
L D Williams	Capt	2nd Life Guards	Member
George Bulkeley	Capt	2nd Life Guards	Member

By the latter half of the 19th century an even more detailed set of forms will be found for a discharged soldier. A series of 21 questions were put to the recruit before enlistment. No. 2167 George Watts, who joined the 13th Hussars in May 1883, gave his birthplace as North Walsham, Norfolk, his age as 21 years, 1 month and 23 days, and reported a five year apprenticeship as a moulder to Messrs Randell of North Walsham (WO 97/4118). He was examined by a magistrate, by both civilian and army doctors, then by two officers. A physical description and religious denomination were also recorded on attestation. A medical history form was compiled on enlistment, scars and marks were noted and he was re-vaccinated. A further medical sheet noted ailments and treatment. During his twelve year service, he appeared to suffer nothing worse than the ague, which kept him in hospital for twelve days in Malta and for ten days in South Africa; quinine effected a complete cure. A Statement of Services form gives details of 'promotions, reductions and casualties'. He was sent 'to cells' for seven days in September 1886; in January 1887 he was held in confinement awaiting trial, then tried and imprisoned for 28 days. Finally, his Military History Sheet included Next of Kin: father, James Watts; brothers (younger), Thomas, Robert and William; sisters, Blanche, Maud and Ethel.

Royal Hospital Chelsea Discharge Documents of Pensioners (WO 121)

It is important to mention here a further series of records of service, which are complementary to those referred to above in WO 97. These are the Royal Hospital Chelsea Discharge Documents of Pensioners in WO 121, for the period 1787 to 1813. Piece numbers 1 to 136 are arranged chronologically by the date of award of pension, and have been name indexed in TNA's on-line Catalogue.

From some cross-checking for soldiers in both WO 97 and WO 121, it appears unlikely that a soldier would appear in both. An example from WO 121/1 is given below.

HIS MAJESTY'S 23RD REGIMENT OF FOOT (OR ROYAL WELCH FUSILIERS) WHEREOF MAJOR GENL RD GRENVILLE IS COLONEL

These are to certify, That the Bearer hereof, William Sample, Private in Major general Richard Grenville's Company of the aforesaid Regiment, Born in the Parish of West Kirk in or near the Market Town of Edingburgh in the County of Midlothian aged Forty Nine and by Trade a Taylor Hath served honestly and faithfully in the said Regiment Seven years and Eight Months; and Twenty Years and Ten Months in the 26th Regiment; but having been wounded in the left cheek at the battle of Guildford in North America the 15th March 1781 and being old and worn out in the Service, he is rendered unfit for further Service and is hereby Discharged, and humbly recommended as a proper Object of his Majesty's Royal Bounty of CHELSEA HOSPITAL. He having received all just Demands of Pay, Clothing, &c, from his Entry into the said Regiment, to the Date of this Discharge, as appears by his Receipt on the Back hereof.

Given under my hand, and the Seal of this regiment, at Tynemouth Barracks, this Seventeenth Day of May 1787

Fredk Mackenzie, Major   *Royal Welch Fusiliers*
Chas Williamson, Surgeon   *23rd Regiment*

The following is a brief summary of the pieces, which are now generally available on microfilm at TNA.

WO 121/		
1-136	Certificates of service, giving disability or reason for discharge, length of service, rank, age, place of birth and trade on enlistment	1787-1813
137-181	Certificates of service and related correspondence	1782-1819
182-222	Certificates of service and related correspondence (Piece number 182 includes some discharge documents from Royal Hospital, Kilmainham, Dublin)	1814-1833
223	General Discharge Registers – Foot Guards to 12th Foot	1871-1879
224	General Discharge Registers – 13th to 30th Foot	1871-1879
225	General Discharge Registers – 31st to 60th Foot	1871-1879
226	General Discharge Registers – 61st to 90th Foot	1871-1879
227	General Discharge Registers – 91st and Miscellaneous Corps (from 1873), Royal Army Reserve (from 1878)	1871-1879
228	General Discharge Registers – 1st Life Guards to 17th Lancers	1871-1879
229	General Discharge Registers – 1st to 35th Brigades	1874-1879
230	General Discharge Registers – 13th to 30th Foot	1874-1879
231	General Discharge Registers – 1st to 14th Brigades Territorial Regiments	1880-1881 1881-1884
232	General Discharge Registers – 15th to 28th Brigades Territorial Regiments	1880-1881 1881-1884
233	General Discharge Registers – 29th to 42nd Brigades Territorial Regiments	1880-1881 1881-1884

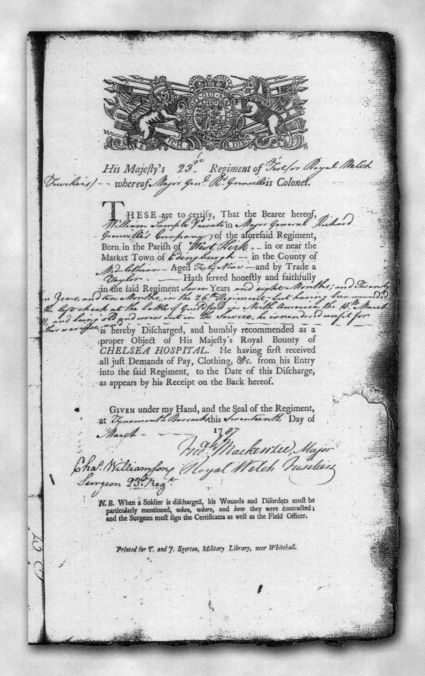

His Majesty's 23*d* Regiment of *Foot (or Royal Welch Fuzileers) — whereof Major Gen.l R.d Grenville is* Colonel.

*T*HESE are to certify, That the Bearer hereof, *William Sample Private* in *Major General Richard Grenville's Company*, of the aforesaid Regiment, Born in the Parish of *West Kirk* — in or near the Market Town of *Edinburgh* — in the County of *Mid Lothian* — Aged *Forty Nine* — and by Trade a *Taylor* — Hath served honestly and faithfully in the said Regiment *Seven Years and eight Months; and Twenty Years, and ten Months, in the 26.th Regiment; but having been wounded the Left cheek at the battle of Guildford in North America the 15.th March, and being old and worn out in the Service, he is rendered unfit for further service,* is hereby Discharged, and humbly recommended as a proper Object of His Majesty's Royal Bounty of CHELSEA HOSPITAL. He having first received all just Demands of Pay, Clothing, &c. from his Entry into the said Regiment, to the Date of this Discharge, as appears by his Receipt on the Back hereof.

GIVEN under my Hand, and the Seal of the Regiment, at *Tynemouth Barracks* this *Seventeenth* Day of *March* — 1787

Fred.k Mackenzie, Major
Cha.s Williamson *Royal Welch Fuzileers*
Surgeon 23.d Reg.t

N. B. When a Soldier is discharged, his Wounds and Disorders must be particularly mentioned, *when, where,* and *how* they were contracted ; and the Surgeon must sign the Certificates as well as the Field Officer.

Printed for T. and J. Egerton, Military Library, near Whitehall.

Figure 14 - Discharge Documents of Pensioners, Royal Hospital Chelsea, Private William Sample, 23rd Foot, 1787, WO 121/1

234	General Discharge Registers – 43rd to 56th Brigades	1880-1881
	Territorial Regiments	1881-1884
235	General Discharge Registers – 57th to 70th Brigades	1880-1881
	Territorial Regiments	1881-1884
236	Cavalry and Foot Guards	1880-1884
237	Royal Artillery and Royal Engineers	1880-1884
238	Miscellaneous Corps	1880-1884
239-253	Register of men discharged without pension	1884-1887
254-257	Alphabetical Nominal Roll of men discharged without pension	1884-1887

Soldiers' Documents for Household Cavalry (WO 400)

Soldiers' Documents for the Household Cavalry, for the period 1799 to 1920, have recently been transferred to TNA where they can be seen in WO 400. These feature surviving records of service for non-commissioned officers and other ranks whose army service concluded in the Life Guards, the Royal Horse Guards and the Household Battalion. The papers are now arranged alphabetically for each of the series listed in the table below.

WO 400/		
1-4	1st Life Guards Series 1	1801-1856
5-55	1st Life Guards Series 2	1859-1920
56-86	2nd Life Guards Series 1	1799-1856
87-166	2nd Life Guards Series 2	1856-1919
167-199	Royal Horse Guards Series 1	1805-1856
200-229	Royal Horse Guards Series 2	1856-1886
230-285	Royal Horse Guards Series 3	1886-1919
286-301	Household Battalion	1916-1919

Microfiche copies of most of the above, as well as some further personnel records for the Household Cavalry, have been retained by them at their Museum at Combermere Barracks, Windsor, Berkshire SL4 3DN.

Footguards Regiments

Soldiers' Documents for three Footguards Regiments (Grenadiers, Coldstream, Scots) are held at TNA in WO 97/150-218. However, further service records have been kept by their respective Regimental Headquarters at Wellington Barracks, Birdcage Walk, London SW1E 6HQ. See the section in Chapter Three relating to Barbara Chambers' Index for 1775-1817, for the 1st or Grenadier Foot Guards.

Muster Books and Pay Lists

Muster Books or Pay Lists form probably the most comprehensive series of army document to have been preserved. They must have been a vital source at the time they were compiled, providing a body of evidence about a soldier's existence to which reference could always be made. As for Soldiers' Documents they are arranged by regiment, so prior knowledge of this is necessary before searching. Muster Books, however, will include soldiers not featured in Soldiers' Documents, for instance those killed in service. Moreover, the Muster Books can be followed through for the whole period of a soldier's service, to give much fuller information than the summary contained in the Soldiers' Documents.

If one has already found a set of Soldiers' Documents for a particular individual, then his dates of enlistment and discharge will be known. If not, but the regiment and approximate dates of service are known, then one must adopt a 'lucky dip' technique, say every five years, until he is located. Each volume usually relates to a single calendar year, although earlier ones often cover a few years.

Muster Books and Pay Lists are to be found in seven series:

WO 10/1-2877	Artillery	1708-1878
WO 11/1-432	Engineers	1816-1878
WO 12/1-13307	General including Cavalry and Infantry	1731-1878
WO 13/1-4675	Militia and Volunteers	1780-1878
WO 14/1- 130	Scutari Depot	1854-1856
WO 15/1-102	Foreign Legions	1854-1856
WO 16/1-3049	New Series covering Artillery, Engineers, Cavalry and Infantry	1878-1898

General Notes:
Service in India is included in all case, except Artillery and Engineers.
For Artillery, see also WO 54, Ordnance Office Registers and WO 69, Artillery Records of Service.
For Engineers, see also WO 54, Ordnance Office Registers.
For Militia and Volunteers, see also WO 68, Militia Records and WO 70, Volunteer and Territorial Records. More details are given in a separate section later.

Muster Books provide a monthly record of a regiment, stating where each man was, his pay and allowances and, in a remarks column, details of any transfers between battalions or regiments, periods of sickness, furlough etc. Each rank is separately

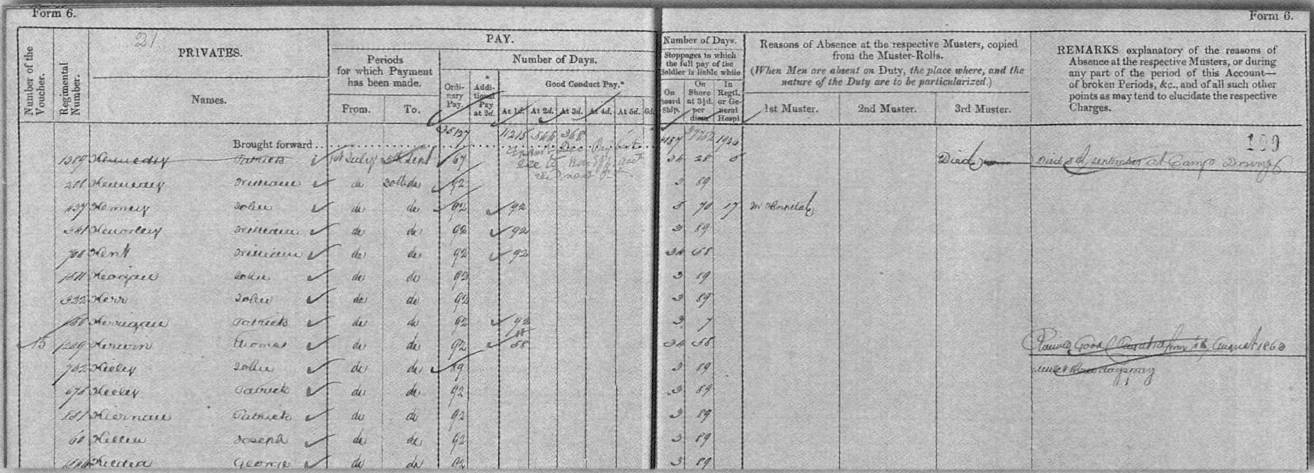
Form 6.

Number of the Voucher.	Regimental Number.	PRIVATES. Names.	PAY. Periods for which Payment has been made. From.	To.	Number of Days. Ordinary Pay.	Additional Pay at 2d.	Good Conduct Pay.* At 1d.	At 2d.	At 3d.	At 4d.	At 5d.	6d.
		Brought forward										

Form 6.

Number of Days. Stoppages to which the full pay of the Soldier is liable while On board Ship.	On Shore at 3½d. per diem	In Regtl. or General Hospl	Reasons of Absence at the respective Musters, copied from the Muster-Rolls. (*When Men are absent on Duty, the place where, and the nature of the Duty are to be particularized.*) 1st Muster.	2nd Muster.	3rd Muster.	REMARKS explanatory of the reasons of Absence at the respective Musters, or during any part of the period of this Account—of broken Periods, &c., and of all such other points as may tend to elucidate the respective Charges.

Figure 15 - Muster Book and Pay List for18th Foot, Royal Irish Regiment, 1862, WO 12/3578 listed, in descending order of seniority. This information is given on a quarterly form covering three monthly musters, for all except the earliest dates. For an individual soldier, therefore, Muster Books can provide a complete month by month account of his service. Initial and final musters may well give birthplace, trade and place of enlistment

In addition, at the end of each batch of musters, further forms may be included, noting, for example, men who became non-effective, allowances to discharged soldiers or fines for drunkenness. Depot Musters can also be extremely useful, sometimes revealing details of allowances paid to men for their wives and children, to enable them to return to their place of enlistment.

The following shows the main features of a Muster Roll for the 1st Battalion of the 6th Foot at the end of 1815 (WO 12/2390).

Pay and additional Allowances

Periods for which Payment has been made; (Table or, where not issued, Periods for which the continued below) respective Persons are considered to be entitled thereto

No Privates		From	To	No. of days	Rate per diem	Amount issued £ s d
912	*Watson James*	25 Sep	24 Dec	91	6d	2 5 6
913	*Watson James*	25 Sep	24 Dec	91	6d	2 5 6
915	*Watts John*	17 Dec	24 Dec	8	8d	5 4
918	*Webster Henry*	25 Sep	24 Dec	91	6d	2 5 6
924	*West James*	25 Sep	24 Dec	91	6d	2 5 6
925	*West James*	25 Sep	24 Dec	91	6d	2 5 6
930	*White William*	25 Sep	24 Dec	91	8d	3 - 8
935	*Wilde Thomas*	25 Sep	24 Dec	91	7d	- - -
936	*Wilde Thomas*	25 Sep	24 Dec	91	8d	- - -

	Reasons of Absence at the Respective Musters			Remarks explanatory of the Reasons of Absence at the Musters... Dates of Inlistment &c.
No	1st Muster	2nd Muster	3rd Muster	
912	-	-	-	-
913	-	-	-	Trade: Labourer of Nilston
915	-	-	Joined from 2nd Battn	Paid by the Detachment Paymaster at Canterbury to 16 December 1815
918	Missing	Missing	Missing	From 28 February 1814
924	-	-	Duty	-
925	-	-	-	Trade: Stone Mason Warwick
930	-	-	-	-
935	Sick Absent	Sick Absent	Discharged	Chelsea Outpension: 24 February 1815
936	Sick Absent	Sick Absent	Transferred	To the 2nd Garrison Bn 25 April 1815

At the time of this muster for the last quarter of 1815, the 6th Foot, or Warwickshire Regiment, were stationed at Lillers in northern France. The first columns of the Muster Book, which give the number of the company and whether the men were entitled to higher pay for periods of service exceeding seven or fourteen years, have been omitted for simplicity. A selection of privates feature in the extract, including John Watts, who had just rejoined the 1st Battalion from the 2nd; he is recorded as having been paid up to the 16th December by the detachment paymaster at Canterbury. The army system ensured that soldiers on the move between units were not paid twice!

It should also be noted that the number quoted in this 1815 example was not the regimental number, but merely a numerical sequence for this particular muster. The regimental number, as introduced in the 1830s, stayed with a man during his time in a particular regiment. (Numbers 914, 916 etc have been omitted in this extract.) Soldiers were listed either by first letter of their surname or strictly alphabetically. There were two James Watsons and two James Wests at this time, so the occupation of one of each of them was included in the Remarks column, in order to distinguish between them.

For John Watts, it was possible to trace his career in the Muster Books of the 99th Foot and the 6th Foot, from 1793 to 1816. Some typical extracts for his service are given opposite.

Year	From To	Location	Regt	Bn	Company	Rank	No of days	Rate per diem	Amount issued £ s d	Remarks	Source WO 12/
1794	17/8 30/9	Dublin Barracks	99th	-	-	Pte	-	-	-	-	9784
1796	1/4 30/9	Killinay Co Galway	6th	1	-	Pte	-	-	-	From 99th 14th April	2382
1799	25/6 24/7	Cork	6th	1	Capt Lee	Pte	30	1s	1 10 0	On board ship 18-24 August	
1799	25/7 24/8	Quebec	6th	1	Capt Lee	Pte	-	-	1 7 6		2383
1806 1807	25/12 24/3	Deal Barracks	6th	1	Capt Edwards	Cpl	90	1/5	6 7 6	On furlough 24 days	2387
1807	25/6 1/9	Gibraltar	6th	1	Capt Robertson	Cpl	69	1/2½	4 3 4½	To Private 1st Sept	2387
1807	2/9 24/9	Gibraltar	6th	1	Capt Robertson	Pte	23	10½d	1 0 1½	From Cpl 2nd Sept	2387
1808	25/6 24/9	In Spain & Portugal	6th	1	No 8	Pte	92	8d	3 1 4	(Rolica 17/8) (Vimiera 21/8)	2388
1808 1809	25/12 24/3	Spain & Aspringe (Kent)	6th	1	No 8	Pte	49 41	6d 1s	4 0 6	(Corunna 16/1) In lieu of beer	2388
1813	1/5 24/6	Jersey	6th	2	No 9	Pte	55	1/2	3 1 2	Transf'd from 1st Battn	2451
1816	25/3 24/4	Camp Neve St Omer	6th	1	No 5	Pte	31	8d	1 0 8	Invalid sent to England	2390

It can be seen that Muster Books provide a very detailed record of an individual soldier's service. However, it is important also to correlate this record against a regimental history or against accounts of battles. Three battles, Rolica, Vimiera and

Corunna, are noted in brackets in the table above; they were not actually mentioned in the Muster Books, but are readily found in the regimental history of the Warwickshire Regiment. A further point concerns rates of pay, which are clearly somewhat variable in the extracts quoted. As already mentioned, slightly higher rates of pay applied for service exceeding seven or fourteen years. Pay would also vary depending on stoppages, for food or clothing, and whether beer was supplied or not. Note the increase to one shilling a day 'in lieu of beer' for the 41 days after arrival in England from the withdrawal at Corunna. Those who check the calculations for total pay at the beginning of 1809 will conclude that the soldier was overpaid by fifteen shillings; there seems to be no ready explanation for this, although it was possibly some compensation for the rigours of the campaign in Spain.

Depot Musters can also be important sources for soldiers not located with the main body of the regiment at any time. For the period 1785 to 1878, there is a good selection of Depot Muster Books in WO 12, piece numbers 12055 to 13288. The coverage is not as complete as for the regimental books, and the depot musters to search must be inferred from gaps in the regimental records for a particular individual, but the results can be very worthwhile. For John Watts, successful searches in Depot Muster Books revealed the following.

Year	From	To	Location of Depot	Remarks	Source WO 12/
1812	25/10	24/12	Cork	Paid by regt paymaster to 24/10 Group of 26 men from 6th Foot 1st Bn quartered at Cork, 'turned over to Detachment Paymaster'	12444
1812	25/12		Cork	John Watts paid 1/2 per day in lieu of beer	12445
1813		24/3			
1815	13/11	16/12	Canterbury	Group of 64 men from 6th Ft 1st Bn 10 days on 124 mile march from Winchester to Canterbury	12208
1816	25/4	24/6	Chatham	Group of 23 men from 6th Ft 1st Bn marched from France to Dover	12302
1816	25/6	1/8	Chatham	Permitted to find own lodgings	12302
1816	2/8	16/8	Chelsea	To Out-Pension on 16/8 (See detailed notes in text below)	12434

The Chelsea Depot Muster Book for 1816 (WO 12/12434) included a separate book, providing an 'Account of Allowances issued to the Wives and Families of Men discharged at Chelsea on Reduction of the Army in the Year 1816, Agreeably to the existing Regulations' and also 'Allowances to Men Discharged'. Such books are sometimes bound in at the end of the main Muster Book. The first account revealed that John Watts had a wife and three children, who were paid a total of £1 5s 1d for the 67 mile journey from Chelsea to Ely. A wife qualified for three ha'pence a mile, each child a penny a mile. Soldiers themselves were expected to travel ten miles a day, so John Watts was given a travelling allowance of five pence a day for seven days, to take him to Ely. For us, the puzzle remains as to why they would travel to Ely rather than to John Watts' home parish of Happisburgh on the coast of Norfolk. The general army rule of paying subsistence to return to the soldier's place of enlistment presumably applied. However, it has not been possible to verify that John Watts enlisted at Ely, either from army records or from local Quarter Sessions records or newspapers.

Muster Books often refer to 'Vouchers' or 'Reports'; these would probably be useful sources of further information but most seem to have disappeared. For example, at the end of 1815, the Muster Book for the 6th Foot referred to Voucher 91: 'a No 1 Report from the Detachment Paymaster at Canterbury showing the period a party from England was paid to'. However, the Report no longer survives.

Muster Books and Pay Lists – some general notes for 1760-1877

The main series of Muster Books which refers to cavalry and infantry from about 1760 until 1877 is found in the 13 305 volumes of WO 12. The List and Index Society has published details of this series. The usual starting date quoted for WO 12 is 1732; however, this early date applies only to the 1st Foot Guards, or Grenadiers. Muster Books for 1732 and 1741 survive for them. For the majority of cavalry and infantry units, the normal starting date is 1760.

While the first 10 000 volumes of these Muster Books relate to the cavalry and infantry in a numerical sequence, the remaining 3 000 or so cover a very wide range of units. These include the African Corps, Army Hospital Corps, Army Service Corps, Canada Fencibles, Canada Rifles, Ceylon Rifle Infantry, Falkland Islands Company, Garrison Battalions, Malta Fencibles, Manx Fencibles, St Helena Regiment, Staff Corps, Veteran Battalions, 1st to 12th West India Regiments and some Garrisons. Some Foreign Corps then follow, such as Corsican Rangers, Dutch Troops, King's German Legion, De Meuron's (Swiss) Regiment and Watteville's. Finally there is a series of musters for depots from Aberdeen to York. As indicated above, the latter should not be neglected as they may well provide some interesting extra information about a soldier when he is not actually based with his regiment.

Prior to 1878, the Muster Books of the Artillery are in a separate series, WO 10; those for Engineers are in WO 11, Militia and Volunteers in WO 13. For the period of the Crimean War, 1854-1856, Muster Books for Scutari Depot are in WO 14 and for Foreign Legions in WO 15. More details about the records for the Artillery and Engineers are given in a later section of this chapter.

The contents of Muster Books did vary considerably over the period 1769 to 1877 but the major features are as outlined in the examples above. A comprehensive survey of the development of army musters is contained in an article by Angela Barlow, using the 47th Foot or the Lancashire Regiment, as an example. Among the many changes the following may be mentioned. By 1825 pay is no longer shown for each man. Around 1830, each set of musters changed from the financial year (based on quarter days) to the calendar year. In the 1830s, regimental numbers were given to a man on enlistment. From 1840, the number of forms began to grow – there were forms for soldiers in confinement, soldiers forfeiting pay, lists of effects and credits of soldiers who had died, been taken prisoner or were missing, lists of soldiers' remittances. The latter include some of the earliest references to soldiers' wives, or perhaps mothers. After the Crimean War, forms multiplied further – a possible 48 by 1865 and 59 by 1875. For recruits, place and date of enlistment, as well as age, were now quoted. Full details were provided for discharged men, where they were enlisted, where to reside, with travel for themselves and families, fares and destinations. From about 1870, the roll of the married establishment is included, giving first name of wife, number and ages, but rarely names, of children and date of being placed on the roll. There were a fixed number of places on the married roll, so a couple might have to wait some time before a vacancy occurred.

It is always important to check the miscellaneous forms at the end of each Muster Book for possible further mention of an individual soldier.

Muster Books and Pay Lists – some general notes and examples for 1878-1898 (WO 16)

The 'New Series' of Muster Books and Pay Lists (WO 16) commenced in 1878 and continued the previous series from WO 10 to WO 13. Thus Artillery, Engineers and Militia, as well as Cavalry and Infantry, are all now included in a single series, namely WO 16. In 1882, and then again in 1888, there were reorganisations of the army. Many of the currently accepted names of regiments were established by the Cardwell reforms of 1881. Pairs of infantry regiments were combined to form the two battalions of a single unit. For example, the East Surrey Regiment was formed in 1881 by the amalgamation of the 31st (Huntingdonshire Regiment) with the 70th (Surrey) Regiment, which then became respectively the 1st and 2nd Battalions of the new regiment. From 1888, WO 16 comprises Muster Books only, without the associated Pay Lists. Moreover, they are arranged in companies and by Regimental District, so that one must obtain the number of this, from Army Lists or from Hart's Army List, before one can gain access to the required Muster Books.

A typical New Series Muster Book contains an extensive range of forms, similar in number and content to those described above for the later years of the period 1760 to 1877. It would be impractical to reproduce full examples of even a few of them, as the forms themselves have become extremely detailed. The following examples are all taken from the 1877-1879 Muster Book and Pay List of the 1st Battalion of the 9th Foot (1st Battalion of the Norfolk Regiment from 1882) (WO 16/1413).

Pay and Allowances are now listed on a standard 'Form 2'; this contains basically the same headings as the Muster Book extract quoted above. In the list of Privates, there were two James Watsons – No 1345 was a labourer from Nottingham, while the other, No 1479, was a seaman from Norwich. Both were paid a shilling a day from 1st April to 20th September and then transferred to the 2nd Battalion of the 9th Foot on 21st September. Good conduct pay, usually a penny a day but occasionally up to fivepence a day, was also payable. Ominously, there were now printed columns to allow for entries relating to soldiers in military prison, in civil prison or in hospital. No 1344 James Watson forfeited his pay from 18th May to 11th June owing to imprisonment, the first six days being in the prison hospital.. (A footnote to Form 2, referring to the Brigade or Regimental Number, reads; 'when pay is charged for the first time for a non-commissioned officer or soldier, transferred from another regiment or corps, his former as well as his present number should be inserted; but the former need to be repeated in subsequent pay lists'.)

Allowances to Discharged Soldiers were recorded on 'Form 24', being a 'Statement of the Amount Paid for Allowances to Discharged Soldiers and their Families to take them Home, together with the Expenses of their Guides and Temporary Allowances to Widows and Children of Deceased Soldiers'. On the 7th August 1878, No 4043 Private John Mahoney, who had enlisted at Limerick and intended to reside at Tralee, was discharged together with his wife Mary, and their three children, respectively aged 14 years 5 months, 10 years 2 months and 4 years 1 month. His unit was based at Dublin at his time of discharge so their railway fares to Limerick, £2 3s, were paid, together with one day's family allowance of 2s 4d and Mahoney's allowance on discharge of 20s.

Fines for Drunkenness were recorded on 'Form 41A'. They were imposed either by order of the commanding officer or by sentence of a court martial; the former dealt in multiples of half-a-crown, while the latter started at £1. No 1160 Private M Tobin was fined 10s by the CO on 29th May 1877, but only 8s 8d had been deducted from his pay before he deserted.

Effects and Credits on 'Form 49' provided a list of officers, NCOs and men who had become 'casualties'; that is, they were lost to the regiment as a result of death, desertion, capture by the enemy, discharge, transfer or going missing. One of those listed for the half-year 12th October 1877 to 31st March 1878 was no 1697 Drummer Charles Newth, born in London, and a musician by trade when he had enlisted on 15th December 1871. He became non-effective at Dublin on 15th December 1877, being discharged to the Army Reserve on completion of his term of service. The form also included columns relating to the forwarding of effects and credits to next of kin of missing, captured or deceased soldiers.

The army had always disapproved of marriage, as detracting from a soldier's loyalty, but had authorised a ratio of six women to one hundred men up to the first half of the nineteenth century. This proportion was strictly applied when regiments embarked for foreign service. These 'on the strength' wives were actually allowed to live with their husbands, usually in an area screened by blankets at the end of the barrack room, in return for the performance of chores, such as cleaning, cooking and mending. 'Off the strength' wives received no rations or allowances. By about 1870, the married establishment had been formally set up, with married quarters, although there was still a limit to places.

Those whose marriages had been officially sanctioned were placed on the Roll of the Married Establishment on 'Form 58'. For example, No 782 Private James Battersby and his wife Johanna had been placed on the married establishment on 5th August 1877; their three children were aged 6 years 6 months, 2 years 2 months and 2 months respectively at the date of the muster in March 1878. In the column provided for changes in the roll, the child's birth on 14th January 1878 is noted as well as Private Battersby's death on 26th January. This column was also used to indicate, 'when a soldier is placed on the roll, the name of whose vacancy he fills'. On this particular, for instance, No 34 Private Edward McMahon and his wife Charlotte were placed on the married establishment on 23rd November 1877, 'Vice Ptes Sullivan and Eames discharged'. (It would appear that at this date a soldier was admitted to the roll only when two had left.)

Description Books

Before the days of photography, it was important for the Army to have a good description of a soldier for various not very flattering reasons. Foremost among these was the need to provide a physical description in the event of desertion, as well as helping to prevent re-enlistment for bounty or the prevention of pension frauds. Description Books give a physical description of each soldier, together with his birthplace, trade, service and enlistment details. The books survive mainly for the first part of the 19th century and are generally arranged by initial letter of soldiers' names in regimental volumes. These can be found in a variety of series:

WO 25/266-688	Regimental Description Books for Cavalry, Infantry, Garrison and Veteran Battalions, Foreign Corps	1756-1878
WO 67/1-34	Depot Description Books	1768-1908
WO 68	includes Militia Description Books	
WO 54/260-309	Royal Artillery Description Books	1749-1863
WO 54/310-316	Sappers, Miners, Artificers Description Books	1756-1883
WO 69/74-80	Royal Artillery Description Books	1773-1876

Some typical examples taken from the **Regimental Description Book**, compiled between 1804 and 1811, for the 6th Foot (WO 25/329) read:

Regimental book of His Majesty's 6th Regiment of Foot

Names		Watts	Welsh	Wilkinson
		John	*Thomas*	*John*
Rank		*Corpl*	*Pte*	*Pte*
Size Feet Inches		*5'6"*	*5'5"*	*5'9"*
Age Years		*31*	*30*	*31*
Description	*Complexion*	*fair*	*fresh*	*fresh*
	Visage	*round*	-	-
	Eyes	*grey*	*blue*	*grey*
	Hair	*brown*	*brown*	*black*
Where Born	*County*	*Norfolk*	*Lancaster*	*Lancaster*
	Parish	*Yarmouth*	*Blackburn*	*Leigh*
Trade		*Mariner*	*Weaver*	*Fisherman*
Former Service		*2 in 99*	-	-

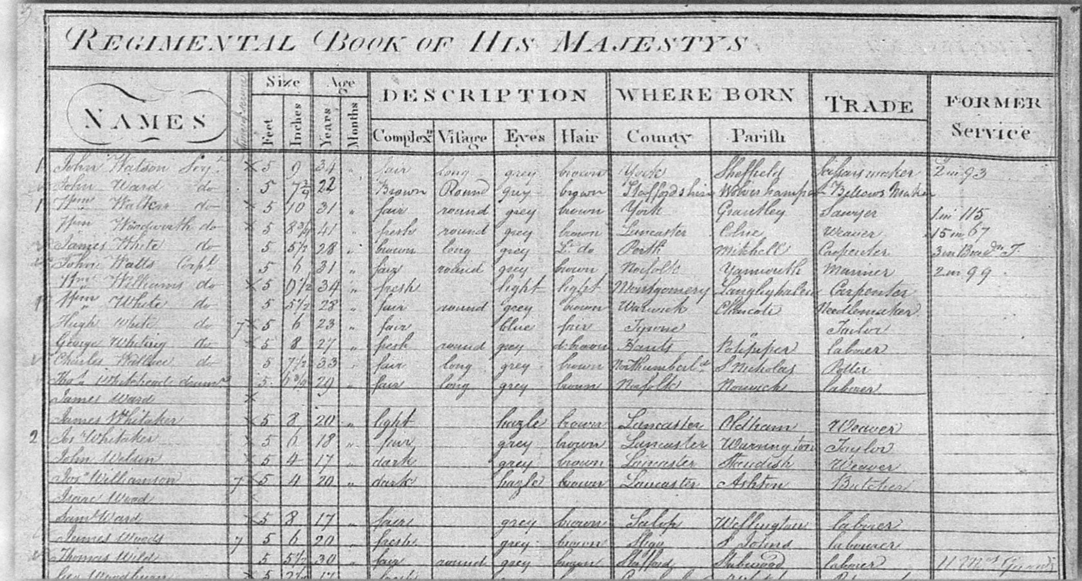

See line 6

John Watts Corpl   Size: 5 feet 6 inches   Age: 31 years

Complexion: fair   Visage: round   Eyes: grey Hair: brown

Where born: County Norfolk   Parish: Yarmouth

Trade: Mariner

Former service: 2 in 99 (2 years in 99th Foot)

Figure 16 - Description Book for 6th Foot, Warwickshire Regiment, 1804-1811, WO 25/329

Enlisted	By whom	Dft fm 99	2 Battn	2 Battn
	Where	Waterford	Gt Baddow	Gt Baddow
	When	14 Apl 96	16 Jun 1806	12 Jun 1806
Casualties	Dead	-	30 May 1811	-
	Deserted	-	-	24 Dec 1806
	Discharged	-	-	-
Observations		-	Prisoner	Returned from
			Spain	desertion
			11 Jan 1809	7 Feb 1807

Hospital Records for Chelsea and Kilmainham

The Royal Hospital at Chelsea was founded in 1682 and opened in 1692, to provide for wounded and disabled soldiers. The corresponding dates for the Royal Kilmainham Hospital, Dublin, are 1679 and 1684. By the early 19th century Chelsea could accommodate about 500 in-pensioners and Kilmainham about 200. The vast majority of eligible discharged soldiers could not therefore be housed within the hospitals, but had instead to become 'out-pensioners'. There were about 3 000 Chelsea out-pensioners by 1711 and 20 000 by 1792. The 'out-pensioner' category was thus really a method of payment of pensions to other ranks, and remained so until 1955, when the Army Pensions Board took it over.

The records of pensioners are not medical ones but relate rather to the granting of a daily pension, based either on length of service or on disability; the award of such a payment, however small it might have seemed to the recipient, was some compensation for his service and/or disability.

It is important to appreciate that soldiers would be discharged either through Chelsea or Kilmainham, depending solely on whether their regiment was on the English or the Irish Establishment (budget). If required, this may be determined from the Army Lists for the relevant period and regiment. After 1822, out-pensioners were only discharged through Chelsea, while both Kilmainham and Chelsea continued to cater for in-pensioners.

Chelsea Hospital

In addition to the Pension Returns (WO 22) and Soldiers' Documents (WO 97, WO 121), which have already been described, there are three other main sets of records relating to pensioners. These are the **Admission Books (WO 116 and WO 117), the Regimental Registers (WO 120)** and what may be loosely described as the **Chelsea Registers (WO 23)**. Taken together these three series will provide a summary of a soldier's service, age, occupation, reason for discharge, rate of pension, place of birth, and a description. Sometimes an entry will be annotated with the date of a man's death. Much repetition of material occurs in these three series. Nowadays it is only possible to guess at the bureaucratic process which brought them into being, but the genealogist will always check every possible source for a further grain of information.

The **Admissions Books (of out-pensioners)** are contained in two series. For cavalry and infantry, pensions awarded between 1715 and 1913 **for disabilities are in WO 116**. Those awarded between 1823 and 1902 for **long service are in WO 117**. The entries are arranged chronologically as soldiers were discharged; as there is no name index, the approximate date of discharge must be known before consulting these series. (Series WO 116 also includes, in piece numbers 125 to 185, a special collection of **Admissions Books for Royal Artillery** pensions from 1833 to 1913.)

A typical example is afforded by the following three entries taken from **Chelsea Hospital Admission Book (Disability)** for 21st June to 27th August 1816 (WO 116/22 fo 126).

Examination of Invalid Soldiers on Friday the 16th of August 1816

Regiment	6th Foot	6th Foot	6th Foot
Name	Prettibier	Watts	Whitcomb
	Josh	John	Saml
Age	45	46	53
Rank	Private	Private	Private
Service (Years Months)			
(in 6th)	16 10	20 4	20 4
(elsewhere)	10 3 (in 60th)	3 1 (in 99th)	2 7 (in 99th)
Total	27 1	23 5	22 11
Rate per diem	1s 3d	1s 1d	1s 1d
Complaint	Worn Out	Worn Out	Worn Out
Where Born	Quebec	Hasbury	Harlington
	N America	Norfolk	Hounslow Middx
Trade or Occupation	Silversmith	Gardiner	Labourer
Remarks			
Height	5' 5"	5' 4"	5' 4"
Hair	black	grey	dark
Eyes	grey	hazle	grey
Complexion	dark	dark	dark

Died 6 May 1830 (Per B 88634)

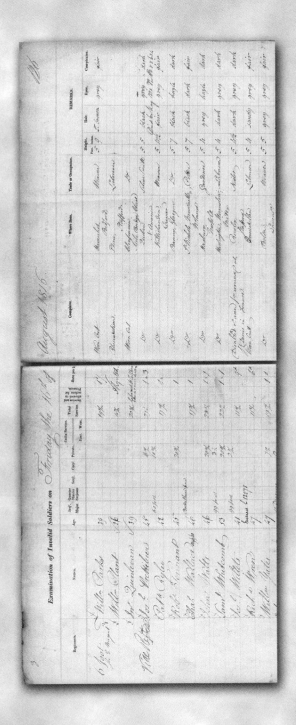

Line 8: Regiment: 6th Foot   Private 20 4/12   99th Foot 3 1/12

John Watts Age: 46   Worn out

Total service: 23 5/12   Rate per diem: 1/1   (Height) 5foot 4 inches   (Hair) grey

(Born) Hasbury Norfolk   (Occupation) Gardiner

(Eyes) hazle   (Complexion) dark

Figure 17 - Chelsea Hospital Admissions Book, Examination of Invalid Soldiers on Friday, 16th August, 1816, WO 116/22

For quite a considerable period, the Admission Books are divided according to cause of discharge, for either disability, as in the above examples from WO 116, or for **long service**. An example of the latter, taken from **WO 117**/1, is quoted below.

Examination of the cases of Invalid Soldiers who have claims to Pensions for Service alone, not being discharged in consequence of disability or the effect of Military Service, and admitted on the Pension List of Chelsea Hospital on 13 April 1824

Sergt Jno McGregor; born Strathspey, (Tomenhout), Banff; age 44 height 5' 10', fair hair, blue eyes, fair complexion, trade, labourer; intended place of residence, Bandon, Cork.

Served as	*Private*	*1 year 1 month*
	Corporal	*1 year 2 months*
	Sergeant	*19 years 5 months*
	Total	*21 years 8 months*

Pension 2s 1½ d per day to commence 12th March 1824

Cause of discharge: appointed Barrack Master at Bandon.
Note: having been appointed Barrack Sergeant, will not be entitled to any pension at present.

The **Admissions Books for Out-Pensioners** are broadly arranged in the following way. (PRO Lists and Indexes, Supplementary Series, Volume VIII, part 1 enables the researcher to check on further details of material in WO 116/1-154 and WO 117/1-36, perhaps before visiting TNA at Kew.)

WO 116/1-124	Disability pensions, for cavalry and infantry arranged by date of admission to pension	1715-1882
WO 116/125-185	Disability and Long Service pensions for Royal Artillery arranged by date of admission to pension	1833-1913
WO 116/186-251	Disability pensions, for cavalry and infantry arranged by date of admission to pension	1883-1913
WO 116/252	Miscellaneous regiments	1762-1802
WO 117/1-76	Long Service pensions arranged by date of admission to pension	1823-1902
WO 117/77	Miscellaneous corps	1872-1920

Turning to the next series, the **Regimental Registers, WO 120**, it should be noted that these include two distinct sets of volumes, although the primary arrangement is by regiment.

The first 51 pieces cover the years from about 1715 to 1843, in six date bands. These are ca 1715-1756, ca 1717-1775, ca 1742-1784, ca 1730-1812, ca 1806-1838 and ca 1839-1843. (Only volumes in the last date band have name indexes within each piece.) Within each piece, entries are by regiment, then chronologically. A piece may contain between 10 and 20 regiments. For example WO 120/23 contains the 1st to 13th Foot for the period ca 1806-1838. The entry we found for John Watts, on folio 254 of WO 120/23, is identical to that quoted on the previous page from WO 116/22. (The Beckett Index to Chelsea Pensioners, covering WO 120/20-30 has already been mentioned in the section on Army Indexes).

The second set of volumes within WO 120 is formed by pieces 52 to 70, which feature pensions being paid between 1845 and 1854, with additions to 1857. An example of the brief entry now given is taken from the Regimental Register for the 1st to 9th Foot (WO 120/55 fo 157).

6th Foot

	Rate	*Date of Admission*	*Residence*	*Died*
John Watts	*1/1*	*16th August 1816*	*Norw(ic)h*	*1/11/1846*
				E42.662/59

Chelsea Registers (WO 23) will now be described more fully – pieces 26 to 65 have already been mentioned above, as a possible regimental finding aid. An example was given there, for John Watts, from WO 23/36. That example virtually duplicates the one just quoted from WO 120/55. Clearly the clerks at the Chelsea Hospital and those keeping regimental records shared and noted the same information.

'Chelsea Registers, &c' (WO 23), therefore, contain much that duplicates the two series just discussed – (Admissions Books and Regimental Registers), but they also house unique and unusual sources. The table below summarises the material available in WO 23. Piece numbers 26 to 65 form the main sequence which duplicates much of WO 120; each piece contains a list of pensioners for about 10 to 15 regiments for a period of about 10 to 20 years. During this period, 1820-1875, the registers, WO 23/26-65, record change of payment district - often a very useful feature. It should also be noted that WO 23 continues beyond WO 120 with two further date bands, namely for 1855-1865 and 1865-1875. (PRO List and Index No 28 gives full details of WO 23 up to piece number 123.)

WO 23/		
1-16	Reports as to invalids admitted to pension (duplicates some material in WO 116 and WO 117)	1830-1844
17-23	Returns of East India Company's Pensioners	1814-1868
24	Returns of Greenwich Hospital Naval Pensions	1868-1870
25	Register of Pensions to Militia and Yeomanry	1821-1829
26-45	'Chelsea Registers' (see notes above)	1820-1854
46-55	'Chelsea Registers'	1855-1865
56-65	'Chelsea Registers'	1865-1875
66-123	Relates to Officers and Widows – see Chapter Two)	
124-131	In-pensioners – Muster Rolls	1702-1789
132	In-pensioners – Muster Rolls	1864-1865
134	List of in-pensioners	1795-1813
135	Pensioners from King's German Legion	1801-1815
136-140	Pensions being paid in 1806	pre 1806
141-145	Ordnance pensions being paid in 1834	pre 1834
147-152	Admission books for pensions payable in colonies	1817-1875
153-159	Lists, registers and admission books of Negro and Cape Corps pensioners	1837-1879
160	Admission book of native and colonial pensioners	1880-1903
162-172	Admission books and rolls for in-pensioners	1824-1917
174-180	arranged chronologically	1824-1917
173	Index to in-pensioners admitted	1858-1933

There is clearly a wide range of information available in these Chelsea Registers. The extracts below are from WO 23/136, the first of four books recording pensions being paid in 1806.

Name	Tarleton Jno	Postleworth Wm
Regiment	6th Foot	6th Foot
Age Years	79	87
Service Years	3	21
Admitted (to pension)	1 Apr 1747	30 Jun 1767
Complaint	Lameness in the Hip	Worn Out
Residence	Kirkby Stephen Westmorland	Cartmel Lancashire

Before concluding this section on Chelsea Pension Records, it is important to refer briefly again to the out-pension records in **WO 121, namely Chelsea Discharge Documents of Pensioners** - also to two similar series in **Chelsea Documents of Pensioners, Foreigners' Regiments (WO 122) and Chelsea Documents of Pensioners Awarded Deferred Pensions (WO 131).**

WO 121 has been discussed already, in the context of the finding the regiment, as pieces 1 to 136 have been name-indexed and are on-line. Sometimes these records are not strictly discharge documents as such, but rather take the form of a petition, recommending a needy soldier for a pension at a later date. A further example from WO 121/1 is that for a Private Donald McDonald.

Discharged 18th June 1787
H M 74th Regt of Foot wherof Col John Campbell is Colonel

Donald McDonald, private in Capt Grant's Company. Born Kilmanivack, in or near the Market Town of Fort William County of Inverness aged 39 years a labourer served near seven years but by an over-exertion in drawing Cannon at the siege of Charlestown and other very fatiguing service at that time, he contracted a violent pain in his breast and spitting of blood, by the continuance of which and consequent long sickness, that has made him very dull of hearing, he is rendered incapable of working and therefore he is hereby discharged and humbly recommended as a proper Object of his Majesty's Royal Bounty of CHELSEA HOSPITAL

Edinburgh 28th March 1787   *John Campbell Col late 74th Regt*

The uniqueness of these Chelsea Pension Records may be confirmed by checking for the same person in WO 97, the normal series of Soldiers' Documents, which supposedly cover the period from 1760 onwards. A search in the appropriate part of WO 97, namely piece number 861 for the 74th Foot, failed to reveal this Donald McDonald. In a Highland Regiment, there were of course several others of the same name. These included a blacksmith born 1790 in Portrea, a wright born 1801 at Inverness and a gardener born 1806 at Armadale. They were not discharged until the years 1829, 1840 and 1849 respectively.

Finally, those discharged from Foreign Regiments in 1816-1817 are covered in WO 122/1-14, while those awarded deferred pensions between 1838 and 1896 are listed alphabetically in the 44 volumes of WO 131.

Kilmainham Hospital

Kilmainham Hospital was opened in 1684 and catered for army pensioners in Ireland. It has recently been renovated and in 1991 it was opened to the public as the Irish Museum of Modern Art. The records of Kilmainham Hospital are contained in series WO 118 and WO 119, but are unfortunately not nearly so extensive as the material for Chelsea. . After 1822, out-pensioners were only discharged through Chelsea, while both Kilmainham and Chelsea continued to cater for in-pensioners.

Kilmainham Admission Books WO 118, for 1759 to 1863, are similar to those already described for Chelsea under WO 116, and cover both in- and out-pensioners. In 1807 existing pensions were re-assessed and these documents became a regular series from that date. Pieces 36, 37, 38, 42 and 43 are entry books of pensioners, containing dates of admission and sometimes death; they are arranged chronologically by date of award of the pension. Piece 13 is a register of pensioners abroad who were transferred to the establishment at Chelsea.

The following example is taken from the Admission Book for 24 February 1819 to 27 June 1821 (WO 118/42).

Soldiers Admitted 27 Oct 1819

Regiment	7th Foot	Service			Years	Days
Name	John Eyers	Marines	20 Oct 1796	13 Jan 1815	18	86
Age	46	7th Foot	28 Aug 1815	22 Oct 1819	4	56
Rank	Private	Total			22	142
Rate	1s 1d per day	Where Born	Marshgibbon Bucks			
Complaint	Worn Out	Trade	Labourer			
Height	5' 9 ¾ '					
Hair	Brown					
Eyes	Grey	DD (Discharged Dead): 26/6/39				
Complexion	Swarthy	D 29477				

Pieces 39 to 41and 44 of WO 118 provide an index to these registers, and also to the **Kilmainham Discharge Documents WO 119**, for 1783 to 1822.

For example, consulting WO 118/44, which indexes admissions between 24 Feb 1819 and 13 Nov 1822, by initial letters, one discovers that both Dr(ummer) James Watts (Discharge Number B 2427) and Pte Michl McMahon (Discharge Number B 2425) had served in the 49th Foot. These entries can then be followed up in the

Admissions Books (WO 118) or in the Discharge Documents (WO 119), which give much fuller information. The Discharge Numbers are checked against the catalogue listing for WO 119, selecting piece number 63 to obtain the full entries. These are as follows (WO 119/63).

Discharge Number	*B 2425*	*B2427*
Name	*Michl McMahon*	*James Watt (sic)*
Rank	*Private*	*Drummer*
Born Parish of	*Dicente*	*Kinsale*
Near town of	*Ennis*	*Kinsale*
County of	*Clare*	*Cork*
Enlisted for	*49th Regt*	*49th Regt*
at	*Cavan*	*Jamaica*
County of	*Cavan*	*W Indies*
on	*6 Jan 1808*	*25 Aug 1795*
at (age of)	*19*	*14*
Served	*13 years 223 days*	*25 years 357 days*
	to 16 Aug 1821	*to 16 Aug 1821*
Discharged	*Reduction of the*	*Reduction of the*
due to	*Establishment and*	*Establishment*
	pulmonary complaints	*weakly state of health*
Conduct	*Good*	*Good*
Age	*32*	*40*
Height	*5' 8¼ '*	*5' 6'*
Hair	*Black*	*Black*
Eyes	*Grey*	*Hazel*
Complexion	*Fair*	*Dark*
Occupation	*Labourer*	*Labourer*
At	*Waterford*	*Waterford*
On	*16 Aug 1821*	*16 Aug 1821*
Paid	*12s to take him to Dublin*	*12s to take him to Dublin*

Prize Records

A soldier may well have qualified for a share in war prize won in military action. The details will be found in the Royal Hospital Chelsea, Prize Records, WO 164, for 1720-1899. These include lists of entitlement from 1779 to 1858, as well as records of unclaimed shares and of payments made to claimants or their agents. The volumes are arranged by action, then by regiment or detachment. Once a soldier's career is known in some detail, a check can be made against particular actions for prize money. For John Watts, the only such bonus was found for the action on the island of Walcheren in 1809 (WO 164/197).

Prize Money for WALCHEREN 1809

6th Foot   Countersigned
WATTS, John   Private 18s 6¾ d   21 Oct 1812   John Campbell

Deserters

If one has evidence, perhaps from Muster Rolls or Casualty Returns, that a man deserted, there are a number of places where this can be followed up. The sources discussed here are Returns of Deserters, Hue and Cry, Newspapers and Bounty Certificates.

Returns of Deserters are to be found at TNA in WO 25/2906-2961 for the period 1811 to 1851. These also include 'Returns of the Prisoners on the Savoy Hulk' from 1799 to 1823. Generally each piece covers a number of regiments, perhaps between ten and thirty, for a number of years. It would be feasible to search a set of these returns if one had definite evidence of desertion from a particular regiment or around a certain date.

A typical entry, taken from the **Returns of Deserters** for the 1st Life Guards – 20th Foot for 1826-1834 (WO 25/2910) reads:

6th Foot
Taylor, John, age 28, 5'8'tall, fresh complexion, brown hair, hazel eyes, deserted 11 Aug 1828 at Canterbury, enlisted 20 Oct 1826 at Manchester; no of report from Regt: 1000;
how disposed of: 14701 24 July 1829
Remarks: Second Time.

The '**Police Gazette**' or '**Hue and Cry**' often contained a much fuller description, as in these examples from the late 1830s. (HO 75/11)

Issue No	1091	1146
Date	30 June 1838	9 Jan 1839
Name	George Fish	George Pratt
Office No	6338	8116
Corps	80th Foot	68th Foot

Parish (birth)	Massingham	Stoke
County	Norfolk	Warwick
Trade	Labourer	Ribbon weaver
Age	20	22 ½
Size	5' 6½ '	5' 8'
Person	w made	v stout
Face	round	round
Eyes	hazel	grey
Nose	prop	prop
Hair	lt brown	brown
Arms	prop	prop
Legs	stout	stout
Mouth	prop	prop
Marks and Remarks	recruit; passed the surgeon	large mole on left arm; seen on way to Cork
Time	20 June	28 Dec
Place	Stamford	Spike Island
Coat	baragan	red fatigue
Trousers	baragan	reg cloth

'Hue and Cry', which was published on Wednesdays and Saturdays, was distributed to all police stations to aid in the apprehension of deserters and other criminals. A large table at the end of each issue contained details of some 50-60 'Deserters from His/Her Majesty's Service'. Copies are available at TNA for 1828 to 1845 in HO 75. It was founded about 1797 as 'Hue and Cry' and later became 'The Police Gazette'. There are good collections of this journal at the British Library's Newspaper Library at Colindale, London, and also at the Cambridgeshire Police Archive.

Some recent publications have extracted and indexed lists of deserters. The names of about 36 500 deserters, featured in the 'Hue and Cry' issues from 1828 to 1840, have been indexed and published on CD by the Manchester and Lancashire FHS. Lists of deserters from British units based in Australia and New Zealand have been transcribed from the Victoria Police Gazette for 1853 to 1870.

Deserters were often mentioned in advertisements in local newspapers, in attempts to secure their recapture. One must of course know the date of desertion from some other source to make it worthwhile searching, unless the newspaper has been fully indexed. The 'Bury and Norwich Post' for 6th March 1793 carried the following advertisement, which is typical; although the Suffolk Militia was based at Hilsea, near Portsmouth, the missing men were all from East Anglia.

HILSEA BARRACKS   Feb 9 1794 WESTERN REGIMENT OF SUFFOLK MILITIA
Commanded by Colonel the Earl of EUSTON

Deserted from the above Regiment the under-mentioned men: Whoever will apprehend and lodge them in any of his Majesty's goals (sic), shall receive TWENTY SHILLINGS reward for each man, by giving sufficient proof of their apprehension and confinement, to
John Spink Esq., Bury St Edmund's, or the Commanding Officer of the Regiment at Hilsea.
T BLOMFIELD Capt and Adjt

WM. PULFORD, aged 22, 5 feet 9 inches high, light brown complexion, light brown hair, grey eyes, by trade a labourer, place of abode, Needham Market, and serving for William Worlidge, Creeting St Peter
STEPH. RANSON, aged 22, 5 feet 5 in. high, light brown complexion, Light brown hair, grey eyes, by trade a blacksmith, place of abode, Shimpling, and serving for George Keddington, Stanningfield
WM. TINGAY, 5 feet 8½ inches high, fresh complexion, light brown hair, grey eyes, place of abode, Brandon, and serving for himself
WM. SMITH, 5 feet 8 inches high, pale complexion, sandy hair, dark eyes by trade a woolcomber, and serving for Robert Hawkins, Hadley
JOHN JACKSON, 5 feet 7 inches high, dark complexion, black hair, dark Eyes, by trade a labourer, and serving for Wm. Cuthbert, Bildeston.

Deserter Bounty certificates were found among the Exchequer Land Tax records in series E 182. These are certificates of arrest of deserters from the army and militia, with orders from magistrates for bounty to be paid to those responsible for arrests. A card index is being generated at TNA, covering initially London and Middlesex for the period 1783 to 1814.

Courts Martial

As in civilian life, further information will be available about an ancestor if he got into trouble. In the 18th century and early part of the 19th century, discipline was of course harsh and was intended to be exemplary so that flogging was the standard punishment. Later in the 19th century, fines and penal servitude were substituted.

For a soldier who committed a minor offence, discipline was often exercised by his Company Commander. More serious cases would come before a soldier's Commanding Officer. He could then be tried by a District Court Martial or a General Court Martial, depending on the severity of the offence. The surviving series of court martial records have all passed through the office of the Judge Advocate General.

The records which survive from the Judge Advocate General's office relate to four types of court martial: General Court Martial, Field General Court Martial, General Regimental Court Martial and the District or Garrison Court Martial. A General Court Martial was the only court which could deal with commissioned officers, but also handled serious cases concerning NCOs and other ranks. A Field General Court Martial dealt with most cases which arose overseas during wartime. A General Regimental Court Martial could try only NCOs and other ranks, and could not deal with capital offences; it was abolished and succeeded by the District Court Martial in 1829. The District or Garrison Court Martial handled lesser offences committed by NCOs or other ranks; it could not pass sentence of death, transportation or floggings of more than 150 lashes.

The verdicts and sentences of courts martial were subject to confirmation, mitigation or remission by higher authority. For instance, a decision overseas to cashier a commissioned officer required the personal confirmation of the sovereign. Other decisions might be confirmed by an area commander-in-chief or by the general officer commanding. Eventually records of all courts martial reached the office of the Judge Advocate General – except for a Regimental Court Martial, whose proceedings should have been retained by the regiment.

Courts martial for commissioned officers are readily found, as they could only be tried by General Court Martial. The three types of record which relate to individual trials are papers, proceedings and registers. Papers were written during the court martial and forwarded to the office of the Judge Advocate General, where volumes of proceedings were generated, together with registers, which provide a tabular summary.

Selected records relevant to a search for the court martial of an **officer** are listed below. For brevity the title 'Judge Advocate General's Office' has been omitted from each line. It should be remembered that many records in these series are closed for 75 years.

WO 93/1-68	Miscellaneous Records	1650-1969
	1A is an index to WO 91 and WO 92	
	1B is an index to trials of officers	1806-1904
WO 71/1-1359	Courts Martial Proceedings	1668-1977
WO 71/121-342	Papers, in date order	1668-1850
WO 71/13-33	Proceedings, entry books, home	1692-1796
WO 71/34-64	Proceedings, entry books, home and abroad	1715-1790
WO 71/65-98	Proceedings, entry books, marching regiments	1756-1789
WO 91/1-51	General Courts Martial confirmed at home	1806-1904
	Proceedings, continuation of series in WO 71	
WO 90/1-9	General Courts Martial Abroad	1779-1960
	Registers of CM confirmed abroad	
WO 92/1-10	General Courts Martial	1666-1960
	Registers of CM confirmed at home	
WO 89/1-5	General Courts Martial	1666-1829
	Duplicates much of WO 92, includes full	
	proceedings for 1666-1698 and 1759-1760,	
	summaries only for 1812-1829	

Examples of entries found, for the 6th Foot, in the Register of General Courts Martial abroad, are as follows (WO 90/1):

Name	Purcell John	Roach Wm	Sayers John
Rank	Ensign	Private	Private
At	Gibraltar	Gibraltar	Almeida
Date	4 Aug 1807	4 Jan 1808	3 Nov 1808
Offence	Being drunk on guard	Neglect of duty etc	Absenting himself from his regt housebreaking etc
Sentence	Hon(ourabl)y Acq(uitte)d	1000 lashes Remitted	To be hanged

It can be seen from these extracts that both officers and other ranks could be tried by a General Court Martial. **NCOs and other ranks** could also be tried by General Regimental Court Martial (before 1829) or District Court Martial (after 1829). Thus searches for the trial of NCOs or other ranks must be made in more than one set of records. In the case of General Courts Martial, the procedure is as described above for officers; one may find papers, proceedings and registers. However, for General Regimental Courts Martial, only registers have survived, for 1812-1829, in WO 89, while for District Courts Martial, the surviving registers in WO 86 span 1829 to

1971. The following table summarises the material, which should be searched for NCOs and other ranks, in addition to the General Court Martial records noted in the previous table.

WO 89/1-5	General Courts Martial	1666-1829
	Includes general regimental courts martial confirmed at home and abroad	1812-1829
WO 86/1-122	District Courts Martial registers confirmed at home and abroad	1829-1971
WO 87/1	District Courts Martial, London	1865-1875
WO 88/1-7	District Courts Martial, India	1878-1945

In our own researches for John Watts, we had found from Muster Books for the Sixth Foot that he was reduced from corporal to private in Gibraltar on 1st September 1807. Accordingly we consulted WO 90/1 for General Courts Martial Abroad, 1796-1825, WO 91/2 for General Courts Martial confirmed at home (July 1807 to September 1808), and finally WO 71/210 for General Court Martial papers (July to September 1807), but without any success. Presumably his offence had been dealt with by normal regimental discipline.

The papers for Ensign John Purcell were available in WO 71/210. His offence occurred on 4th August 1807 also in Gibraltar, and it might have been that John Watts' demotion on 1st September was in some way connected. In the papers for John Purcell, we found no reference to John Watts, although evidence was given there by several other soldiers of the 6th Foot. •

The death sentence on Private John Sayers appears to have been that confirmed by Sir John Moore, as noted by Fortescue.

The next day he (Moore) entered Almeida, where an unpleasant duty awaited him. The Sixth Foot, which had occupied the town since the evacuation of the French, was suffering from the misrule of a bad commanding officer, and was in a disgraceful state. The officers had been negligent; the conduct of the men had been infamous, and one private was actually under sentence of death by court-martial. Moore confirmed the sentence, and then called the real culprits – the officers – before him ..... He now addressed the officers of the Sixth with great severity, told them that they were unworthy to go on active service, and passed the hardest sentence which he could inflict – that he should leave them behind ... The fact must therefore be recorded, not from any malignancy towards a regiment which has long since recovered and enhanced its fair fame, but in justice to a great commander.

This episode casts an interesting light on the regiment in which an ancestor served and leaves one wondering whether Private John Sayers deserved his fate.

Artillery, Engineers, Other Corps, Militia and Volunteers

Most soldiers will have been found in the two largest categories of the army, namely infantry and cavalry (including foot guards). However, there were and are several other major groups in which fighting men have served. These include artillery, engineers and other corps, militia and many categories of volunteers. Each group merits a chapter, if not a book, but there is only space here to summarise records which exist exclusively for them.

Artillery

The Royal Regiment of Artillery, formed in 1722 (together with the Royal Engineers, formed in 1716 but not actually 'Royal' until 1787), were separate from the rest of the army, being under the Board of Ordnance and not the War Office, until 1855. The Royal Horse Artillery (RHA) was founded in 1793. In 1899 there was a reorganisation of the Royal Artillery, which formed two separate branches, the Royal Horse and Royal Field Artillery, and the Royal Garrison Artillery. A single corps was then formed in 1924, although the Royal Horse Artillery retained its title and its distinctive badge. Extensive records exist exclusively for soldiers in the artillery and are summarised in the table below. (Note that Soldiers' Documents for the Royal Artillery are arranged alphabetically for each of the three periods between 1760 and 1882.)

WO 10/1-2876	Artillery Muster Books and Pay Lists	1708-1878
WO 54/1-948	Ordnance Office Registers	1594-1871
260-309	Royal Artillery Description Books	1749-1859
317-328	Artillery Discharges, Transfers and Casualties	1740-1859
338-481	Registers of Artillery Pensions	1816-1840
672-755	Artillery Miscellaneous Pay Lists	1692-1860
WO 69/1-905	Artillery Records of Services etc,	1756-1911
	includes records of service for RA	1791-1855
	and records of service for RHA	1803-1863
63-73	Registers of baptisms and marriages for RHA	1859-1877
74-80	Description Books	1773-1876
551-582	Registers of baptisms and marriages	1860-1877

583-597	Registers of deceased soldiers for RA (see also pieces 644-646)	1821-1873
779-782	Indexes and posting books for Artillery records of service in WO 69	
WO 97/ 1210-1271	Soldiers' Documents – Royal Artillery	1760-1854
1306-1358	Soldiers' Documents – Royal Artillery	1855-1872
1763-1848	Soldiers' Documents – Royal Artillery	1873-1882
WO 116/125-154	Chelsea Admissions Books (Disability) RA	1833-1882

Engineers

The Corps of Royal Engineers grew from an officer corps of engineers, established by the Board of Ordnance in 1716, and a corps of Royal Military Artificers (non-commissioned ranks), formed in 1787. The title of the Royal Artificers was changed in 1813 to Royal Sappers and Miners, which led eventually to the 'Sappers' nickname, by which the Royal Engineers are known. When the Board of Ordnance was abolished in 1855, the two corps, like the Artillery, were placed under the War Office. The two separate corps of officers and other ranks were then merged into a single Corps of Royal Engineers in 1856. The RE dealt with military aviation, then with aircraft, until the formation in 1912 of the Royal Flying Corps. Similarly the RE Signal Service was the precursor of the Royal Corps of Signals, formed in 1920.

The following records apply exclusively to engineers. As for the artillery, Muster Books and Pay Lists continue from 1878 to 1898 in the new series of WO 16.

WO 11/1-432	Engineers Muster Books and Pay Lists	1816-1878
WO 12/	Muster Books and Pay Lists	
10916	Military Artificers	1798
13291	Sappers and Miners	1831-1832
13292	Discharges without pension	1833
WO 54/1-948	Ordnance Office Registers	1594-1871
310-316	Description Books for Sappers, Miners and Artificers	1756-1833
329-337	Engineers Discharges, Transfers, Casualties	1800-1859
482	Returns of Sappers and Miners entitled to pension	1830
WO 97/1148-1152	Soldiers' Documents – Corps of Sappers	1760-1854
1359-1364	Soldiers' Documents – Royal Engineers	1855-1872
1849-1857	Soldiers' Documents – Royal Engineers	1873-1882

Other Corps

Beside the two senior corps of the pre-1914 army, the artillery and the engineers, there were numerous other corps, most of which have undergone several changes of title. A detailed study cannot be given here and the reader is referred to Brereton's authoritative guide for historical information and for order of precedence. (The Royal Armoured Corps is omitted here, having been formed in 1939 from mechanised units of Cavalry of the Line and the former Royal Tank Corps.)

Corps which existed in some form before 1914 are mentioned briefly below, in order of precedence of their present-day successors. The following table then gives information about individual soldiers' records, which are unfortunately not nearly as extensive as for soldiers already discussed.

The Royal Corps of Signals (formed 1920) derived from the Royal Engineers Signal Service. The Royal Army Chaplains' Department (1919) originated with the department formed under a Chaplain-General in 1796. The Royal Corps of Transport (1965) has a complex family tree, among its progenitors being the Commissary General (pre 1794) under Treasury control, Royal Waggon Corps (1799), Royal Waggon Train (1802), Land Transport Corps (1855), Military Train (1856) and the Army Service Corps (1869), which became Royal in 1918.

The Royal Army Medical Corps (1898) sprang from the Medical Staff Corps (1855), Army Hospital Corps (1857), Army Medical Staff (1873) and once more the Medical Staff Corps in 1884. The Royal Army Ordnance Corps (1918) has a pedigree stretching back, like those of the artillery and engineers, to the Board of Ordnance. (The RAOC took over the RASC supply tasks in 1965.) Field Train (1792), Military Store (1857) and Ordnance Store are among the many titles of earlier units.

The Corps of Royal Military Police (1926) had its origins in the Provost-Marshal and the Provost Service. The Military Mounted Police (1855/1877) were followed by the Military Foot Police (1885), combining into a single corps in 1926. The Royal Army Pays Corps (1920) derived from civilian clerks in the 17th century, forerunners of agents such as Cox's, and from commissioned Paymasters with the rank of Captain. By 1893, soldier-clerks assisted these officers in the Army Pay Corps, briefly joined by a Corps of Military Accountants (1919-1925).

The Royal Army Veterinary Corps (1918) started as the Army Veterinary Department (1881). From about 1796 qualified 'vets' had been appointed to each cavalry regiment by the Head of the School of Veterinary Medicine in London. The Royal Military Academy Sandhurst Band Corps (1923/1947) descended from a band at Sandhurst in 1815; with no more than 39 members, it could claim to be the smallest corps in the British Army.

The Small Arms School Corps (1919) derived from the School of Musketry at Hythe in Kent (1854). The Military Provost Staff Corps (1906) started life in 1901 as the Military Prison Staff Corps. The Royal Army Educational Corps (1946) was preceded by a Corps of Army Schoolmasters (1846) and an Army Educational Corps (1920). The Army Physical Training Corps (1940) followed the Army Gymnastic Staff (1860) and the Army Physical Training Staff (1918).

Lastly we come to Queen Alexandra's Royal Army Nursing Corps (1949), which derived from the Army Nursing Service, and followed the legendary work of Florence Nightingale in the Crimea. Queen Alexandra was patron of Queen Alexandra's Imperial Military Nursing Service (1902), amalgamated with the Territorial Army Nursing Service (1907) in 1949. (The authors' aunt, Major Phyllis Heymann, served in both QAIMNC and QARANC. See Chapter Seven -World War II Records for her service papers. We would have been intrigued to hear her response to Brereton's statement that QARANC are 'of course nurses rather than soldiers'!)

The relatively small number of records available at TNA for various corps are summarised in the following table.

WO 12/	Muster Books and Pay Lists	
1522-1535	Royal Wagon Train	1799-1833
1535	Staff Corps Cavalry	1813-1818
10365-10451	Army Hospital Corps	1860-1876
10453-10490	Army Service Corps	1870-1878
10655-10681	Commissariat Staff and Transport Corps	1860-1870
10823-10834	Land Transport Corps	1855-1856
10910-10915	Medical Staff Corps	1855-1861
10917-10943	Military Labourers (mostly Mauritius)	1837-1875
10947-11015	Military Train and Horse Transport	1856-1870
11065-11090	Staff Corps	1799-1837
12970-	Depots – School of Musketry – Hythe	1854-1878
-12996	Depots – School of Musketry – Fleetwood	1861-1867
WO 16/	Muster Books and Pay Lists (New Series)	1878-1898

WO 25/233-258	Chaplains, Payments and Certificates of Service	1805-1843
/582-602	Military Train Description Books	1857-1869
WO 67/32	Commissariat Staff Depot Description Book	1859-1868
33-34	Military Train Depot Description Books	1837-1868
WO 97/	Soldiers' Documents	
1153	Wagon Train	1760-1854
1174-1177	Royal Staff Corps	1760-1854
1183	Corps of Military Labourers	1760-1854
1698	Army Hospital Corps	1855-1872
1702	Land Transport, Army Hospital and Medical Staff Corps	1855-1872
1703-1704	Military Train	1855-1872
1720-1721	Military Labourers, Commissariat Staff Corps, Military Store Staff Corps and School of Musketry	1855-1872
2148-2153	Army Service Corps	1873-1882
2154-2156	Army Hospital Corps	1873-1882
2157	Military Staff Corps	1873-1882
2170	Corps of Armourers, Military Labourers, School of Musketry	1873-1882
2171	Military Mounted Police	1873-1882
WO 111/1-13	Army Ordnance Corps	1901-1919

Militia

Militia, the oldest of English auxiliary forces, should properly be the subject of a complete book. A full account of their development is contained in Dr I F W Beckett's study of the British auxiliary forces, including militia, volunteers and yeomanry. Two booklets provide a detailed listing of muster rolls and other militia records on a county by county basis, noting material held at TNA, in numerous county record offices as well as in other locations. These are Gibson and Dell's 'Tudor and Stuart Muster Rolls' and Gibson and Medlycott's 'Militia Lists and Musters, 1757-1876'. The later material held at TNA is described by William Spencer in 'Records of the Militia and Volunteer Forces, 1757-1945'; this book also contains much interesting background on the formation of these forces and elucidates the somewhat complicated collection of militia records. Printed Militia Lists are available in the library at TNA for various dates in the 18th and 19th centuries.

Able-bodied men over 16 had long been required to do military service, usually in their own shires or counties. In an emergency, these men would be available as soldiers. In Tudor times, trained bands were organised at parish expense. Militia were much more strongly established by an act of 1757, following the Seven Years' War. Extensive records listing men were created, and exist for the whole period until 1829, when the militia ballot was suspended. Voluntary enlistment continued through the nineteenth century, leading to the formation of a Special Reserve, the Territorial Force or Army, just before the first World War.

For the Tudor and Stuart period, the introduction to the booklet by Gibson and Dell gives the historical basis of the Muster Rolls and Militia Lists. The earliest rolls date from 1522, when Wolsey ordered a muster, which may be seen as a pretext for a detailed valuation of property. The arrangement of documents is by parish within the hundred. Extensive lists exist for the period up to 1580, with a few further examples up to 1640, in several series of both Exchequer records and of State Papers Domestic.

For the period of resurgence of the militia, from 1757 onwards, the introduction to the booklet by Gibson and Medlycott provides a detailed survey of the several types of list produced. As Medlycott has pointed out, in an earlier article entitled 'Some Georgian 'Censuses', the militia ballot lists from 1757 to 1831, and the 'defence' lists for 1798 to 1804 form a group of records which may be said to take the place of censuses. Clearly they should be consulted by every family historian, once the parish of origin has been determined, and not just by those tracing a military ancestor.

By the time of the Napoleonic conflicts, Britain was maintaining a constitutional home defence force, the militia, which could not be sent out of the country; a militiaman who joined the regular army at this time was liable to six months' imprisonment. By the Ballot Act of 1802 most men aged between 18 and 40 could be drafted into the militia. If there were insufficient volunteers in an area, lists were compiled of able-bodied males, following which ballots were held to select some of them for service. Those selected, if unwilling to serve, but able to pay a fine of £15, could buy immunity for five years. Alternatively, if they could find a substitute, they could acquire immunity for life – the initial going rate was £25. It is important to distinguish between the initial lists, termed Ballot Lists by Gibson and Medlycott but often called Militia Lists in other sources, and the lists which followed the ballot, called Militia Muster Rolls or Enrolment Lists.

An example of a militia enrolment list, dated 23rd October 1779, shows that men were sworn for the Westmorland Militia at Appleby. William Whitehead, a tailor aged 17, height 5' 5', born at Orton, was serving as a substitute for Robert Bowman of Orton. On the other hand, Thomas Nelson, a cooper aged 18, born at Ravenstonedale, was serving on his own behalf for that parish. Some even volunteered, such as Thomas Gibbins, a cooper aged 21, born at Scattergate, who served for the village of Hoff. These examples are from the Lonsdale papers at the Cumbria Record Office, Carlisle, and are typical of many such lists which are available at County Record Offices, whether in Lieutenancy papers or in private collections.

Very similar to the earlier militia ballot lists are what Medlycott has called 'Defence Lists'. This term covers the Posse Comitatus lists of 1798 and the Levee en Masse lists of 1803-4. With the very real threat of invasion in early Napoleonic times, orders were given to compile lists of men not already serving in any military capacity. Again, these lists should be sought for the relevant area by any family historian, not just one interested in a particular military ancestor.

An example of the value of such lists is afforded by the publication of the Levee en Masse for the Wapentake of Staincliffe with Ewcross in the West Riding of Yorkshire, under the title 'The Craven Muster Roll 1803'. We were interested in the Willan family in the Dent township of Sedbergh parish, and the males aged between seventeen and fifty-five could be identified. In class 1, unmarried men under thirty with no child living under ten years of age, there was John Willan, a labourer. Class 2, unmarried men between thirty and forty-nine, with no child living under ten years of age, included George Willan, a farmer. Thomas Willan, a labourer, was in class 3, married men between seventeen and twenty-nine with not more than two children living under ten. Another John Willan, labourer, was in class 4, which comprised all those not in the first three classes.

As well as the units mentioned above, an Army of Reserve was raised by the Additional Forces Act of 1803, in an attempt to increase recruitment into the regular army. This reserve was raised by ballot in the same way as the militia. There was never conscription as such, but considerable pressure was now brought to bear in the ranks of the militia and reserve to transfer to the regular army. An interesting commentary on this complicated area is contained in Glover's 'Wellington's Army'.

The families of men who served in this Army of Reserve were entitled to a 'Family Allowance' of 1s 6d per week for the wife and for each child under ten years of age. The records of these payments are contained in the Exchequer Receivers' Accounts of Land and Assessed Taxes, Subsidiary Documents, E 182 at TNA. A most interesting article on these accounts for the Basingstoke area of Hampshire has been published by Edward Lawes. For example, one of the 42 families listed for Stockbridge in May 1804 was that of James and Eleanor Gornall, with their children Eleanor 8, Ann 4, Philip 3 and William 1, (E 182/922, Part 2). While discussing E 182, it is worth noting that this series contains deserter bounty certificates for militia, as well as for the regular forces. A partial card index of deserter bounty certificates is available at TNA, and also a partial index on microfiche from 1803 (see TNA Catalogue for E 182).

For the period from 1757 onwards, many militia records are kept at TNA. Documents such as muster rolls, description books, returns of officers' service, are available. The major sources held at TNA are listed in the table below, but the researcher is well advised to consult Spencer for further detail. As mentioned earlier, the Militia Papers of WO 96 are currently (2008) being digitized and should be on-line by 2010. It must be noted, however, that much material relating to the militia was never collected centrally and should be sought in County Record Offices and private collections.

WO 13/1-4675	Muster Books and Pay Lists Militia including Supplementary Militia and Local Militia, Fencible Infanty and Cavalry, Yeomanry and Irish Yeomanry and Volunteers	1780-1878
WO 68/1 –568	Militia Records Including enrolment books, description books, casualty books, court martial books	1759-1825
WO 96/1-1522	Militia Attestation Papers	1806-1915

Volunteers and other Auxiliary Forces

Volunteer groups had of course arisen at various times in the history of the country, usually when invasion threatened. A very brief summary will be attempted here. The Volunteers were usually infantry, and were raised in 1794 as a supplement to the Militia. Similarly the Yeomanry, or cavalry, commenced in 1804. Local Militia were formed in 1808 but had disappeared, along with the Volunteers, after Waterloo in 1816. A new Volunteer Force, or Rifle Volunteers, was formed in 1859. The Yeomanry, meanwhile, had continued in existence but combined with the Volunteer Force in 1907 to form the Territorial Force. In 1908 the Militia was given the title Special Reserve.

(Following World War I, the Territorial Force became the Territorial Army in 1921, and the Special Reserve again became the Militia. From 1924 until disbandment in 1953, the Militia survived as a Supplementary Reserve. From 1940 to 1945 the Home Guard, or Local Defence Volunteers, were in charge of home defence.)

Fencible infantry and cavalry were in fact regular regiments raised for service at home but they were often classed with the militia. When the army was reorganised on a regional basis in 1882, many county militia regiments and volunteer units became third, fourth and even fifth battalions of local regiments.

The expression 'auxiliary forces', at the time of the Army Discipline and Regulation Act of 1879, in fact referred to the militia, the yeomanry and the volunteers. At this date, when the pay and allowances of the regular land forces at home and abroad totalled nearly £5 million, it is interesting to note the following expenditure on auxiliary and reserve forces:

	£
Militia, not exceeding 132,526 men, including	*495,200*
30,000 militia reserve	
Yeomanry cavalry	*47,900*
Volunteer corps	*512,400*
Army reserve first class, not exceeding 22,000	*203,000*
and army reserve second class	

The Imperial Yeomanry was raised in 1899 especially for the South African War. Officers' service must be sought in Army Lists around that date, as individual records have not survived. Documents for other ranks are noted in the table below.

A list of nearly 40 000 men who served in the Imperial Yeomanry, Lovats Scouts and Scottish Horse, in the Boer War of 1899-1902, has been published by Kevin Asplin. He quotes names, ranks and numbers, units, clasps to Queens South Africa medal and casualty status. Further indexes and lists for Boer War soldiers have been published by the same author. See the following website:
http://hometown.aol.co.uk/KevinAsplin/home.html

The following table presents a list of some of the material related to personal information on officers and soldiers available at TNA. It should be stressed, as for militia, that much material is preserved elsewhere in archives, private collections and regimental museums - see for example the compilation for 'Military History in the North West' by Terry Wyke and Nigel Rudyard.

WO 13/1-4675	Muster Books and Pay Lists Militia including Supplementary Militia and Local Militia, Fencible Infanty and Cavalry, Yeomanry and Irish Yeomanry and Volunteers	1780-1878
WO 13/3726-3785	Fencible Cavalry	1794-1802
WO 13/3786-3791	Fencible Provisional Cavalry	1794-1802
WO 13/3968-4159	Yeomanry	1803-1853
WO 13/4160-4621	Volunteers	1797-1814
WO 23/25	Pensioners discharged from Yeomanry regiments	1821-1829
WO 23/89-91	Pension Payments to Volunteers, Yeomanry, Local Militia	1868-1882
WO 97/	Soldiers' Documents	1760-1854
1091-1112	Local Regiments (Militia) – alphabetical by name of soldier	
1173	Fencible Volunteers	
WO 127/1-23	South African War, Local Armed Forces, Nominal Rolls	1899-1902
WO 128/1-165	Imperial Yeomanry Soldiers' Documents South African War (index in WO 129)	1899-1902
WO 129/1-12	Imperial Yeomanry Registers, South African War	1899-1902

CHAPTER FIVE
Other sources - prior to 1914

There are of course many other sources of information on officers and other ranks outside the War Office and associated series at TNA. Some of these are outlined in this section for the period preceding 1914. The topics covered are Indexes, Army Museums, Medals and the Army Medal Office, Vital Records – that is records of births, baptisms, marriages, deaths and burials, Archives Abroad, the London Gazette and Indian Armies. Various other useful sources are listed in a final section.

Army Indexes

Many 'army indexes' have already been mentioned in Chapter Three on 'Other Ranks – prior to 1914 – Finding the Regiment'. Some other smaller and more specialised indexes are noted here.

Nowadays, of course, many indexes and listings (that is, possibly incomplete lists) may be accessed on-line, for instance via GENUKI. Another tactic used by surfers is to 'google' (or 'dogpile') the area of interest to see what is currently available. One must be aware also that websites may change names or become unavailable.

Sussex Military Marriages 1750-1812 have been extracted from parish registers by Michael Burchall and published by the Sussex Family History Group. The Group has also published a listing of military baptisms, marriages and deaths, 1793-1840, for Brighton St Peter, Preston Village. (www.sfhg.org.uk)

Researchers and late-night browsers alike are indebted to Stephen Lewis of Cheltenham. His website may be found via www.members.tripod.com /~Glosters/memindex3.htm

A remarkable series of listings, mostly to **those who died in service,** can be found there under Military Records, in two categories, **Officers Died** and **Soldiers Memorials**

Officers Died includes listings for:

North America & Canada	1750-1782
Peninsula Campaign (from A History of the Peninsula War, Vol VIII, John Hall - a listing of officers who died in action as well as of 'natural causes', with separate list for the King's German Legion)	1808-1814
Quatre-Bras & Waterloo (from 'The Waterloo Roll Call' by Charles Dalton) Peninsula & Waterloo Veterans	1815
Afghanistan	1838-1842
Gwalior	1843
Sutlej Campaign	1845-1846
Punjab Campaign	1848-1849
Indian Mutiny (above items from 'Soldiers of the Raj' by G de Rhe-Phillipe, 1912, 'The Mutiny Casualty Roll' by I Tavender and 'Hodson's Index')	1854-1856
Crimean War (from 'The Crimea Casualty Roll' by F Cook)	1854-1856
Afghanistan (from 'The Afghan Campaign' by S Shadbolt and 'Soldiers of the Raj')	1878-1880
The Boer War (from 'The Last Post' by M Dooner, 'With the Flag', 'After Pretoria')	1899-1902

The website also lists (many of) those killed in service, or those who died as a result thereof, in the Irish Rebellion of 1916, Malaya 1948-1960, Korea 1950-1953, Northern Ireland 1969-1999 (for NCOs and Men), Falklands 1982, Kosovo 1999, Afghanistan and Iraq 2003-2008.

Soldiers Memorials includes listings from graves and other memorials in many countries, for most of the campaigns noted above for officers, as well as the following:

Crimean War (from grave inscriptions recorded in 1858 by Capt John Colbourne (60th Rifles) and Capt Frederic Brine (Royal Engineers))	1854-1856
South Africa (from 'South Africa Campaign' by Mackinnon and Shadbolt, 'Zulu' by I Knight)	1879
Egypt	1882
Sudan (from 'Egypt 1882' by M Mawson, 'Egyptian Soudan' by Halford & Sword)	1896-1897

'Lives of the Light Brigade' is the title of the E J Boys archive, where many details of those involved in this famous encounter may be found. A full listing of soldiers is in progress on the website: www.chargeofthelightbrigade.com

The **Crimean War Society** welcomes new members and publishes a wide range of material related to that conflict. See www.crimeanwar.org

A **'Great Crimea War Index'** is being compiled by Major Brian Oldham, although no recent information could be obtained about it. It is an index of all British soldiers who took part in the Crimean War and covers those regiments who went to the Crimea between 1854 and 1856. Admiralty sources have not been used, so naval and marine personnel are not included. However, those British soldiers who served with the Ottoman Army will feature if they were awarded the Crimean War medal (listed also in WO 100/22-34).

Further information may be sought by application to Major Brian Oldham, 21 Malting Close, Stoke Goldington, Buckinghamshire MK16 8NX.

West Kent and East Kent Settlement and Removal Indexes - although not strictly military, this series of indexes produced by Miss Gillian Rickard for the county of Kent includes references to soldiers, their wives and children. Many soldiers passed through Kent on their way to or from the mainland of Europe, and there are often examinations of soldiers and militia men stationed at Hythe, Ashford, Chatham and Woolwich. Sometimes wives and children were examined with a view to removal to their home parish, after their husbands had been posted overseas. Two examples are given from the parish of Hythe.

Exam: of John WALKER, one of the Dragoons in Sir Charles Howard's Regiment of Dragoon guards, dated 2 May 1753 - he was born in the parish of Kirkenswell Cumberland where he remained till he was about 10 years old, from which parish he went to the City of York and in the parish of Peter the Little in the City of York he was bound apprentice to Jeremiah Hall, tailor, deceased, for seven years, where he remained three and a half years and was about twelve years old when bound apprentice and departed without his Master's consent and afterwards went to the town of Hull, Yorkshire where he worked as a weekly servant with Francis Sommerscale in Trinity House Lane Hull for one year or so and when about fifteen years old inlisted himself into General Winyard's regiment of foot and worked as a servant with Joseph Wallis of Portmahon tailor for about twelve months and remained at Portmahon four years and returned to Portsmouth to England when he was about twenty years old and was there about twelve weeks and worked as a servant for about eleven weeks there but with who he can't say and afterwards went to the parish of St Anne's Soho and worked with Jno Darby tailor for sixteen or seventeen weeks and then went to the City of York where he inlisted himself into Sir Charles Howard's Regiment of Dragoon guards and was at that time about 22 years old and when about 23 years old married Eleanor Taylor at the City of Norwich by whom he has one child named John - signed John Walker. Dated 2 May 1753

The examination of Ann CUMMINGS wife of Thomas Cummings, a musician in the 1st Battalion, 95th Regiment now in Portugal, dated 7 December 1811. Her father Anthony Simonson by trade a weaver lived in Pepper Corn Lane in the City of Kendall Westmorland, he belonged in the said city but what parish she cannot say, he was afterwards adjutant of the 3rd Regiment called the Buffs and when lying at Chatham she was born, he afterwards went to the West Indies and died there abt eleven years since, she has not gained a settlement in her own right, she was lawfully married to Thomas Cummings at Colchester and has one child born in wedlock aged about two and a half years - signed Ann Cumming (7 December 1811)

Information about these indexes and fees for searches may be found at www.kentgen.com or by email to GRickard@kentgen.com.

In Memoriam: Roll of Honour - Imperial Forces - Anglo-Boer War 1899-1902, University of KwaZulu-Natal Press, 2001. Compiled by Steve Watt, this is a comprehensive reference and definitive listing of every individual who died serving with the Imperial forces in the Anglo-Boer War 1899-1902 (including civilians), as well as of those who died during the period of occupation up to 1913. The listing covers over 25 000 who died with details of which unit they were attached to, where and how they died, and where they are buried. Where possible the religion of each casualty and record of exhumation, age, grave number and monument listing are included.

National Army Museum

The National Army Museum, Royal Hospital Road, London SW3 4HT, houses the national collection of British army relics and 'the story of the British soldier through five centuries'. There is also a reading room where books, archives, photographs and prints relating to the history of the British, Indian and colonial armies may be consulted. Although it is unlikely that one will find material relating to a particular soldier ancestor, it is certain that one can find many interesting documents and equipment, which should bring to life the conditions he faced. Website: www.national-army-museum.ac.uk

At the National Army Museum, material is generally arranged by regiment, but there are also bibliographical indexes to books and archives. The collection is extensive and varied; the following items were among many in an exhibition there entitled 'Only a Scrap of Paper?'.

Regimental Hospital Register	19th Foot	1789
Regimental Punishment Register	Monmouth and Brecon Militia	1793
Payments to relatives of officers and men killed	87th Regt	July 1807 to April 1814
Roll of Soldiers' Families	9th Queen's Royal Lancers	Oct 1906

The National Army Museum has preserved an important series of documents, previously held by the Ministry of Defence, relating to **deceased soldiers' effects**. These records cover the period 1901-1990.

The records of deceased soldiers' effects are particularly valuable as they cover soldiers who died or were killed in service between 1901 and 1990; it will be recalled that the main material for 1901-1914, Soldiers' Documents (WO 97), only relates to discharged soldiers. The record books may contain useful genealogical information.

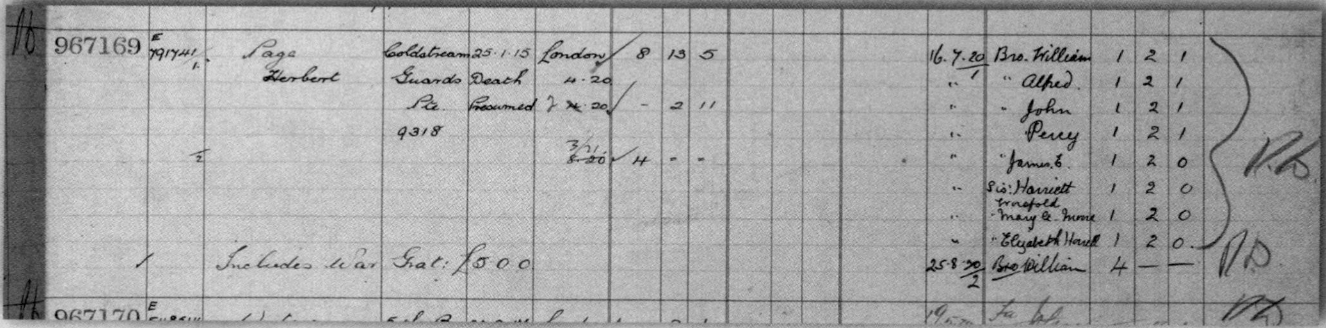

967169 E 791741 1. Page Herbert Coldstream Guards Pte. 9318 25.1.15 Death Presumed London 4.20 7.4.20 8 13 5 - 2 11 3/21 8.20 4 - -
16.7.20 Bro. William 1 2 1
" Alfred 1 2 1
" John 1 2 1
" Percy 1 2 1
" James E. 1 2 0
" Sis: Harriett 1 2 0
" Mary A. Ironfold 1 2 0
" Elizabeth Hall 1 2 0
25.8.20 Bro William 4 — —
Includes War Grat: £5 0 0

Reproduced by permission of the National Army Museum

Figure 18 - Deceased soldiers' effects, Private Herbert Page, Coldstream Guards, death presumed 25 January 1915

The name and relationship of recipients of a deceased soldier's estate are given, as well as service details, such as unit, regiment, rank and regimental number.

Record No	661911	Account and Date	London 6/18
Registry No	E/616225/1	Credits	£19-5-10
Soldier's Name	Watts, Reginald	Charges	£19-5-10
Regt	25 Bn MGC	Account & Date	MO 8/18
Rank No	Pt 143035	Date of Authority	21-8-18, 26-11-19
Place and	France, Action	To whom authorised	Fa: Henry G
Date of Death	21-3-18	Amount Authorised	£19-5-10, 9s 10d

These records are currently held off-site at Stevenage by the National Army Museum. There is no public access to them but an official search will be made at a cost of £10 per entry.

The archivist at NAM commented as follows to our recent enquiry:
'Despite the misleading title of this run of records, enquirers will not be able to discover what personal effects a soldier left. Rather, it is a record of how much money was owing to a soldier upon his death and to whom it was paid. Up to 1914 other details are recorded such as date of enlistment and trade on enlistment; for WW2 there are often addresses. The chief value of the records is to First World War genealogists who, finding that their ancestor's service record was destroyed, want to identify whether a certain Fred Bloggs is their Fred Bloggs by discovering the name of the next of kin.'

Regimental Museums

Regimental Museums, and their associated records and archives, are often located in those towns and cities traditionally linked with particular units. For example, the Royal Warwickshire Regiment Museum is at St John's House in the centre of Warwick. However, with the Cardwell reforms of 1881, and the defence reductions of 1968 and 2005, one must not expect to find a museum for every single 'old' regiment. For example the Regimental Museum, Queen's Lancashire Regiment, at Fulwood Barracks, Preston, contains the archives of several predecessor regiments, namely the East Lancashire Regiment (30th and 59th Foot), the South Lancashire Regiment (Prince of Wales's Volunteers) (40th and 82nd Foot) and the Loyal Regiment (North Lancashire) (47th and 81st Foot).

There is no known listing of documents and archives held throughout Britain at regimental museums and headquarters. However, much very useful material is preserved in regimental archives, especially for the twentieth century. Regimental journals and photographs are to be found, along with regimental histories and personal reminiscences. Although the primary sources of personal information have been retained centrally, in the War Office department records at TNA, it is always worth enquiring from a Regimental Archivist or Curator what relevant material is held locally. Reference has already been made to a very useful bibliography for the North West of England, by Terry Wyke and Nigel Rudyard.

At the archives of the Royal Regiment of Fusiliers, Wellington Barracks, Bury, an enlistment book for the Lancashire Fusiliers, 1881-1903, is preserved, including a full description of soldiers. A similar nominal roll for the 80th Foot, 1804-1881, is kept at the Staffordshire Regiment HQ, Whittington Barracks, Lichfield.

An excellent listing is contained in 'A Guide to Military Museums and other places of Military Interest' by Terence and Shirley Wise.

The Army Museums Ogilby Trust (AMOT) Guide to Military Museums has produced a website which is approved by the Ministry of Defence as the definitive guide to the regimental and corps museums of the British Army spread throughout the United Kingdom. A printed version of the information available on the website was published in March 2007 as 'Military Museums in the UK', Third Millennium Publishing, 2007. Website: www.armymuseums.org.uk

Medals and the Army Medal Office

Medals have been mentioned earlier in the context of the search for the regiment of a soldier ancestor. Once a soldier's service is known, it is tempting to see if he received a campaign or service medal. He may even have received one of the more famous medals for gallantry or for meritorious service.

The primary sources for medal awards are the medal rolls now kept at TNA. Campaign medal rolls are in WO 100, and a brief summary of relevant campaigns is contained in Appendix 1. Meritorious Service Awards are in WO 101/1-7, for the period 1846 to 1919; Long Service and Good Conduct Awards are in WO 102/1-16 for 1831 to 1902.

Awards for individual gallantry date from the Crimean War. Published books list recipients of the more famous, the VC, DSO and DCM. The original records for the VC are in WO 98 at TNA, WO 32 for the DSO and MC, WO 146 for the DCM. Recipients of the DCM, for the period 1855 to 1909, are also listed in a volume of the original PRO Lists and Indexes.

The Army Medal Office was located for about sixty years at Droitwich Spa in Worcestershire. In 2005 it moved to MoD Medal Office, Building 250, RAF Innsworth, Gloucester, Gloucestershire GL3 1HW. It administers the award of Honours, Decorations and Medals for the Ministry of Defence. Website: www.mod.uk/DefenceInternet/DefenceFor/Veterans/Medals.

It is no longer possible to replace campaign medals for service before 1920, although replacement of service medals after 1920 is still permissible. Replacement of medals is only offered to the recipient or the immediate next of kin, and then only when clear and documented proof of loss is provided.

Reference has already been made to Battle Honours of the British and Indian Armies, 1695-1914 by N B Leslie and Spink's catalogue of British and associated decorations and medals by E C Joslin. The collecting of medals, ribbons and clasps is in itself a highly specialised activity, and further titles relating to this are contained in the bibliography.

'Vital Records'

Family historians will of course follow up the traditional lines of research, in church and civil registers, in the UK and abroad. These records are vast, and even when partially indexed, they may not give a direct lead to soldier ancestors. However, if all else has failed to reveal a soldier's marriage, or baptisms and burials of family members, then it is necessary to follow him 'round the world'. Some pointers are given from the authors' and others' experiences, to encourage researchers not to give up.

Registers of Births, Baptisms, Marriages and Deaths and Burials

Soldiers travelled the world as part of their experience of life in the army. This did not stop them from getting married or having children, despite the many limitations imposed by the army when they were on active service overseas. Mention has already been made above of the usefulness of army records of birth, marriage and death in tracing a soldier's regiment. However, it is clear that the military made much use of civilian churches wherever the army of the time happened to be. Once one knows where an ancestor served, for instance from regimental muster books, it is logical to check in the parish registers of nearby churches to see if any records are available of his family. A first check would of course be made in the relevant sections of the IGI.

Before 1837, many births and baptisms in England and Wales were recorded in non-parochial and non-conformist registers, which were later transferred to the Registrar General. These are now available at TNA in classes, RG 4, RG 5 and RG 6. A new partnership project is underway between TNA and S&N Genealogy Supplies to digitise and place these records on-line. Basic searching will be free, with a charge for advanced searching and to download images,

Below we give some examples of events relating to the military, although it must be emphasised that these are random finds picked from small localised indexes.

Sussex Military Marriages, 1750-1812, were assembled by Michael Burchall from entries in 86 parishes. Stray military marriages in Cornwall have been collected by HN Peyton.

Marriages at St Peter's, Tiverton in Devon for 1795-1800 were extracted by Sheila Pike, for example:

James Cumming	*Sergt*	*62nd Foot*	*St Catherines Edinburgh*
Mary Lee			*Of this parish*
17 Oct 1798 by licence			
Andrew Townsend	*Soldier*	*11th Foot*	*Ealms Co Derry*
Elizabeth Cornish			*Of this parish*
11 Aug 1796 by licence			

The frustration of searching for a soldier's missing marriage can only be lessened by hoping that it may turn up one day in a collection of 'strays', such as those noted in the marriages registers of St Helier, Jersey between 1815 and 1824 :

George Lowe	*57th Foot*	
Martha Berryman		*of Guernsey*
13 Aug 1815		
Peter Faddy	*Captain Royal Artillery*	
Margaret Dutron		*of St Peter's Port Guernsey*
16 Sep 1815		*now living in St Helier*

Marriage Licence Bonds, which are increasingly being indexed nowadays, may also provide a soldier's marriage far away from home. This example is from Norwich Archdeaconry bonds for 1813-1837:

Thomas Fitzgibbon s 33   Sergeant 5th Regiment Dragoon   Yorkshire
*   Guards   Huddersfield*
Ann Willoughby s 30   King's Lynn St Margaret
14 Sep 1818 – to marry at King's Lynn St Margaret or St Nicholas

For our own searches, involving Private John Watts of the 6th Foot, we knew that he had left the army in August 1816 with a wife (first name Catherine) and three children. He had presumably married and had these children during the last six or seven years in the army, unless he had married the widow of a comrade, as frequently happened, and 'acquired' the latter's children. We had searched the IGI and also the indexes to Regimental Registers and Chaplain's Returns without success. In fact the Regimental Registers for the 6th Foot do not survive before 1837, and so the only remaining course was to see whether his marriage or children's baptisms took place in parishes near where he was stationed.

John Watts had served in Canada with the 6th Foot, from about 1800 to 1806, and it proved possible to borrow a microfilm copy of the register of Holy Trinity Anglican Church, Quebec, from Library and Archives Canada in Ottawa. Many events relate to British soldiers, for example:

2 Nov 1799
John Egan, age 20, Private of the 6th Foot, died 2 Nov 1799, was buried; present, from 6th Foot, Sgt James Robinson and Cpl Robert Nash

26 Nov 1799
Catherine Smith, daughter of John Smith, Sergeant of the 6th Foot, and Francoise, his wife, was baptised

11 Jun 1800
Catherine Firty, daughter of John Firty, Private of the 6th Foot, and Elizabeth, his wife, was buried

29 Sep 1800
Samuel Parke, age 32, Corporal of the 6th Foot, executed for murder 29 Sep 1800, was buried

John Watts had been based in Gibraltar during 1807 to 1808, so we asked for searches to be made of appropriate registers there. The Military Chapel, or King's Chapel, holds records of baptisms from 1769, marriages from 1771 and burials from 1786. An Army Chaplain is still based at King's Chapel and has care of their registers. Despite continuing efforts, especially in the Cork and Kinsale area around 1810 to 1812, we must sadly note that so far there has been no trace of any relevant record of either the marriage of John Watts and Catherine, or of the baptisms of the three children born by 1816.

'The British Overseas'

At this point it is worth mentioning another potential source of information on the records of birth, baptisms, marriages, deaths and burials of 'The British Overseas', compiled by Geoffrey Yeo.

The important feature of this booklet is that it lists records which are now held in the UK, either at TNA, by the General Register Office or by the Guildhall Library, London.

Most of these registers were kept for any British overseas, not solely for the armed forces, but it would clearly be worth trying to find a specific event or family in them, depending on one's knowledge of their whereabouts at a particular time. The researcher is advised firstly to consult 'Tracing your Ancestors in the National Archives, the website and beyond', by Amanda Bevan. This deals with a very complicated topic and provides an extensive table of the overseas birth, marriage and death records held at TNA.

A brief summary of **registers, originating with the Registrar General, but now held at TNA** is given here:

RG 32/1-35	Miscellaneous Foreign Returns	1831-1953
RG 33/1-160	Miscellaneous Foreign Registers & Returns	1627-1958
RG 34/1-9	Miscellaneous Foreign Marriages	1826-1921
RG 35/1-69	Miscellaneous Foreign Deaths	1830-1921
RG 36/1-13	Registers and Returns of Births, Marriages and Deaths in Protectorates of Africa and Asia	1895-1950
RG 43/1-19	Miscellaneous Foreign Returns of Births, Marriages and Deaths Indexes	1627-1947

Entries in RG 32 to RG 36 are largely indexed in RG 43, and copies of this are held at TNA.

The National Archives also hold some **Foreign Office registers**, containing records of births, baptisms, marriages, deaths and burials. These registers formed the basis of consular returns to the Registrar General; it would appear that some material is unique and is not duplicated in the Consular Returns now held by the Overseas Section of the General Register Office. As Amanda Bevan points out, one is able to browse through these Foreign Office registers at TNA; the GRO material is indexed, but certificates must be bought in the usual way to gain fuller information. A few examples from the Foreign Office list of registers are given below.

FO 446/3-6, 28-30	Argentina, Buenos Aires	marriages	1826-1900
FO 681/13-22	China, Chefoo	births	1861-1943
		marriages	1872-1940
		deaths	1906-1933

TNA also holds a few registers for the West Indies, preserved in the records of the **Colonial Office** department. Examples are given below.

CO 152/21, 25	West Indies, Antigua	baptisms and burials marriages	1733-4, 1738-45 1745
CO 152/18, 25	West Indies, Montserrat	baptisms, burials, marriages	1721-1729

Yeo also refers to some records of Forces chaplains abroad which are now held at the **Guildhall Library, London,** namely those for the Cape of Good Hope Garrison, 1795-1803, and for the Gibraltar Garrison, 1807-1812. These are indexed in a composite index of Foreign Registers at the Guildhall. The volume for the Gibraltar Garrison would seem to have been the personal register of one Thomas Tringham, serving as 'Chaplain of Brigade to the Forces in Gibraltar' at that time. A typical entry reads

John Cameron Harvey Wilman, son of Harvey Wilman, Captain in the 2nd Battn of the 9th Regiment of Foot, and Abigail his wife, born at Warrington, County of Lancaster on the 6th day of January 1810, baptised at Gibraltar on the 5th day of April 1812 by me Thomas Tringham

Chaplains' Returns have been mentioned in Chapter Two; however, it would appear that there is no certainty that all registers compiled by army chaplains have actually been returned to the appropriate authority and entered with the records currently available through the General Register Office. For instance, the **Archives Nationales du Quebec** has the original Garrison Registers for Quebec for 1797-1800 and 1817-1826. The first set related to soldiers of the 24th and 26th Foot, being kept by Rev James Henderson and Rev Alex Spark, while the later registers were the work of Rev

Joseph Langley Mills, Chaplain of HM Garrison in Quebec. These are also available on microfilm loan from Library and Archives Canada in Ottawa.

Some Garrison Registers for 'events occurring abroad' are currently held by the Overseas Section of the General Register Office and it is likely that most names from them are indexed in with the main series of Chaplains' Returns. However, since Yeo refers to these **Garrison Registers** but does not include details, a list of them is provided here.

Garrison and Station Registers (Original Registers) now held by the GRO

Garrisons of Cork	births baptisms	1886-1910
	births baptisms	1913-1914, 1921
Garrison of Cologne	baptisms	1920-1929
	marriages	1919-1929
Antwerp and places in Dutch Brabant	births baptisms marriages	1810-1815
Ostend, Martinique, Trinidad	births baptisms marriages burials	1812-1816
St Jean de Luz and Toulouse (France) and Vera (Spain)	baptisms (one) marriage	1813-1814
Valenciennes (France)	births/baptisms	1809-1818
Valenciennes (France)	marriages (two only)	1817
Ionian Islands, Kingdom of Naples and elsewhere	births baptisms	1809-1864
Army of Black Sea and British Salonika Force	marriages	1916-1923
Garrisons of Egypt	marriages	1886-1924
Guadaloupe and North America	baptisms marriages burials	1813-1815
Madeira	baptisms marriages burials	1814
Garrison of St Lucia	baptisms marriages burials	1898-1905
Barbados (Windward and Leeward Islands Command)	deaths burials	1804-1906
Garrisons of Halifax, Nova Scotia, Quebec,	baptisms	1823-1906
Toronto and Kingston	marriages	1813-1871
(Upper Canada)	burials	1847, 1866-1869, 1793-1870

This somewhat haphazard presentation of lists of registers for the 'British Overseas' may be continued with **another collection of military registers held at TNA.** Those in WO 68 and WO 69 cover baptisms and marriages. Material for the period after 1918 is included here for completeness.

WO 68/	formerly militia		
439	Rifle Brigade 6th battalion	114th West Meath	1834-1904
441	Somerset Light 3rd & Infantry 4th battalions	Somerset Militia	1836-1887 1892-1903
497	West Norfolk Regiment		1863-1908
499	King's Own Yorkshire Light Infantry 3rd battn	1st West Yorkshire	1866-1906
499	West Yorkshire Rifles 3rd battalion	2nd West Yorkshire	1832-1877

WO 69/		
63-73	Royal Horse Artillery	1817-1827
551-582	(most entries relate to the period 1860-1877)	1859-1883

WO 156/			
1	Dover Castle	baptisms	1865-1916
2	Shorncliffe and Hythe	baptisms	1878-1939
3	Dover	baptisms	1929-1940
4	Buttevant	baptisms	1917-1922
5	Fermoy	baptisms	1920-1921
6	Jerusalem and Palestine	Command baptisms	1939-1947
7	Sarafand, Palestine	baptisms	1940-1946
8	Sarafand	marriage banns	1944-1947
9-10	Canterbury Garrison	burials	1808-1811, 1859-1884, 1957-1958
11-638 See below, under Garrison church registers			

RG 4/		
4330-4332, 4387 Royal Chelsea Hospital	baptisms marriages burials	1691-1856

RG 4 entries of baptism and marriage should also be found in the IGI (www.familysearch.org). However, as noted above, these registers are being digitized under a joint project between TNA and S&N Genealogy Supplies.

Finally we come to **garrison church registers.** Anglican registers were held until quite recently by the Royal Army Chaplains' Department (RAChD), who were based at Bagshot Park, Surrey, but now at the Armed Forces Chaplaincy Centre, Amport House, near Andover. Their registers have been transferred to TNA, in class WO 156, comprising 638 volumes of baptisms, confirmations, deaths/burials and marriages for both UK and overseas garrisons.

Garrison church registers for Catholics are still preserved by the Bishop's Office (Diocese of Portsmouth), Wellington House, St Omer Barracks, Thornhill Road, Aldershot, Hampshire. The archivist may be approached via www.portsmouthdiocese.org.uk

Civil Registration in the British Isles and at Sea

The Registrars General in London, Edinburgh, Dublin and Belfast hold a variety of records, including the familiar civil registers, which are of direct relevance to military ancestry. Many of these have already been introduced and described in the section on 'Finding the Regiment before going to the National Archives'.

Soldiers will clearly be mentioned in the normal records of births, marriages and deaths. These date from 1837 in England and Wales, but there is no specific or separate index here to personnel in the armed forces. However, from about 1880, there are separate indexes to soldiers of Scottish or Irish origins.

At the General Register Office, Edinburgh, there are records for soldiers of Scottish birth or origin. **'Service records (from 1881)' include Army Returns of Births, Deaths and Marriages of Scottish persons at military stations abroad during the period 1881-1959.** There are also certified copies of entries relating to marriages solemnised outside the UK by Army Chaplains since 1892, where one of the parties is described as Scottish and at least one of the parties is serving in HM Forces. 'War registers (from 1899)' cover the deaths of Scottish soldiers in the South African War (1899-1902); World War I (1914-1918), the deaths of Scottish persons serving as Warrant Officers, Non-commissioned Officers or Men in the Army or as Petty Officers or Men in the Royal Navy; World War II (1939-1945). Also there are incomplete returns of the deaths of Scottish members of the Armed Forces.

The General Register Office, Dublin, has records, required under the Births, Deaths and Marriages (Army) Act, 1879, of Irish persons serving throughout the British Commonwealth up to 1921. There are index entries at the back of each normal annual index volume, running from 1888 to 1930 for births, and to 1931 for marriages and deaths. There is also a separate index of deaths of Irish soldiers for the Boer War, 1899-1902.

Further details of the civil registration arrangements for Scotland and Ireland are to be found in **'Tracing Births, Deaths and Marriages at Sea'** by the present authors. In relation to Service Registers, the comment is made that 'it is unclear as to whether deaths of service personnel at sea, from 1881 onwards, would be recorded in the Marine Deaths Register or in one of the various service or, if appropriate, war death registers, so it would be wise to check both'. Therefore, if a birth in a soldier ancestor's family is known to have occurred at sea, it would be worthwhile to check the various records described in the above book. A podcast based on this topic may be found on the National Archives website at www.nationalarchives.gov.uk/rss/podcasts.xml/army-bmd.mp3

Some Irish sources

The **1901 and 1911 censuses for Ireland** are of course available for public research. They are currently being indexed by surname, with free online presentation planned. However, if one knows that an ancestor was serving in a particular regiment that was based in Ireland at the time, then useful information may be gleaned from this census return. For example, the 2nd South Lancashire Regiment was based at the Military Barrack of Buttevant, South Cork in 1911 and included the following.

Henry Broadhurst *Religious profession: Church of England*
Sgt Major 2nd S Lancs Regt
Education: (can) Read and Write age 39 *Occupation: clerk Married*
(Where Born) England

George Riddock
Sergt 2nd S Lancs Regt *Religious profession: Methodist*
Education: (can) Read and Write age 27 *Occupation: clerk Single*
(Where Born) Co Antrim)

Charles Ashley
L Cpl 2nd S Lancs Regt *Religious profession: Church of England*
Education: (can) Read and Write age 21 *Occupation: musician Single*
(Where Born) England

The above entries were made on a Form H, 'Return of Military, RI Constabulary or Metropolitan Police, in Barracks'. Each married man, if 'residing with his wife in Barrack', was also required to fill in a separate Form A, as used by the 'Community at large', for his family members.

(Website: www.census.nationalarchives.ie)

Military cemeteries have recently attracted the attention of family and local historians in Ireland.

British Military Graveyard, Ballincollig, Co Cork, Ireland, 1810-1922 by Anne Donaldson, published by the Ballincollig Enterprise Board in 2003, ISBN 0-9545075-0-9, provides an interesting history of the army serving in this small town about six miles west of Cork city. Regiments represented in the burial registers, as well as family names, are listed. Many well-researched accounts are given of the events surrounding the deaths of soldiers and members of their families.

Memorial Inscriptions of Grangegorman Military Cemetery, Dublin, Ireland, published by the Genealogical Society of Ireland, 2006, ISBN 1-898471-47-9, is another important contribution to knowledge of British army personnel in Ireland. Grangegorman Military Cemetery, on Blackhorse Avenue, Dublin has been in use since the 1870s as a burial ground for British and Commonwealth military service personnel and their families.

Among the burials are soldiers who took part in the Crimean War, the First and Second World Wars, the 1916 Easter Rising and those who perished on the 'RMS Leinster' when it was sunk in the Irish Sea by a German torpedo in 1918. This publication is a valuable source for military, family, local and social historians, containing the transcriptions of over 1,300 headstones and memorials, providing such details as rank, regiment and date of death together with a surname index. Copies of 'Memorial Inscriptions of Grangegorman Military Cemetery' are available from: Genealogical Society of Ireland, 11 Desmond Avenue, Dun Laoghaire, Co. Dublin, Ireland The Society's website is www.familyhistory.ie The Commonwealth War Graves Commission website includes the following note about Grangegorman Military Cemetery:

'The cemetery was opened in 1876 and was used for the burial of British service personnel and their near relatives. It contains war graves from both world wars.

Some of the graves were re-located to this site at a later date (nine from King George V Hospital grounds, two from Trinity College grounds, three from Portobello (Barracks) Cemetery, two from Drogheda (Little Calvary) Cemetery and one from Oranmore Old Graveyard). The 'Leinster' graves are in several trenches in the different denominational plots. A Screen Wall Memorial of a simple design standing nearly two metres high and fifteen metres long has been built of Irish limestone to commemorate the names of those war casualties whose graves lie elsewhere in Ireland and can no longer be maintained. Arranged before this memorial are the headstones of the war dead buried in Cork Military Cemetery but now commemorated here. There are now 613 Commonwealth burials of the 1914-1918 war, 2 of which are unidentified, and 12 of the 1939-1945 war, 1 of which is unidentified, commemorated here.'

An incomplete listing of names may be found at www.interment.net/ data/ireland/dublin/grangegorman

Archives and Sources Abroad

Australia

'How to Trace your Military Ancestors in Australia and New Zealand' by RH Montague gives an overview of the activities (pre 1914 of course) of regiments of the British Army in Australia. This booklet provides a list of the units stationed there, with covering dates. Although there are no major series of original records in Australia for the soldiers who served there, many muster books and pay lists are available on microfilm for research in Australia, under the Australian Joint Copying Project (AJCP).

SAG's index to Soldiers and Marines 1787-1830

The Society of Australian Genealogists provides free access to an index of soldiers and marines who were stationed in New South Wales in the early Colonial period, 1787-1830. They give the following background to this index.

'From the beginning of the Colony of New South Wales in 1788 until 1870 various British Military Regiments including the Marines arrived on our shores. Their role was to protect the inhabitants by acting as a police force and to keep law and order, especially when it came to bushrangers. The 3rd Regiment was the first to provide men for the Mounted Police.

It was not only New South Wales which felt the military presence, as their command spread over the other colonies - Van Diemen's Land, Victoria, South

Australia, Western Australia and Moreton Bay (now Brisbane). In 1860 the 40th Regiment saw service in one of the Maori Wars in New Zealand.

At the end of their term in the colony the Regiments usually travelled on to the various British India establishments such as Madras and Calcutta. A soldier was usually given the option of staying on in the colony if he wished to settle here. Thus there are many Australians who have British Military ancestors. Their names may be found in this index.

The names have been obtained from one selected Quarter of a Regimental Paylist and Muster and Admiralty Muster. The original material for the later regiments is to be found in The National Archives, Kew, London and forms part of the War Office records which are identified as series WO12.'
The regiments featured in the index are 3rd Foot (Buffs), 39th Foot (Dorsetshire), 40th Foot (2nd Somersetshire), 46th Foot (South Devonshire), 48th Foot (Northamptonshire),73rd Foot (Highland), 102nd Foot (New South Wales Corps).

Their website is www.sag.org.uk

James Hugh Donohoe's 'The British Army in Australia, 1788-1870, Index of personnel' is now available in book, microfiche and CD formats.

'Between 1945 and 1995, the Australian Joint Copying Project (AJCP) microfilmed material in the Public Record Office, London and elsewhere relating to Australia, New Zealand and the Pacific. Among the documents was War Office correspondence and returns. Donohoe has indexed the personnel in the War Office Muster Books and Pay Lists. He has listed the full names of 34,139 officers and men. The names are in alphabetical order, three columns per page and each name is referenced to the unit in which the soldier served. Each unit is referenced to the AJCP Reel Numbers and Piece Number.

If a British soldier served in Australia between 1788 and 1870 then his name is most likely to be listed by Donohoe. With the AJCP Reel Number and Piece Number the unit muster rolls and pay lists can be examined. Copies of the AJCP are held by the National Library, State Libraries and some University libraries. Reels can be ordered through inter library loan.'

Reference has been made above to the **War Office Pension Returns** (WO 22), which are available for the period 1876-1880 for Australia, for New South Wales 1849-1862 and then 1871 to 1880, and for Queensland, Tasmania and Victoria from

1876 to 1880. There is a complementary set in the State Records of South Australia for the period July 1843 to December 1844.

Their website:is www.archives.sa.gov.au

Army Deserters from HM Service in Australia have been transcribed from the Victoria Police Gazette by Yvonne Fitzmaurice. Volume I covers 1853 to 1858; Volume II for 1859 to 1870 also includes deserters in New Zealand.. A typical example reads:

Rank	Pte	Enlisted Place	Warrington
Regt No	707	Date	7 7 1855
Name	Joseph Beckton	Birthplace	Manchester Lancs
Age	37 y 4 m	Occupation	Silk-weaver
Height	5' 5'	Regiment	50th
Complexion	Fresh	Place of desertion	Sydney
Hair	Sandy	Date of desertion	19 3 1869
Eyes	Grey	Remarks and Brands	(see VPG = more information is available from the source or the author)

Another publication, listing military and naval deserters in Australia and New Zealand from 1800 to 1865, has been compiled by Rae Sexton.

Nominal rolls are now accessible on-line for people who served in the following conflicts:

Sudan War - NSW contingent to the Sudan, 1885
Boer War - personnel in Australian units, 1899-1902
Boxer Uprising - China, 1900-1901
Website: www.awm.gov.au/database/nroll.asp

Canada

Library and Archives Canada, Ottawa, hold, in Record Group 8, a surprisingly large series of original records relating to the British Army. This Record Group, 'British Military, Ordnance and Admiralty Records, 1757-1903', relating of course to activities in Canada, consists of four series. Series I (formerly the 'C' Series) comprises British Military Records, Series II covers Ordnance Records, while

Series III and IV relate to Admiralty Records. There is a name index to much of the material; this index and Series I have been microfilmed and may be borrowed for study elsewhere.

In our search for John Watts, who served in Canada with the 6th Foot from 1800 to 1806, we looked at three volumes of depositions, memorials, returns and correspondence for this regiment. Many soldiers are named, although John Watts did not feature in the records. For example, for the 1st June 1801, there is a return of fifteen men, giving their names and origins, who had deserted three days earlier. The CO requested permission to try them before a General Court-Martial. Thirteen of them were apprehended within the next ten days, heading for the USA, and it was assumed that the others had probably perished in the woods. On 19th May 1801, it was reported that Captain Martin Alves and a detachment of the 6th Foot, which had sailed from Portsmouth on the 'Sovereign' on the 22nd April, had been shipwrecked on Cape Breton island. The twenty men, five wives and three children were all safe but had lost clothes and equipment. Names, ages and heights of the men were given, as were the names of the women.

Further military material is available at Library and Archives Canada in various manuscript groups (MGs). MG 13, War Office, London, comprises an extensive collection of copies and microfilm of War Office records kept at TNA, selected to relate to the activities of the British Army in Canada. MG 18, Military and Naval Documents, includes copies of some Muster Rolls of New England troops serving against the French between 1710 and 1760. (The original rolls are in the Massachusetts Archives, Boston.) MG 23, Late Eighteenth Century Papers, and MG 24, Nineteenth Century Pre-Confederation Papers, both contain interesting military items. For example, there is a record book of punishments ordered by courts martial at the Quebec Garrison between 1777 and 1784. All manuscripts are well calendared by the Manuscripts Division.

War Office Pensions returns in WO 22 are available at TNA, for Canada for the period 1845 to 1862 and for Nova Scotia for 1858 to 1880.

France

This section concentrates on archives, in both France and Britain, which may be searched for information on **British soldiers during the French Revolutionary and Napoleonic wars,** that is from 1793 to 1816. Much material has survived, but few indexes exist.

There are extensive sources, in France, for British prisoners of war and internees during some periods of the French Revolutionary and Napoleonic Wars. These were described by the late Mme Margaret Audin in the Genealogists' Magazine (Volume 20 Number 8 pp 274-277 December 1981). Her research was sparked off by two baptismal entries in the parish registers for St Ann, Turton (Lancashire) in 1811 and 1813. These were for Mary and Edward Fairbrother, children of Edward and Dinah Fairbrother, and the baptisms were performed by William Gorden, 'vicar of Dunsten, Oxfordshire and Chaplain to the British Prisoners of War in Verdun-sur-Meuse'. The latter town had been designated by Napoleon as the assigned residence for English citizens living in France during the Continental blockade.

Edward Fairbrother, a labourer, was born in 1782 at Edgworth (near) Manchester. Muster rolls for the 2nd Foot Guards in 1809 are annotated 'Prisoner War' against his name. (Private Communication from Mrs Marjorie Pollard, based on her research and that of Captain Erik A Gray for Mr A Fairbrother of Bramhall, Stockport). An enquiry to the Archives Communales de Verdun resulted in the supply of birth certificates for the two children, Mary and Edward Fairbrother. Civil registration had been ordered by Napoleon both in France and in other areas temporarily under his rule, for example Holland.

The birth entry for Mary Fairbrother read (in translation):

No 226 Marie Ferbrother

The year 1811, the 30th May at 10 o'clock in the morning. Known to us Louis Gaud, mayor of the town of Verdun, being the Registrar of the Registry Office of the said town.

Appearing at the Town Hall, Edward Ferbrother, soldier in the service of His British Majesty, English prisoner of war at the depot of Verdun, aged 27 years, billeted in the house of one Nicolas Pierre, locksmith, in this town in Mongaud Street, who presented to us an infant of feminine sex born in his billeting the 28th May precisely at 3 o'clock in the afternoon, declaring it to be of him and of Danna Bradshaw his wife and to whom he declared to give the first name Marie.

The said declaration and presentation made in the presence of the said Nicolas Pierre, locksmith, aged 36 years, of Mongaud Street, and of one Jean-Baptiste Burthé, journeyman carpenter aged 65 years of Dancuraux Street in the said Montgaud and the said witnesses signed with their names the presented birth certificate, the said

Edward Ferbrother, father of the infant having declared neither knowledge of writing nor of signing of this certificate after a reading of it was made.

Mme Audin's searches in the Verdun registers revealed more than 600 births, marriages and deaths concerning English prisoners. She estimated the number of PoWs and hostages in France at between twelve and twenty thousand. Sadly her planned name index of British personnel was never published.

The late Jim Beckett has written about 'British Prisoners in France 1808'. While sorting through some parish documents for Cartmel, north Lancashire, he had discovered lists of over 1800 persons held prisoner at various places in France: Verdun, Valenciennes, Arras, Sarrelibre and Bitche. There appears to be no clear reason for their being filed with Cartmel parish papers. (Reference at the Lancashire Record Office, Preston PR 2712/4 - see also Manchester Genealogist, Volume 15, No 1, January 1979)

Recently, considerable information on **centrally held records of British PoWs in France** has kindly been provided by another researcher in France. These are held at three archives in Paris. A brief summary of material is given below.

French Army Archives, Château de Vincennes

This archive holds much material on British PoWs for the 'Premier Empire' (1804-1814), but none for the Revolutionary Wars of 1793-1802. There is an alphabetical list of names for the forty-eight boxes of correspondence between the prisoners and the French authorities.

Other archive groups feature:

YJ 28	General correspondence, including lists of British captives and authorizations for their travel, with itineraries.
YJ 29	Yearly lists of British PoWs captured on ships, 1806-1815
YJ 30	Lists of British PoWs by prison depot, 1804-1814
YJ 31	Further name lists of British people captured on various ships
YJ 32	British PoWs at Verdun, Sarrelouis, Valenciennes
YJ 33	British PoWs, lists of names and correspondence

French Navy Archives, Château de Vincennes

These include:

FF2-61	Alphabetical lists of British prisoners exchanged	1797-1798
FF2-62	Name lists of British PoWs	1802-1808
FF2-71	Name lists of British PoWs exchanged	1798-1799
FF2-67		1799-1800
FF2- 95		1798-1802

The following examples are taken from Register FF2-95, entitled *'Prisoners of War exchanged Year VII to Year X (22 September 1797 to 22 September 1802) in accordance with Articles 2 and 3 of the Cartel concluded 14 September 1798'*. Most of those listed were in fact from merchant navy vessels.

Date	Ship or place of capture	Names	Rank	Weighting according to tariff
22/11/98	at Ostend	Wiltshire Wilson	Artillery Captain	2
28/02/99	the 'Betsy' merchant ship	Wm Wilson	Mate	2
15/07/99	the 'Maria'	Henry Wilson	Master	3
11/01/00	49th Regiment	Richard Johnson	Lieutenant	3
11/01/00	4th Regiment	Thomas Wilson	Lieutenant	3
13/07/01	'Stork' sloop of war	John Wilson	Master	6

A description of the Ostend expedition of 1798 is given by Iain Swinnerton in Prisoners of War, Part 3, the rate of exchange, Family Tree Magazine, October 2005.

French Foreign Ministry Archives, Quai d'Orsay

This holds much general information on the subject of PoWs in the political correspondence files. Laws were passed from 1793 ordering the arrest of all British subjects in France. However, agents were appointed on both sides to organize the exchange of some prisoners. By the peace treaty of Amiens in March 1802, which marked the end of the Revolutionary Wars, all prisoners and civilian internees were to be released within six weeks of its ratification. Dated 1806, there is a list of English prisoners freed, following the outbreak of the Napoleonic wars in 1803.

135

The National Archives (TNA) at Kew also house records of this period. There is no single finding aid or index but the following may be searched for a specific individual. Some lists in ADM 103 do contain an index for that piece.

ADM 30/63/12-17	Pay lists for British PoWs at Givet, Verdun, Arras, Bitche	1806-1807
ADM 103/467-481	British in France, prisons, British released from France	1787-1820
ADM 103/630-633	Deaths of prisoners, British in France	1794-1815
ADM 105/44-66	Prisoners' applications, misc. reports	1795-1820
WO 25/2409	PoWs at Valenciennes	1805-1813
WO 28/11	Orders, letters and returns - PoWs held at Lille	1798-1799

An example from these papers is given below, for John Drought of the 12th Hussars. Extensive research by his descendant, Dr Michael Stratford, revealed that John Drought had been taken prisoner by the French in Spain on 27 September 1811. The casualty list for the 12th Light Dragoons (WO 25/1437) recorded this date for him, while the Muster Master General's Office index (WO 25/1205) noted that he had been *'struck off 24 December (1811) having been taken by the enemy. Rejoined 29 April (18)14'.*

The original in ADM 103/480 is in French - an English translation is provided here.

1. Port of St Servan (St Malo)
List of English Prisoners returned to their country from the port of S'Servan since the hostilities have ceased

Ships on which they effected their departure and date
John Drought   soldier   12th Dragoons Gunboat No 90 (26 April)

2. Gunboat No 90 (Le Parliementaire), Captain Wm Cudenet Ens de Vaiss

Nominal list of the English passengers who have obtained passports to return to their country and embarked at St Servan with Wm Cudenet, at this moment in harbour, and are to return to Jersey

Depot
No 81   John Drought   12th Dragoons Briancon

Order: the present list of the 153 English prisoners of war who W Cudenet (Captain of .... No 90) will transport to Jersey where he will obtain a receipt from the Governor of that island.

'**British Prisoners of Napoleon**' is a project organized by Professor Peter Clark, collecting information for a period of almost 11 years, from the Collapse of the Peace of Amiens in May 1803, to the First Abdication of Napoleon on 6 April 1814. He has written to the authors as follows: 'the total number of the names of PoWs from the British Army (all ranks) adds up at present to 2 173. They come from two major sources; at first soldiers captured in transport ships, and then later from the Peninsular War, as the struggle progressed in the period 1810 to 1814.'

'One weakness is the names of men who were captured after March 1812; they do not appear on the Lloyd's Relief Lists, and it seems that all lists from depots were destroyed shortly after the end of the war. At a guess those 'missing names' may number several hundreds. Another hiatus is the absence of the names of men who were captured in the brief period after Wellington and his Army crossed from Spain into the South of France. We know that many British soldiers and stragglers were captured, but the battles of Orthez and Toulouse took place in so short-lived and disruptive a period for the French that British men who were captured never got marched as far as the Depots where their names could have been recorded. I have not found any lists for such short term PoWs, and doubt if any exists, and their number would be in the region of a few hundreds.'

'At present I am in the final stages of completing a database, for the names of all known prisoners (hostages, detenus, travelling gentlemen and families, naval officers and seamen, army officers and soldiers, merchant masters, mates, and merchant seamen, and some unfortunate passengers). The list currently contains 14,881 named individuals, with their forenames, surnames and any known alternative spellings, their titles, rank or profession, ships they served in, or regiments they belonged to, their home towns if known, any special notes (for example if mentioned in contemporary diaries, newspaper reports, published narratives, and if for any reason their names were reported in the Daily Secret Police Reports to Napoleon, if any wives and children were with any of them, the various escapes, successful and unsuccessful, special releases, if they died in captivity in France, if named in the SHAT Archive at the Chateau de Vincennes, if they fathered any known children in France), the depot or depots where they were held, and especially if any known living descendants have been traced.'

'My current work is now focusing on PoWs who managed to escape. They are one of the most difficult categories to trace, since they often elude any of the known lists or more obvious sources. I am steadily working my way through the many internal police reports, and at a guess there are perhaps another two hundred or so individuals to add to the database which will bring the total number of named British prisoners up to 15 000 or so. A detailed and annotated bibliography for all published works on the subject of the prisoners now runs to 225 pages.'

Professor Clark is happy to check requests from any enquirers to see if any potential names are included in the data base, but will not undertake major pieces of research, unless the enquiry happens to be particularly important, or of wider significance than an individual's own family interest. He may be reached at 66 Lancaster Road, London, N4 4PT, or by email at bpn1803to1814@mac.com   (BPN = British Prisoners of Napoleon).

New Zealand

'How to Trace your Military Ancestors in Australia and New Zealand' by RH Montague gives an overview of the activities (pre 1914 of course) of regiments of the British Army in New Zealand. This booklet provides a list of the units stationed in NZ, with covering dates. British forces were based there, mainly in the period 1840 to 1870, during the Maori wars.

As for Australia (see above), there are no major series of pre 1914 original records kept in NZ , but many muster books and pay lists are available on microfilm, under the Australian Joint Copying Project (AJCP), at all Australasian National and State Libraries.

If a soldier forebear was discharged in New Zealand between 1840 and 1870, then a most useful source has been provided by Hugh and Lyn Hughes. From muster rolls they have transcribed names, and birthplaces where given, of all soldiers of the 'Imperial Foot Regiments' discharged there. Those involved were foot regiments numbers 12, 14, 18, 40, 43, 50, 57, 58, 65, 68, 70, 80, 96 and 99. Over eight hundred soldiers of the 58th Rutlandshire regiment took a New Zealand discharge.

Five hundred army pensioners recruited from Great Britain settled as the Royal New Zealand Fencibles between 1848 and 1853 at Howick, Otahuhu, Onehunga and Panmure. The names of these military colonists have been extracted from sailing lists and indexed by Shirley Kendall in the 'Pensioner Gazette', which records personal accounts of the settlers and their descendants.

Montague gives further interesting details of military settlement schemes in NZ in the 1860s. Many of those involved were born in Britain or Ireland. Nearly two thousand recruits, many from the goldfields of Victoria and Otago, were attracted, between 1863 and 1866, to join the four regiments of Waikato Militia by the prospect of free land. There are also roll books for these regiments. A similar settlement was tried between 1863 and 1869 at Taranaki and Hawkes Bay. Archives New Zealand hold enlistment details and particulars of land grants.

The following information appeared recently on the New Zealand government website, about the personnel records of soldiers who served in the Boer or South African War:

'The military personnel files of those who served in our Defence Services during the South African (Boer) War (1899-1902) have been transferred to Archives New Zealand from the New Zealand Defence Force, Personnel Archives.

In recognition of the enduring historical value of these records, an agreement was signed in 2005 by the Chief of Defence Force and the Chief Archivist of Archives New Zealand to transfer these files into the permanent care of Archives New Zealand. In so doing both parties acknowledged the significance of these records to our national and family histories. The records transferred are for personnel whose service ended prior to 31 December 1920. Archives New Zealand will keep and care for the records in perpetuity. They will undergo conservation treatment as required, and be located in a special temperature and humidity controlled environment. The records have open access and can be accessed by families, researchers and the general public. Archives New Zealand now holds 6425 personnel files for New Zealanders who served in the South African (Boer) War. Note that the personnel files of ninety two (92) Boer War servicemen who were still serving in New Zealand's military forces after 31 December 1920 have been retained at NZDF Personnel Archives at Trentham. These will not be transferred to Archives New Zealand until further notice.'

Archives New Zealand's website is: www.archives.govt.nz and their on-line index to New Zealand government archives is www.archway.archives.govt.nz

War Office Pension returns (WO 22) are available at TNA, for New Zealand for the periods 1845 to 1854 and from 1875 to 1880.

South Africa

The following information has been gleaned from the internet and could be helpful to those wishing to find servicemen in South Africa since the Boer Wars.

The Documentation Centre (Department of Defence Archive) is the custodian of the archives of the Department of Defence/SANDF since its inception in 1912 as the Union Defence Force. All records of offices of the Department of Defence are transferred to the Department of Defence Archives when they are ten years old or older.

The Department of Defence Archives specializes in military history. It houses the official records of the Department of Defence as well as a collection of unique publications, unit history files, photographs, maps and pamphlets pertaining to the Department of Defence/SANDF and its predecessors dating from 1912. The Personnel Archives and Reserves (PAR) which also forms part of Documentation Centre, houses the personnel records of all former members of the SANDF and its predecessors. These personnel files are invaluable as a source for biographical details.

The Documentation Centre currently houses approximately two million files consisting of 1 607 different archival groups and approximately 250 680 personnel files. The most frequently consulted archival groups are as follows: Adjutant General. Chief of the General Staff. Commandant General. Director General Air Force. Divisional Documents. Naval Ships Logs. Chief of the Navy Ships Logs. Quartermaster General. Secretary for Defence. Union War Histories. Various War Diaries for the First and Second World Wars.

Address: Documentation Centre of the SANDF, Department of Defence, Private Bag X289, PRETORIA. (e-mail info@mil.za)

A very useful guide to South African military history, with bibliography and sources, by Rowena Wilkinson may be found on the website of the Military Museum at Johannesburg:

http://www.militarymuseum.co.za/ANCESTORS.html

USA

The National Archives of the United States hold extensive records of volunteer soldiers who fought in various wars, in the Federal Government's interests. The so-called compiled military service records date from 1775 to 1902, from the Revolutionary War to the Philippine Insurrection. The National Archives Building also houses service records for US Regular Army Officers, 1789-1917, and for enlisted men 1789-1912. There is clearly very little material available for soldiers who served in the British Army, unless an ancestor changed his allegiance during the revolutionary period.

Those interested in American military records will find a full description in Chapter 8 of Eakle and Cerny's 'The Source'. A section covers the period of the 'colonial wars 1675-1763', and an extensive bibliography lists published muster rolls from this period. The National Archives' own guide to genealogical research also gives full details of records for volunteers and the regular army.

Website: http://www.archives.gov/genealogy/military/

Other useful sources for army research pre 1914

London Gazette

The London Gazette, dating from 1666, is England's oldest surviving newspaper. 'Published by Authority', it is the official newspaper of government, carrying acts of state, proclamations and appointments to offices under the Crown in its weekly editions and extensive supplements. Full series may be found in the State Papers Room of the British Library, and at TNA in ZJ 1/1-1430, as well as in many major libraries in the UK and overseas.

The London Gazette publishes details of all Army Commissions, in both the Regular Army and in the Militia, and indexes may be used to trace such events for officers. Other ranks are less frequently mentioned, although full lists of Casualties were published during the Crimean War as well as a list of amounts due to the dependants of deceased soldiers following that conflict. During the siege at Sevastopol, for example, regular reports and nominal lists were published. The Second Supplement to the London Gazette, of Tuesday the 27th of November 1855, published on Thursday 29th November 1855, reported the following among the wounded on the 15th November:

Nominal Return of Non-Commissioned and Privates
WOUNDED on the 15th November 1855
WOUNDED, by the explosion of magazines
in camp (of French siege-train)
19th Regiment of Foot
1214   Corporal James Doorly, severely
2987   Private Jeremiah O'Brien, severely
2693   John Caldwell, contusion
3319   Robert Sommerville, slightly
3596   John Gearedd, slightly
2763   Edwin Herwood, severely
887   William Beech, slightly

The website. www.gazettes-online.co.uk, gives free searchable access to the London Gazette, the Edinburgh Gazette and the Belfast Gazette and is therefore particularly useful for tracing commissions and awards during the World War periods of 1914-1920 and 1939-1948.

Records of officers and men of the East India Company's armies, 1708-1861 and of the Indian Army, 1861-1947, are to be found in an extensive collection, formerly at the India Office Library, and now part of the British Library in central London. A fully detailed listing of India Office military records has been produced by Anthony Farrington while Fitzhugh has provided a general introduction to the subject of East India Company ancestry. Peter Bailey has written more recently with 'Researching ancestors in the East India Company armies' while Ian Baxter's guide to biographical sources in the India Office Records has now reached its third edition.

A brief guide to biographical sources at the former India Office Library provides summaries of material available on European Officers, Departmental and Warrant Officers, European NCOs and Privates, Medical and Veterinary Officers, Indian Officers and Other Ranks, and Bandsmen, for both periods listed above. There is also much material for officers and other ranks of British Army regiments stationed in India. For example, lists of officers in British Army regiments are given in the series Military Statements for Bengal 1785-1858, Madras 1794-1858 and Bombay 1791-1858. These are then continued in the Bengal Army list 1819-1889, the Madras Army list 1810-1895 and the Bombay Army list 1823-1895, followed by the Indian Army list 1889-1947.

Pension records are also available. For example, for other ranks in British Army regiments in India, the collection features Chelsea Pension Accounts 1870-1942 as well as Lists of Chelsea Out-Pensions drawn in India from 1873-1914. Ecclesiastical Returns should of course be searched for baptisms, marriages and burials.

Ian Baxter has written as follows about the 'reorganization of 1859-1861': 'after the government of India had been transferred from the East India Company to the Crown in 1858, the EIC European troops amalgamated with the British army, the infantry becoming regiments of the line and the artillery and engineers part of the Royal Artillery and Royal Engineers. Those officers who had been serving with the EIC European corps either followed them into the British army or obtained extra-regimental employment under the Government of India. Meanwhile the EIC native army, after extensive reorganization continued in being as the Indian Army, largely with the same officers as pre-1859.'

If one is aware of a soldier ancestor's service at some stage in India, then it is important to search both in the India Office collection at the British Library and also at the National Archives. Most service records for officers and men of the British

Army stationed in India will be found at TNA among the regimental and other records described in previous sections.

Additionally at TNA there are Pension Returns (WO 22) for Bengal 1845-1880, Bombay 1855-1880 and Madras 1849-1869; also Chelsea Registers (WO 23) for East India Company Pensioners 1814-1868. Muster lists for Victoria Hospital, Netley, give details of men discharged between 1863 and 1875, in WO 12/13017-13105. Further discharges are noted between 1875 and 1889 in the musters of the depot at Gosport, in WO 16/2282, 2888-2915.

The 'India Office Family History Search' database contains around 300 000 records for British and European people in India between 1600 and 1949. Website: http://indiafamily.bl.uk/UI/

A Soldier's Journey, by Sue Woods, is a most entertaining account of thorough research, at both TNA and the British Library, into an ancestor, Robert Joseph Gledhill. He had served in the British army in India, where he married and had children. (Manchester Genealogist, Volume 40, Number 4, 2004.)

A most useful list of 'Open access microfilms in the Asia, Pacific and Africa collections, in the Reading Room of the British Library' has been compiled by Emma Jolly. This gives a good overview of the material available in the Ecclesiastical Returns (N Series) as well as military records for the Bengal and Madras armies. (Genealogists' Magazine, September 2008.)

Journal of Society for Army Historical Research

The Society for Army Historical research, founded in 1921, produces a quarterly journal which is probably the major publication dealing with historical matters relating to the British Army. The first forty volumes (1921-1962) are indexed in an exemplary manner, first in a Subject Index, then in an Index to Regiments, Corps and Formations. Finally, there is a Concordance of Numbered and Named Regiments, which should settle most disputes about the precise dates and titles of the units of the British Army.

An occasional series of Special Publications will cover a topic in more detail or fully reproduce an important source. For example, Special Publication Number 3 is a reprint of the earliest known printed Army List, of 1740.

The Society for Army Historical Research may be reached via its Editor or its Secretary, c/o the National Army Museum, Royal Hospital Road, Chelsea, London SW3 4HT.

Army Records Society

The Army Records Society was founded in 1984 with the object of publishing documents relating to the military history of Britain. Each year the Society issues an edited volume illustrating some aspect of the Army's past. Membership of the Society is open to all – the Secretary's address via the National Army Museum, Chelsea as given above.

Waterloo Committee

The Waterloo Committee was founded in 1973 by His Grace the Duke of Wellington and is a charitable trust with a Belgian counterpart in Brussels. There is an Association of Friends, whose objectives are 'to promote public education and appreciation of the wars between Great Britain, her allies and France known as the Napoleonic wars, to preserve and safeguard the site of the battle, to encourage a better understanding of events which preceded the Battle of Waterloo and the course of military operations in the campaign of 1815 and its consequences and to encourage research on all matters pertaining to the campaign and to assist in the publication of such research'. Membership of the Association of Friends is open to all and entitles free entry to Stratfield Saye House and the Wellington Museum at Waterloo, as well as receipt of three journals per year. The current Honorary Secretary is John S White, 23a Wylde Green Road, Sutton Coldfield, B72 1HD.

An index of all men who fought at Waterloo has been compiled by Derek Saunders. He is a former Chairman of the Association of Friends, and also used to operate a small Waterloo Museum at Broadstairs. He welcomes enquiries from those who are reasonably certain that their soldier ancestor was actually involved at Waterloo. An initial application, with reply paid envelope, may be made to Mr D P Saunders, 15 Waldron Road, Broadstairs, Kent CT10 1TB.

We enquired on behalf of a friend researching the name Bradbury in Marsden, West Yorkshire, about soldiers of that name who had fought at Waterloo. Family tradition and letters recorded that two Bradbury brothers had lost their lives in the service of their country, one in the last charge of the French at Waterloo. Derek Saunders sent the following details:

Bradbury	Daniel	Driver	Royal Horse Artillery G Troop
Bradbury	Emmanuel	Sergeant	1st Dragoon Guards Wallace's No 3 Troop
Bradbury	Francis	Private	2nd Life Guards
Bradbury	George	Private	1st Dragoon Guards Elton's No 1 Troop

Bradbury	John	Private	1st Dragoon Guards Elton's No 1 Troop
			Killed in action 18th June
Bradbury	Randle	Private	52nd Foot
Bradbury	Thomas	Private	33rd Foot No 3 Company
			Wounded 18th June
Bradbury	William	Private	15th Light Dragoons

More recently, David Milner has been compiling a register of all those who fought at Waterloo and Quatre Bras. He welcomes information, and is willing to check specific queries provided you have good reason to believe a soldier was at the Battle, but neither he nor Derek Saunders can undertake 'one name' or 'blanket' searches. Website: www.waterloocommittee.org.uk - email for David Milner: battle.veterans@btinternet.com

Naval and Military Press

The Naval and Military Press specialises in books, CDs and related material for the 'serious student of conflict'. Their CDs of soldiers who died in the Great War, 1914-1919, and the Army Roll of Honour for World War II, 1939-1945, are justifiably well-known. Also most useful is the CD, Armies of the Crown, giving a comprehensive bibliography of regimental histories. Recently, Fortescue's History of the British Army, compiled between 1899 and 1930, has been reprinted by N&MP.

Their regular booklist may be obtained by applying to Unit 10, Ridgewood Industrial Park, Uckfield, East Sussex TN22 5QE, England. Online access is via www.naval-military-press-com.

The Society of Genealogists, London

The Society's Library has a growing collection of material on the British Army: at present, over 2 700 titles. As well as long runs of the Army List and of the Indian Army List, the Society has an almost complete set of the Journal of the Society for Army Historical Research with indexes. The earliest 'army list' held is a copy for 1588 but, prior to that date, there are a number of rolls of arms which may be of use. The Society holds an extensive collection of published regimental histories and medal rolls. These are all listed on the library catalogue. The document research notes and manuscript special collections include genealogical notes on many soldiers and their families and these include a lot of ephemeral items of military interest as well as containing much biographical information - including letters and diaries of soldiers.

The Society holds most of the books, fiche and CDs titles cited in this work. Where an item mentioned in the bibliography is also available at the Society, the shelf mark is shown in [square] brackets. The Society is also developing a database of all items mentioning the British Army, including magazine articles, held in its Library. This database can be consulted in the library of the SoG. After nearly a hundred years, the Society's collections are considerable so its Library may well be worth a visit: see the front pages for addresses etc. The Library Catalogue is freely available on-line at www.sog.org.uk

CHAPTER SIX
World War I Records

The Great War, nowadays usually termed World War One (WWI below), was the first conflict in which complete nations were engulfed in the struggles and horrors of war, which had previously been confined to battlefields. Almost all family historians discover that family members were involved in some way. There are countless examples of family mementoes kept by relatives, such as letters, post cards, photographs and medals, and oral traditions have also preserved links with that time.

Many **service records** are now available for soldiers who participated in WWI. In the period of almost fifteen years since the first edition of this book, the surviving service records for soldiers have been microfilmed, and may be searched at TNA. Despite the collection there of over twenty eight thousand reels of microfilm, this represents the records of perhaps only forty per cent of soldiers, since many papers were completely destroyed by bombing during World War Two. The first three sections below deal with service records for **other ranks, officers and women.**

For soldiers who were killed, there are three sources which may readily be searched for further details. Foremost are the indexes and website provided by the **Commonwealth War Graves Commission**. The publication **'Soldiers died in the Great War'**, initially in eighty one volumes, may now be searched on CD, and on the internet. The separate **indexes to war deaths compiled by the General Register Office** can lead the researcher to an official certificate, which may be purchased from them.

There are many other lesser sources of information for soldiers of WWI. Although none is likely to give a very complete picture of his service, it is well worthwhile following up every small lead for clues to a soldier's experiences. The items and sources included in this chapter are listed below:

Army Service Records for Other Ranks
Army Service Records for Officers
Army Service Records for Women
Royal Flying Corps
Commonwealth War Graves Commission
Other War Memorial Projects
Soldiers died in the Great War
Index to War Deaths at General Register Office
Service Medal and Award Rolls
Gallantry Medals and Mentioned in Despatches
War Diaries
Imperial War Museum
Regimental Museums
London Gazette
Absent Voters' Lists
Western Front Association
Red Cross and Prisoners of War
Service Records held by families and Personal Accounts
Disability and other Pensions
'Local' Newspapers and Books
'National Roll of the Great War'
Memorial Plaque and Scroll
Courts Martial

Finally there is a brief section devoted to the involvement of soldiers from **Australia, Canada, India, New Zealand and South Africa.**

Army Service Records for Other Ranks

TNA holds two series of service records for other ranks. The first is termed the 'burnt' series (WO 363) and these relate either to those who died in service or to those who actually survived through the war. The second or unburnt series (WO 364) is for soldiers discharged to pension, including a medical discharge. The latter papers were brought together for administrative reasons, usually for pension purposes. Only about 40% of relevant papers survived the bombing in World War Two.

In total, service records have survived or have been reconstructed for about 2.8 million soldiers. The burnt documents now occupy nearly twenty four thousand reels of microfilm at TNA, while the unburnt documents take up nearly five thousand reels. Each series was formed by arranging the papers in alphabetical order of soldiers' names prior to microfilming.

The service records, WO 363 and WO 364, are all in the process of digitization. These records will then be available free on TNA computers, and on a paid basis through www.ancestry.co.uk (At August 2008, WO 364 has been completed, as has much of WO 363.)

Household Cavalry service records for WWI have all survived and have been transferred to TNA as WO 400. (As noted above in Chapter Four.)

Guards regiments service records for WWI are held still at their Regimental Headquarters, Wellington Barracks, London. No copies are currently held at TNA.

If a search is successful, then there is a wide range of papers and army forms, which may feature in a soldier's service record. These may include: attestation form, medical history, casualty form, statement as to disability, medical reports prior to discharge or transfer to the reserve, regimental conduct sheet and proceedings on discharge.

Examples are given below of some of the service records for **Private Percival John Watts.** The main form was of course the attestation paper on enlistment.

Army Form B 2505 Short Service (For the Duration of the War)
Attestation of 6071 Watts P J Royal West Kent Regiment

The first section featured 'Questions to be put to the Recruit before enlistment'

What is your name?	*Percival John Watts*
What is your full Address?	*8 Vanbrough Park Rd Blackheath SE*
Are you a British Subject?	*Yes*
What is your Age?	*19 years 90 days*
What is your Trade or Calling?	*Designer*
Are you Married?	*No*
Have you ever served in any branch	
of His Majesty's Forces.... ?	*No*
Are you willing to be (re-)vaccinated?	*Yes*

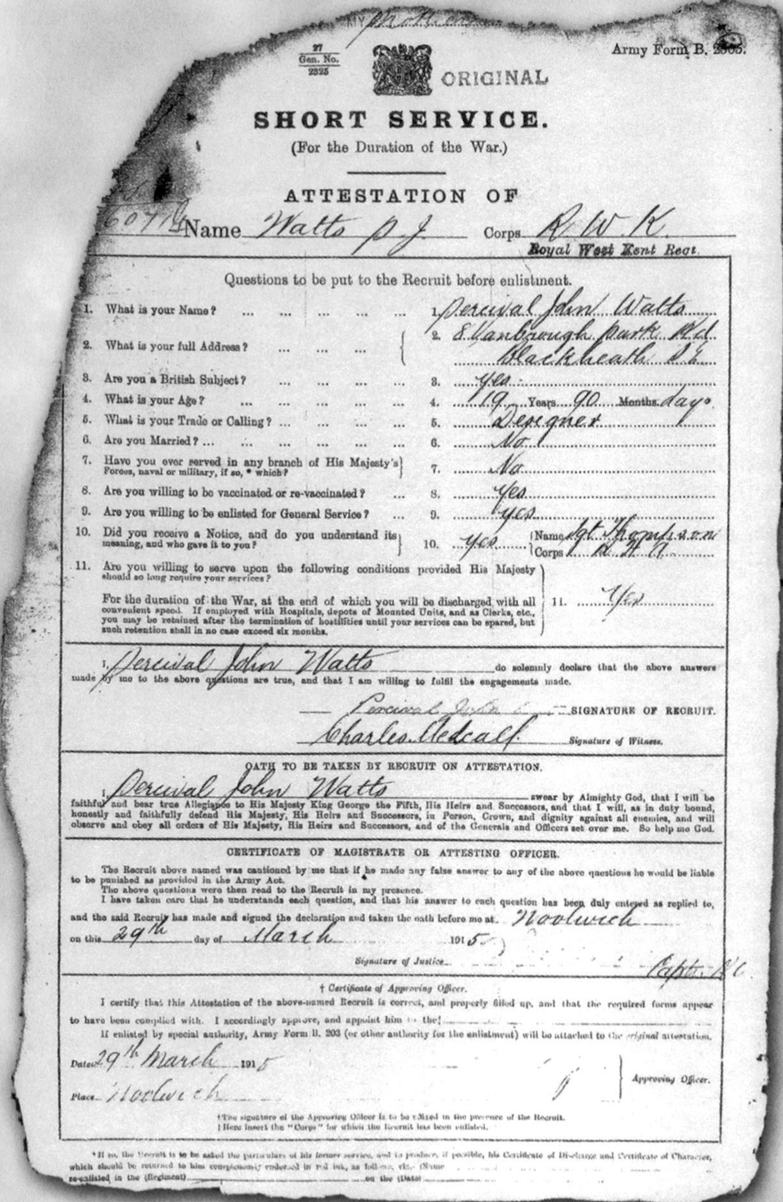

27
Gen. No.
2325

ORIGINAL

Army Form B. 2505.

SHORT SERVICE.

(For the Duration of the War.)

ATTESTATION OF

6071 Name *Watts P. J.* Corps *R. W. K.*
Royal West Kent Regt.

Questions to be put to the Recruit before enlistment.

1. What is your Name?	1.	*Percival John Watts*
2. What is your full Address?	2.	*8 Vanbrugh Park Rd, Blackheath S.E.*
3. Are you a British Subject?	3.	*Yes*
4. What is your Age?	4.	*19* Years *90* ~~Months~~ *days*
5. What is your Trade or Calling?	5.	*Designer*
6. Are you Married?	6.	*No*
7. Have you ever served in any branch of His Majesty's Forces, naval or military, if so, * which?	7.	*No*
8. Are you willing to be vaccinated or re-vaccinated?	8.	*Yes*
9. Are you willing to be enlisted for General Service?	9.	*yes*
10. Did you receive a Notice, and do you understand its meaning, and who gave it to you?	10.	*yes* Name *Sgt. Thompson* Corps *R. W. K.*
11. Are you willing to serve upon the following conditions provided His Majesty should so long require your services? For the duration of the War, at the end of which you will be discharged with all convenient speed. If employed with Hospitals, depots of Mounted Units, and as Clerks, etc., you may be retained after the termination of hostilities until your services can be spared, but such retention shall in no case exceed six months.	11.	*Yes*

I, *Percival John Watts* do solemnly declare that the above answers made by me to the above questions are true, and that I am willing to fulfil the engagements made.

Percival John W... SIGNATURE OF RECRUIT.

Charles Medcalf *Signature of Witness.*

OATH TO BE TAKEN BY RECRUIT ON ATTESTATION.

I, *Percival John Watts* swear by Almighty God, that I will be faithful and bear true Allegiance to His Majesty King George the Fifth, His Heirs and Successors, and that I will, as in duty bound, honestly and faithfully defend His Majesty, His Heirs and Successors, in Person, Crown, and dignity against all enemies, and will observe and obey all orders of His Majesty, His Heirs and Successors, and of the Generals and Officers set over me. So help me God.

CERTIFICATE OF MAGISTRATE OR ATTESTING OFFICER.

The Recruit above named was cautioned by me that if he made any false answer to any of the above questions he would be liable to be punished as provided in the Army Act.
The above questions were then read to the Recruit in my presence.
I have taken care that he understands each question, and that his answer to each question has been duly entered as replied to, and the said Recruit has made and signed the declaration and taken the oath before me at *Woolwich*
on this *29th* day of *March* 191*5*

Signature of Justice ... *Capt. R.E.*

† *Certificate of Approving Officer.*

I certify that this Attestation of the above-named Recruit is correct, and properly filled up, and that the required forms appear to have been complied with. I accordingly approve, and appoint him to the ‡ ...
If enlisted by special authority, Army Form B. 203 (or other authority for the enlistment) will be attached to the original attestation.

Date *29th March* 191*5*

Place *Woolwich*

Approving Officer.

† The signature of the Approving Officer is to be affixed in the presence of the Recruit.
‡ Here insert the "Corps" for which the Recruit has been enlisted.

* If so, the Recruit is to be asked the particulars of his former service, and to produce, if possible, his Certificate of Discharge and Certificate of Character, which should be returned to him conspicuously endorsed in red ink, as follows, viz.:- (Name ... re-enlisted in the (Regiment) ... on the (Date) ...

Figure 19 - Army Service Record for Private Percival John Watts, Royal West Kent Regiment, 1915, 1) Attestation page.

Are you willing to be enlisted for   Yes
General Service?
Did you receive a Notice, and do you understand   Yes
its meaning, and who gave it to you?   Sgt Thompson RHA
Are you willing to serve upon the following
conditions provided His Majesty should so long   Yes
require your services? For the duration of
the War......

The recruit signed to confirm that the above statements were true, he then took an oath on attestation, and a magistrate or attesting officer countersigned, followed by a further check from an approving officer. For Private Percival John Watts, this all took place at Woolwich on 29th March 1915.

Medical History Form B 17d

Surname	Watts	Christian Name	Percival John	
Birthplace	Parish	Charlton	County	Kent
Examined	on 29 day of March 1915			
Declared Age	19 years 90 days			
Trade or Occupation	Designer			
Height	5 feet 11 inches			
Weight	113 lbs			
Chest Measurement	34 ½ inches when fully expanded			
	2 ½ inches range of expansion			
Physical Development	Good			
When vaccinated	Infancy			
Vaccination marks	4			
Vision RE-V	6 / 9			
LE-V	6 / 9			
Approved by	W L Cassells Lieut RAMC			
Enlisted	29 March 1915			

Information supplied by the Recruit

Name and Address of next of kin:
James Watts 8 Vanbrough Park Blackheath SE
Relationship: Father

Statement of the Services

Service towards limited engagement reckons from				29 3 15
Joined at Woolwich				30 3 15
RWKent	D	Posted	Pte	30 3 15
	3rd	Posted	Pte	7 4 15
	8th	posted B E Force	Pte	30 9 15

Killed in Action	5 11 15	
Total Service towards Engagement to	5 11 15	222 days

Casualty Form Army Form B 103

Regimental Number	G 6071
Name	Percival John Watts
Enlisted	29 3 / 15
Terms of Service	Duration of War
Report Date	6 11 15
From	O C Battn
	Killed in action

Office copies of some letters have been preserved. One such letter related to the forwarding of personal property of the deceased to his father, at Blackheath, in February 1916. Sometime before 1920, the parents of Percival John Watts had moved to 38 Belgrave Road, Pimlico, SW; they signed a form to that effect in response to a request from No 2 Infantry Record Office, Staines Road, Hounslow, who wished to 'be enabled to dispose of the plaque and scroll in commemoration of the soldier named overleaf in accordance with the wishes of His Majesty the King'. However, a letter of July 1922 to the Pimlico address, from the Imperial War Graves Commission, noted that forms in reference to the grave of 6071 Pte P J Watts 8th Bn Royal West Kent Regt (died 5-11-15 Elzenelle Brasserie Cem Plot 7 Row B) had been returned by the Post Office authorities. Finally, a handwritten letter dated 10th September 1925 from Mrs K Watts has been preserved, notifying the Infantry Records Office of their latest address, at 16 Lind Street, St. Johns, SE8. The memorial plaque and scroll were then sent to the bereaved parents, James and Kate Watts.

The major book for this topic is 'Army Service Records of the First World War' by William Spencer, Public Record Office Readers' Guide No 19, 3rd edition 2001.

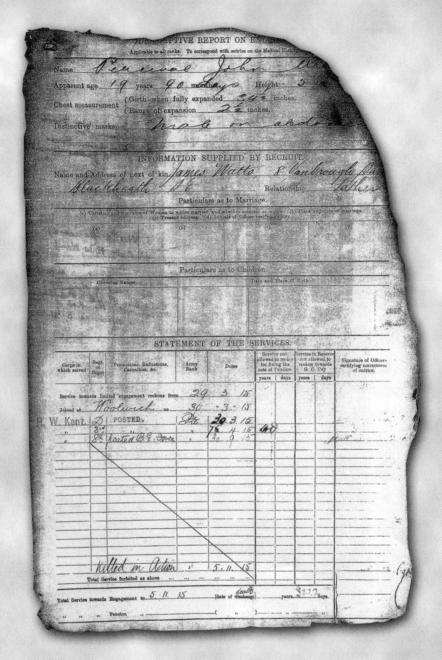

Figure 20 - Army Service Record for Private Percival John Watts, Royal West Kent Regiment, 1915, 2) Statement of Services

More details of the search procedure are outlined in TNA Research Guide, British Army: Soldiers' Papers: 1914-1918, First World War.

Army Service Records for Officers

All the main files containing service records for officers in WWI were destroyed in the bombing of Arnside Street in September 1940. However, supplementary files containing 'weeded' material had been kept elsewhere, and these are now available at TNA. This surviving material covers nearly 220 000 officers, estimated to be about 85% of the number involved. (It is known that records are missing for RAMC officers with a temporary commission.)

There are two main series of service records for officers, contained in WO 339/1-11072 and WO 374/1-77799, and a single index series in WO 338/1-23.

WO 339 holds the records of nearly 140 000 officers who ceased serving before 1922, and who were in the Regular Army or the Emergency Reserve. That is, they would come into one or more of three categories: a regular army officer pre-war, given a Temporary Commission in the regular army or commissioned into the Special Reserve of officers.

WO 374 forms the records of nearly 80 000 officers, who had either a Territorial Army commission and/or a temporary commission.

The records in WO 374 are indexed by name in TNA's Catalogue (accessible online), but unfortunately many entries only give the surname and a single initial. The records in WO 339 are arranged by 'long number'; again TNA's Catalogue often only gives the surname and a single initial. There is a contemporary nominal index in WO 338, on film at TNA, which gives full names, units and the 'long number'. This index includes references to officers' files that have not survived. Additionally references are contained therein to files still retained by MoD; these have the initial letter P and refer to files created after March 1922.

The procedure given above should enable one to find most officers although the usual difficulties may be experienced when searching for someone with a common name. In this case, it is sensible to begin one's search by first checking Army Lists.

Examples are given here of some of the service records for **Lieutenant George William Henry Potter** - known in the family as Harry Potter.

Short Service Attestation Form (Army Form B. 2512) records his initial service as a sapper with the Electrical Department of the Royal Engineers in Glamorgan, commencing January 1916.

He applied in 1917 for a commission in the Royal Garrison Artillery, but found himself ordered to report to an Infantry Training School at Crookham. A letter written by his father, John A C Potter, to the War Office, presumably added weight to an appeal against this development.

Casualty Form - Active Service (Army Form B. 103) records his subsequent moves, not 'casualties' as we might imagine in the sense of injuries.

Regiment or Corps	216th Siege Battery R.G.A.	
Rank	2/Lt	
Surname	POTTER	
Christian Name	G.W.H.	
	Place of Casualty	Date of Casualty
Embarked	Southampton	15.11.17
Disembarked	Havre	16.11.17

Report			
Date	From whom received		
1.12.17 O.C. 216 SB	Joined 216 SB	Field	27.11.17
8.12.17 (ditto)	Missing		30.11.17
17.3.18 SM List 307	Prisoner of War in Germany		PC via Frankfurt Red Cross
20.12.18 WO List	Arrived at Leith and		Scot Gen Hosp
	Conveyed to Edinburgh		17.12.18

There are a few more official letters and also a full copy of GWH Potter's birth certificate, entered on Army Form B. 2.

Possibly the most interesting record is a handwritten:

'Statement regarding circumstances which led to capture' (Form 2A. Confidential)

Reference P.O. 360 (A.G.3)	Dated 16/1/19	
Name in Full:	George William Henry Potter	Rank at time of capture: II Lt
Date of Capture:	30.11.17	
Place of Capture:	Villiers Guislain	
If wounded or otherwise:	Not wounded	

Company etc:	216 Siege Battery
Unit:	R.G.A. (S.R.)
Whether escaped or repatriated:	Repatriated
Date of escape or repatriation:	11/12/18
Date of arrival in England:	19/12/18
Present address	Oban House, Park St, Pembroke Dock

Statement:

The Battery position was at Villiers Guislain and my dug-out (which I shared with 3 other officers) was about 100 x (yards) from that of the B.C. About 7.30am Nov 30th we were awakened by the enemy's shelling. As soon as possible we dressed and I left the dug-out with Lt. Cole and proceeded at once to the Mess which adjoined the B.C.'s dug-out. We were astonished to see it had been hit, and finding no officers about, immediately went to see the guns. Only a few men were to be seen, both Section Posts were abandoned and all the guns had been put out of action. We at once realized the seriousness of the situation especially as no message had been sent to us by the B.C. We then endeavoured to work our way back. We struck a small lane and had just gone a few yards when we saw the Huns approaching 'en masse', and we realized we were surrounded. Being unarmed we were unable to offer resistance and were obliged to surrender.

The B.C. and the majority of the men got away safely but we received no information whatever with regard to the situation.
G.W.H.Potter II Lt R.G.A. (S.R.)

In this statement, Lt Harry Potter was asked whether he escaped or was repatriated, and answered the latter, as he did not return to England until after the November 1918 armistice. However, he had no official reason or requirement to record the details of his escape attempt. Fortunately he later wrote an account of a nine day long escape, with a Captain H. P. Churchouse, Royal Warwicks, from a PoW camp at Heidelberg. They were recaptured and sent to the more secure camp at Clausthal, under the direction of a somewhat stern Commandant Niemeyer. Some details of his time at Clausthal are given in the section below on 'Service Records held by families and Personal Accounts'.

The major book for this topic is 'Army Service Records of the First World War' by William Spencer, Public Record Office Readers' Guide No 19, 3rd edition 2001.

More details of the search procedure are outlined in TNA Research Guide, British Army: Officers' Records, 1914-1918, First World War.

Army Service Records for Women

The Women's Army Auxiliary Corps (WAAC) was founded in March 1917, and renamed Queen Mary's Army Auxiliary Corps in April 1918. Over 57 000 women served in the Women's Army Auxiliary Corps between 1917 and 1920. However, the records of service were severely damaged in the 1940 air raid, and the remaining WAAC records of service are at TNA in WO 398/1-240 for only about nine thousand personnel. These surviving records may now be obtained online; index searches are free.

The Service Medal and Award Rolls (WO 329) include the award of the British and Victory Medals, as well as the Silver War Badge, to women. There is a separate index as part of WO 372, and further details and examples are given in the section below on Service Medals and Award Rolls.

Records of army nurses may be found in WO 399/1-9349 for Queen Alexandra's Imperial Military Nursing Service (QAIMNS) and in WO 399/9350-15789 for the Territorial Force Nursing Service (TFNS). The series list is itself an index of persons, and so may be searched by name using the catalogue or TNA website; however, the time period 1914-1920 is entered against all names.

Examples are given in Chapter Seven, World War II Records, of some of the service records for Major Phyllis Heymann in QAIMNS and QARANC.

See also two TNA Research Guides, First World War: Women's Military Services and Nurses and Nursing Services: British Army.

Royal Flying Corps

The Royal Flying Corps was formed in 1912 and remained an army unit until it was merged with the Royal Naval Air Service (RNAS) to become the RAF on 1st April 1918. Records of service for those in the RFC who survived to that date should now be found in AIR 76, AIR 78 and AIR 79. However, some mention of those persons could still be found amongst the army records, in particular the Medal Index Cards and Medal Rolls.

See TNA Research Guide: Royal Air Force (RAF), RFC & RNAS: First World War, 1914-1918: Service Records, and also William Spencer's Air Force Records for Family Historians, 2000.

Commonwealth War Graves Commission

'Some 1 700 000 Commonwealth servicemen and women died in the two world wars, 1914-1918 and 1939-1945, and to this day are remembered in the war cemeteries and Memorials to be found all over the world. In an overall index, held at Commonwealth War Graves Commission Head Office in Maidenhead, the names of these war dead are recorded in alphabetical order by surname and include Number, Rank (Service), date of death and location of grave or Memorial'.

The above extract, from an early information sheet of the Commission, indicates the care and dedication which they have always brought to their task. Those who have visited the cemeteries and memorials in various parts of the world will recognise their unique achievement. In earlier years, the CWGC responded most helpfully to written enquiries, and their supervisory staff would take pictures of graves when visiting certain cemeteries. Nowadays, in the era of the Internet, the Commission has provided a first class service to all those researching the last resting place of those killed in these conflicts.
Website: www.cwgc.com

A typical example is taken from the index to those buried at Dozinghem Military Cemetery, Westvleteren, Belgium.

> HAYMAN, Lt. J. H. 29th Mechanical Transport Coy. Royal Army Service Corps, attd. 29th Siege
> Bty. Ammunition Col. 'B' Siege Park, II Corps. Died of wounds (gas) 18ty July 1917.
> Age 23. Son of Henry and Elsie Hayman of 48, Cheniston Gardens, Kensington, London.
> I. J 1.   (Plot, Row and Grave references)

A photograph is included of the Dar Es Salaam War Cemetery and the associated casualty details for Lance Corporal Arthur T Giffin. His service medals are discussed in the relevant section below.

The Commonwealth War Graves Commission has reached an agreement with the **War Graves Photographic Project**. Its aim is to photograph every war grave, individual memorial, MoD grave and family memorial of serving personnel from WWI to the present day and make these available within a searchable database. This is a voluntary project and a donation is requested for the provision of a photograph of a headstone or a memorial.
Website: http://twgpp.org

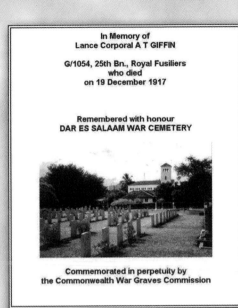

In Memory of
Lance Corporal A T GIFFIN

G/1054, 25th Bn., Royal Fusiliers
who died
on 19 December 1917

Remembered with honour
DAR ES SALAAM WAR CEMETERY

Commemorated in perpetuity by
the Commonwealth War Graves Commission

Reproduced by permission of
the Commonwealth War
Graves Commission

Casualty Details

Name:	GIFFIN
Initials:	A T
Nationality:	United Kingdom
Rank:	Lance Corporal
Regiment:	Royal Fusiliers
Unit Text:	25th Bn.
Date of Death:	19/12/1917
Service No:	G/1054
Casualty Type:	Commonwealth War Dead
Grave/Memorial Reference:	4. C. 11.
Cemetery:	DAR ES SALAAM WAR CEMETERY

View Details

Figure 21 - Lance Corporal A T Giffin, G/1054, 25th Bn, Royal Fusiliers, Remembered with honour, Dar Es Salaam War Cemetery, 19 December 1917

The **UK National Inventory of War Memorials** is a registered charity working to compile a record of all war memorials in the UK and to promote their appreciation, use and preservation. There is a searchable database of names. This project is in partnership with the Imperial War Museum. Websites: www.iwm.org.uk and www.ukniwm.org.uk

The **British War Memorial Project** is a recent volunteer project intended to build an online International War Memorial to British service personnel from 1914 to the present day. Its website is www.britishwargraves.co.uk

War Memorials on the Web by Stuart Raymond is a new directory which refers to over 2 000 webpages. The directory has been published in two parts, Part 1 for Southern England, the Marches and Wales, Part 2 for the Midlands, Northern England and East Anglia. (Stuart Raymond, Genealogical Bookman, PO Box 35, Exeter EX1 3YZ.) Website: www.stuartraymond.co.uk

Roll of Honour 'This site is dedicated to those men and women who fell fighting for their country. Recorded here are various war memorials within a variety of counties, - it is fully intended to complete as many war memorials in the United Kingdom as possible. The counties and the war memorials completed for each are listed on a separate page. Photographs have been taken of the majority of the memorials, details of the men included and their photographs where possible.' Links to many interesting databases are included on this website: www.roll-of-honour.org

Local projects - there are many of these in place around the country. **The North East War Memorials Project** aims to record every War Memorial between the river Tweed and the river Tees. Beside the traditional memorials, many other sources have been located, such as memorial books for local businesses and plaques in churches and clubs. Website: www.newmp.org.uk

Ireland's Memorial Records: World War I 1914-1918 was compiled by the Committee of the Irish National War Memorial and first published in eight volumes in 1923. It provides many details of about 49,000 individuals who died during WW1. It is now available on a fully searchable CD from www.eneclann.ie

Soldiers died in the Great War

The publication 'Soldiers died in the Great War 1914-1919' is in eighty parts, arranged by Regiment or Corps, then by Battalion and then alphabetically by soldiers' names. There is a single volume of 'Officers died in the Great War 1914-1918'.

The entry for Percival Watts was found in the list for the 8th Battalion of the 53rd or Royal West Kent Regiment and reads:

> *Watts, Percival John, b. Charlton, Kent, e. Woolwich, Kent (Blackheath, Kent), G/6071,*
> *Pte., k. in a., F. & F., 5/11/15*

Places of birth, enlistment and residence (in brackets) are given, followed by number, rank; killed in action in 'France and Flanders'.

The complete publication was issued on CD in 1998 and this format allows full searches of approximately 700,000 records. Contact www.naval-military-press.com or The Naval and Military Press Ltd, Unit 10, Ridgewood Industrial Park, Uckfield, East Sussex TN22 5QE. The same database, for Soldiers Died in the Great War 1914-1919, is now on-line at www.military-genealogy.com . The index may be searched free while a charge is made to see each soldier's details.

Index to War Deaths at General Register Office

The Index to War Deaths for the whole period 1914-1921 is held by the General Register Office but is now accessible to researchers world-wide on microfiche and online. A typical index entry would read:

> *Watts, Percival J Pte 6071 RWKR 1915 Vol 1 72 p 84*

The corresponding death certificate confirmed that Private Percival J Watts, Regimental Number 6071, had served in the Eighth Battalion of the Royal West Kent Regiment, that he had been born in England and had been killed in action aged 19 in France on the 5th November 1915.

Entries relating to Scottish and Irish soldiers were sent to the GROs in Edinburgh and Dublin, where separate indexes have been made.

Campaign Medals

The Service Medal and Award Rolls, War of 1914-1918, comprising 3 273 volumes, were transferred around 1988 to TNA, from the Army Medal Office, Droitwich.

They are now available in series WO 329. They relate to the award to officers and other ranks of the Army and Royal Flying Corps of the British War Medal, the Victory Medal, the 1914 Star, the 1914-1915 Star, the Territorial Force War Medal and the Silver War Badge.

What makes this series of great significance to any researcher of a WWI soldier is that there is an alphabetical card index to these Medal Rolls in WO 372. At Kew this is available on microfiche or computer; researchers using the internet site for DocumentsOnline may search the index free and then pay to download a copy of the specific card of interest. (In 2008: ancestry.co.uk is currently adding the same cards to its website, with the addition of the reverse of the card. In a small number of cases, there may be additional details on the reverse, such as a family address, or a note about sending out the medals.)

This indexed series of medal cards then forms an excellent starting point for research of a soldier. There is a separate microfiche card index to women during WWI. Of course, with so many individuals involved in the conflict, there are inevitably many of the same name. Exact initials have not always been used in the index, and entries may be slightly out of order on the fiche, so some perseverance may be necessary.

An example from a medal card in WO 372 contains the following information:

GIFFIN, Arthur	*Corps 8/R Fus, Rank L/Cpl, Regtl No G/1054*
Medal: Victory	*A 761, Roll T.P./104 B page 50*
Medal: British	*ditto*
Medal: 15 Star	*C 632, Roll T.P./58 B page 24*
Theatre of War first served in	*(1) France*
Date of entry therein	*31-5-15*
Remarks	*Died 19-12-17*

The references to the Medal Rolls may then be followed up in WO 329. One entry was located on page 50 of a Roll of Individuals from the Royal Fusiliers entitled to the Victory Medal and the British War Medal, and further details of service could be deduced from this:

G. S/1054 A/Cpl GIFFIN Arthur Thomas			
8/R Fus A/Cpl GS/1054	*1 (a)*	*1.6.15 to 10.11.15*	
25/R Fus	*5 (a)*	*23.7.17 to 19.12.17*	
Notes	*Died*	*19.12.17*	

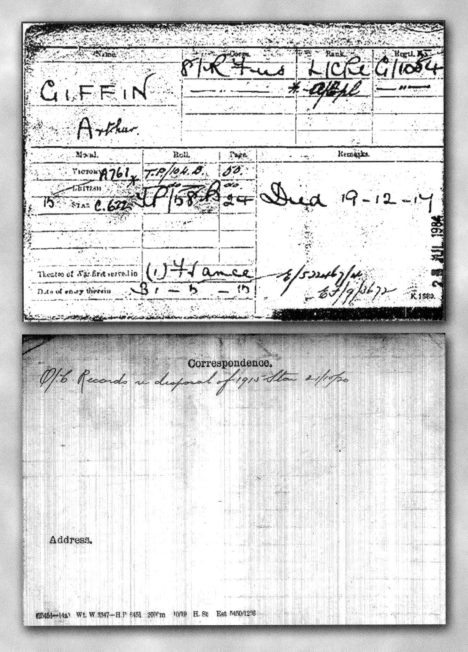

Figure 22 - Service Medal and Award Rolls Index, World War I, L/Cpl Arthur Giffin, 8/Royal Fusiliers, WO 372

In the above example, the Medal Rolls also indicated service in another theatre of war, area 5 or East Africa, a detail which was not shown on the medal card.

More details are given in TNA Research Guide: Medals: British Armed Services: Campaign and other Service Medals.

Gallantry Medals and Mentioned in Despatches

Gallantry awards, and mentions in dispatches, were very numerous during WWI; many books have been published about the recipients of the more 'famous' medals. While almost all awards would have been published in the London Gazette (see below for online details), this may not be the best place to begin a search, especially for a common name. Indexes are available at TNA and in fact these will quote the relevant issue of the London Gazette, which may then be consulted for possible details of the citation or recommendation of the commanding officer.

At TNA, the Victoria Cross Register is in WO 98/8, and an alphabetical list of recipients from 1914 to 1920 is in WO 98/6.

For officers, the Distinguished Service Order (DSO) and Military Cross (MC) may have been awarded. The DSO register is in WO 390, and a name index of those awarded the DSO or MC between 1915 and 1938 is in WO 389/9-24.

Lieutenant Michael Guthrie was awarded the Military Cross. His service record (WO 339/70740) shows that he had enlisted as a student, being a candidate for Holy Orders, in October 1915, in the Inns of Court OTC, based at Berkhamsted. Following promotion from private to lance-corporal in May 1916, he was then commissioned into the 3rd (SR) Battalion of the Northumberland Fusiliers in December 1916. He saw active service in France and Flanders, but no further details have been found, for instance in war diaries of his units (WO 95/2477). He was released from military duty on 5th March 1919.

The Military Cross index card (WO 389/14) refers to T/Lt Michael Guthrie, 19th (Pioneer) Bn Northumberland Fusiliers, gazetted to MC on 3rd June 1919, and decorated on 1st January 1921. The Supplement to the London Gazette, 3rd June 1919, lists his award, along with many others, but with no citation.

Citations for gallantry awards appear rarely to have survived; the same applies for those Mentioned in Despatches. It was found that Lt Guthrie's service record contained no mention of his MC award. This would probably be because it had been recorded in his current file, which was subsequently destroyed in the WWII bombing.

For NCOs and other ranks, gallantry awards included the Distinguished Conduct Medal (DCM), Military Medal (MM) and Meritorious Service Medal (MSM). There are various card indexes at TNA to these medals, with cross-references to the London Gazette. The cards normally give surname, forenames or initials, unit, rank and number of an individual.

Mentions in Despatches (MiDs) indexes are also kept at TNA, in three distinct alphabetical sequences.

Permission to accept and wear foreign decorations may be found in HO 38, Warrant Books and further details may also be located in Foreign Office Correspondence.

The definitive book, for the above two sections, is William Spencer's Medals, The Researcher's Guide, TNA 2006.

More details are given in two TNA Research Guides: Medals: British Armed Services: Gallantry, and Gallantry, Further Information.

War Diaries

War diaries can give very useful background information on the activities of units on active service. They can provide useful information relating to the award of a gallantry medal or to the casualty or death of a soldier. At TNA they are preserved in WO 95, with some material for Field Hospitals in WO 106. Much material was lost in the 1940 bombing of the Arnside Street depository, and the surviving war diaries at TNA (5 500 boxes) are in general those used when the official history of WWI was compiled. War diaries may often include cross references to Trench Maps, available at TNA in WO 297, 298 and 300-303, and at the Imperial War Museum.

Some war diaries may be in the possession of regimental museums, as it appears that at least one carbon copy was made at the time of writing. For example, the Queen's Lancashire Regimental Museum (at Fulwood Barracks, Preston) , which now houses records from the East Lancashire Regiment, the Loyal Regiment (North Lancashire) and South Lancashire Regiment (Prince of Wales's Volunteers), has several examples relating to these units. These include the following war diaries.

War diary 1st East Lancashire Regiment	Oct 1914	846/1.2.70
2/5th Bn E Lan R war diary	Feb 1917- July 1918	846/1/2/172

1 Loyals in France war diary	Sep 1914	846/2.2
Army book 153 Ref Capt Nimmo RAMC MO 1 Loyals war diary	4 Aug 1914- 3 Oct 1914	846/2.2.88
9 Loyals (duplicate) war diary	Sep 1915-Jun 1918	846/2.2.205

South Lancs Regiment		
1/5th Bn war diary, summary	WWI	846/3.2.216
2/5th Bn war diary	1915	846/3.2.217
2/5th Bn war diary	1916	846/3.2.218
2/5th Bn war diary	1917	846/3.2.219
7th Bn war diary	7 Jul 1915-31 Jan 1916	846/3.2.236
7th Bn war diary	29 Jun 1916-1 Feb 1918	846/3.2.236
8th Bn war diary	Sep 1915- Jan 1918	846/3.2.236
9th Bn war diaries	1915-1918	846/3/2/244

The above details were extracted from the 'Access to Archives' website, www.a2a.org.uk. It includes the contents of a catalogue for the Queen's Lancashire Regimental Museum.

Similar extensive war diaries are held for the various battalions of the Northumberland Fusiliers at their Archives in Alnwick Castle. Copy lists in these indicate that several copies were made for distribution. The Archives also hold many years of the St George's Gazette, which was the monthly Northumberland Fusilier Newsletter; this contains full lists of casualties during WWI.

War diaries of smaller units, such as companies or platoons, may give a detailed hour-by-hour account of events. Officers are often referred to by name, not usually the case for other ranks. A brief extract is given from a neatly typed war diary kept at TNA, for the 25th Royal Fusiliers at 2.15 (am/pm?) on 11th June 1915 (WO 95/5235).

...crept up to within 30 paces with 3 Machine Guns and strong force of rifles. They opened a very heavy fire which was immediately returned by the Company in this vicinity. Our Machine Guns also promptly took up position within 30 paces and after a severe exchange of fire assisted by a charge made by A.Company the enemy drew off leaving 2 Machine Guns in our hands. The action lasted about 1½ hours.

Our casualties were

Officers	*Lieut Robinson*	*Killed*
	Capt Sutton Page	*Wounded*
	Capt M Ryan	*Wounded*

Rank and File

Killed 3

Wounded 11

Missing 2 Signallers attached to GHQ

Captain Isaacson, Staff Captain, Lindi Column was badly hit and died shortly afterwards.

The lightness of our Casualties was due to the fact that the men lay low and still throughout.....

A further example from War Diaries is given below in the section about Canada under Commonwealth Forces in WWI. This is important for researchers of British regiments if they were under Canadian command.

A published set of orders of battle, The History of the Great War, HMSO, may be used at TNA to find the location of all units. The link for 'army organization' on the 'Long, Long Trail' website www.1914-1918.net may also be used to find the whereabouts of a known regiment or corps during WWI.

TNA Research Guide: British Army: Campaign Records, 1914-1918, First World War

Imperial War Museum

The Imperial War Museum, Lambeth Road, London SE1 6HZ holds major collections of material relating to the two World Wars, and also to conflicts since 1914 involving Great Britain or other members of the Commonwealth. These include manuscript papers, personal diaries, printed publications, photographs, maps, medals and uniforms. The Department of Photographs is housed in All Saints Annex, about ten minutes walk from the main museum; the Annex was once the Bethlehem Royal Hospital for the Insane, often known as 'Bedlam'. The Department of Printed Books maintains a large collection of regimental and other unit histories. (website www.iwm.org.uk)

The Imperial War Museum Book of The First World War, by Malcolm Brown, was the first of a distinguished series of books (from IWM) about the two World Wars.

It was reprinted by Pan Books in 2002 and provides in a single volume a brief account of the many aspects of the conflict. Further books in this series relate to the Somme, 1918, and the Western Front.

The UK National Inventory of War Memorials, based at the IWM London, holds information about war memorials in the UK. The majority of the archive relates to WWI, but memorials for the Crimean, Boer War and earlier conflicts are covered, as are those from WWII to the present day. The database of an estimated 50 000 - 60 000 war memorials is located at the Department of Printed Books in London, with a copy at IWM North, and it is planned to make this accessible on the Internet.

Imperial War Museum North was opened in 2002 at The Quays, Trafford Park, Manchester. Apart from being a stunning architectural sight, the focus of its displays and events is on how war shapes lives.

Regimental Museums

The reader is referred firstly to the section in the previous chapter (Other Sources – Prior to 1914) on the usefulness of Regimental Museums.

The significance of Regimental Museums is in fact greatly increased from 1914 onwards, in view of the much more extensive range of material available. Many more artefacts, and associated records and archives, have been kept in more recent years. Regimental Journals and photographs have been produced and preserved in much greater profusion in the twentieth century than in earlier times.

There appears to be no full listing of documents and archives held throughout Britain at regimental museums and headquarters. The National Register or Archives has provided a very useful summary in its report NRA 20951, Regimental Museums, a Survey of Manuscript Collections. This is available at TNA for personal study.

Local holdings in the north-west of England are excellently summarised in 'Military History in the North West', compiled by Terry Wyke and Nigel Rudyard, 1994, Volume 15 of Lancashire Bibliography.

The 'Access to Archives' website, www.a2a.org.uk. also includes details of catalogues for some Regimental Museums, eg the Queen's Lancashire Regimental Museum at Preston, Lancashire. (See above section on War Diaries.)

London Gazette

The reader is referred firstly to the section in the previous chapter (Other Sources – Prior to 1914) on the usefulness of the London Gazette.

The London Gazette publishes details of all Army Commissions, in both the Regular Army and in the Militia, and indexes may be used to trace such events for officers. Other ranks are less frequently mentioned. Military promotions are subdivided into Commands and Staff, Regular Forces, Territorial Force, Volunteer Force, Overseas Contingents and Indian Army.

There are quarterly indexes which list awards under 'State Intelligence'; names are given for recipients of the DCM, DSM, DSO, Foreign Orders, MC and MM. Those mentioned in despatches are then listed under 'War Office'.

The London Gazette itself (but not its original indexes) contained alphabetical lists of 'Soldiers' Balances Undisposed of', together with the sums due to those 'supposing themselves entitled as Next of Kin'. For instance, the issue for 30th November 1917 contained 'List CCCCCIX of the names of deceased Soldiers whose Personal Estate is held for distribution..... Effects 1916-1917', as well as the '1st Re-publication of List CCCCXCIX' of the names of deceased Soldiers for 1915-1916'. One wonders whether the relatives of Private R Clarke, Northamptonshire Regiment, ever claimed his £5/15/4, or if Cameron Highlander Corporal J Cameron's next of kin benefitted from his £30/4/4.

The website. www.gazettes-online.co.uk, gives free searchable access to the London Gazette, the Edinburgh Gazette and the Belfast Gazette and is therefore particularly useful for tracing commissions and awards during the World War periods of 1914-1920 and 1939-1948. (See also section in this chapter on Gallantry Medals.)

Absent Voters' Lists

It is often possible to trace some initial information about a soldier, if he was qualified to vote, from Absent Voters' Lists. The Absent Voters' List for 1918, preserved with other Electoral Registers at Stockport Library, gave the following details for some members of the Maggs family living at 5 Brentnall Street, Stockport.

MAGGS, Edwin	21601	Pte., R.Marines
MAGGS, Christopher	9816	Stkr., Submarine
MAGGS, James	16051	Pte., 12th Cheshires

Accrington 1918 Absent Voters List
Abbott to Barnes

Surname	Other Names	Number	Rank	Unit	Address	P.D.	Nr.
Abbott	James	35138	Pte.	East Lancs.	6 Westwood Street	B2	1025
Abbott	James Kirby	7/19452	Pte.	S.W.B.	26 Marlborough Street	C	1179
Abbott	James Kirby	19452	Pte.	7th S.W.B.	25 Plantation Street	E1	2708
Abbott	Richard	88285	S/Sgt.	R.F.A.	60 Primrose Street	H1	4101
Abbott	William	353917	Pte.	A.S.C.	78 Water Street	D1	2109
Abraham	Frederick Noble	L85	Gnr.	R.F.A.	96 Manor Street	D1	1965
Acklam	Ernest Kirby	197451	Pnr.	R.E.	66 Exchange Street	H1	4040
Ackrill	Fred	17928	Pte.	2nd East Lancs.	14 Burnley Road	D	1715
Ackrill	William	94215	Pte.	12th King's Liv.	14 Burnley Road	D	1716
Adams	George	24054	L/Cpl.	K.O.R. Lancs	422 Manchester Road	F2	3280
Adamson	John Richard	118777	Pte.	R.A.M.C.	21 Owen Street	C	1207
Adderley	Harold Davis	283108	Pte.	R.E.	22 Portland Street	B	691

World War I Absent Voters List - Issued October 1918
Example from Accrington, Lancashire. (from website www.pals.org/avl/index.htm)

Figure 23 - Absent Voters List - extract of Accrington list, October 1918

170

Clearly such information can be extremely useful in determining the unit and service, particularly in the case of a fairly common name. However, one should not expect to find such records for every electoral district.

Western Front Association

The Western Front Association was formed to maintain interest in a key period of history, 1914-1918. Its main aim is to perpetuate the memory, courage and comradeship of all those, on both sides, who served their countries in France and Flanders. It is non-political and welcomes members of all ages.

The WFA has produced a thrice-yearly journal 'Stand To!' since 1981. These journals are now being reprinted in batches of twelve by the Naval and Military Press.

In May 2005, the WFA was granted custodianship of the originals of the mens' Medal Index Cards, which are in the process of digitization by ancestry.

Website: www.westernfront.com

Red Cross and Prisoners of War

The **British Red Cross** (Archives Section, Barnett Hill, Wonersh, Guildford, Surrey GU5 0RF) has good records of its own personnel and will search these for enquirers; a donation to such work is welcomed. In this way we found that Henry Hayman (father of the Lt John Hayman, whose death in action was quoted above) had received the War Medal, for his work under the Joint War Committee of the British Red Cross and Order of St John during WWI. The only records of British military personnel available date from WWI and are contained in the British Red Cross and Order of St John Enquiry Lists for wounded and missing. The Archives has such lists only for February 1915; 18 May 1915; 26 June 1915; 17 July 1915; 24 July 1915; 7 August 1915; 4 September 1915; 18 September 1915; 1 September 1916; 15 September 1916. The regiment should be known in order to search these lists. A further Enquiry List, Number 14, 1917, containing all enquiries up to and including 20 July 1917, is available and has been published by Sunset Militaria.

The **International Committee of the Red Cross** (Geneva) holds some records of British prisoners of war, for both World Wars. Enquiries may be directed through the British Red Cross or direct to the Archives Division, 19 Avenue de la Paix, CH-1202, Geneva. A search fee is charged. A typical reply gave details of 29074 Prisoner William Hughes, born at Birkdale on 5 October 1896; his unit was the 13th

King's (Liverpool Regiment), he was captured on 28 March 1918, interned in Langensalze camp at 10 August 1918 and had received wounds in the right arm and shoulder.

The United Nations has now (2007) designated the Red Cross archive as having the status of a World Heritage Site, so that it is to be incorporated into Unesco's Memory of the World programme. It has been reported that their records, held on six million fiche, relate to two million PoWs of WWI. (Tribune de Genève, 19 Nov 2007.) Plans are afoot to digitize and make the records public by 2014, the anniversary of the commencement of this conflict.

There is no comprehensive list at TNA for British and Commonwealth **Prisoners of War**. For officers, the library at TNA holds a List of British Officers taken prisoner in the various Theatres of War between August 1914 and November 1918, compiled by the military agents Cox and Co in 1919. (This list has also been published by the Naval and Military Press.)

At TNA one may also consult a guide entitled 'Researching British and Commonwealth Prisoners of War, WWI'. This gives the sources most likely to give some personal details, as well as copies of name indexes extracted from WO 161/101. The latter source is now available through Documents Online. However, the WO 161 database only features about 7 000 individual cases, a relatively small proportion of those involved; it is estimated that over 7 000 officers and 174 000 other ranks of the British army were captured by the enemy.

A major Cataloguing Project of FO 383 has recently been completed and placed online. The record series FO 383 comprises 547 volumes of correspondence of the Foreign Office Prisoners of War and Aliens Department during World War One. Throughout the project the emphasis was placed on the inclusion of individual names. Hence an online search may well turn up references to military prisoners, civilian internees or to relatives enquiring about the whereabouts or welfare of prisoners or missing persons.

More details of other possible sources at TNA, mainly for background information, are outlined in the TNA Research Guide: Prisoners of War, British, c1760-1919.

Service Records held by families and Personal Accounts

Many papers and personal accounts from the World War One have survived within families and every family historian will make extensive enquiries from distant relatives to see what might be available.

'The Small Book', or Army Form B 50, should have been held by each soldier. That for **George Vernon No 21358 in the 22nd (S) Manchester Regiment** has been treasured in the family since WWI. Attestation details were entered at the front of the book:

George Vernon enlisted at Manchester on the 12-1-16 at the age of 24 years 2 months.
Born in or near the Town of Hyde in the County of Chester
Trade or calling: *Hatter*
Last permanent residence: 116 Manchester Road Hyde
Height: *5 feet 5 ½ inches*
Marks: *scar right elbow*
Religion: *C of E*

The next page listed 'The Soldier's Next-of-Kin Now Living'. In this case only parents' names and address were given, but spaces were provided for wife, children, brothers and sisters, and other relations.

On discharge from the army, the soldier would also receive a sheaf of papers. For example, **17189 Gunner William Weeds, 38th Siege Battery, Royal Garrison Artillery**, was transferred to the Army Reserve on demobilization on 6 February 1919. This fact was recorded on Army Form Z 21, which gave his date of first enlistment as 27 October 1903.

He also received Army Form W 5065, a Soldier's Demobilisation Account. This showed that he was due over £42, which included a War Gratuity of £25, a Pay Warrant Gratuity of £5, paid leave and ration allowance for 28 days and £2.12s 6d allowance for 'plain clothes'. £25 of the sum due was deposited in the Post Office Savings Bank, with the remainder then divided out over a few weeks

A most remarkable album has been kept by the family of **2nd Lieutenant G W H (Harry) Potter, 216 Siege Battery, Royal Garrison Artillery.** He was taken prisoner about 30 November 1917 and spent the rest of the war in PoW camps at Heidelberg and Clausthal. The family album features newspaper cuttings, telegrams and cards/letters, as well as many photographs depicting life in an officers' camp. Although conditions were doubtless not comfortable, the recreational facilities seem to have been quite sophisticated. The album includes many photographs and printed programmes, for plays and concerts, by both a British Amateur Dramatic Society and by French PoWs. As mentioned in the press cutting from a local newspaper, reproduced here, Harry Potter was an accomplished violinist. In fact his instrument was sent out to Germany for him, so that he was able to join in concerts and other productions.

Pembroke Dock Officer Missing.

SECOND-LIEUT. G. W. H. POTTER, R.G.A., (son of Mr. and Mrs. C. Potter, Balmoral House, Park Street, Pembroke Dock), who has been missing since November 30th.

Sec.-lieut. Harry Potter, R.G.A., who is reported as missing. He hails from Pembroke Dock.

Figure 24 - Local Newspaper, reporting 2nd Lt GWH (Harry) Potter, RGA, missing, 1917

Pembroke Dock Officer Missing

We regret to hear that Second-Lieut. G W H (Harry) Potter,
RGA, has been missing since November 30th. His parents, Mr
and Mrs C Potter, Balmoral House, Park Street, Pembroke Dock,
have received a telegram from the War Office to this effect, and
it is to be hoped that he has been taken prisoner. Mr Harry Potter
was formerly employed on the clerical staff in Pembroke Dockyard,
but after repeated application to the Admiralty was given permission
to join the Glamorgan Royal Engineers, and was stationed for some
time at the Harbour forts. He then went through a cadets' course at
Bexhill, and received a commission in the RGA in October last, being
posted to the 216 Siege Battery. He had only been in France about a
week before he was reported missing.

Mr Potter was a clever violin player, and was much in demand at
concerts in South Pembrokeshire. He also, until he left the district,
regularly assisted in the orchestra at the Sunday evening concerts
at Pembroke Dock Market Hall.

Various official camp notices were collected by Lt Harry Potter. These included a printed form on which the meals of the week were listed. Although it appeared to be in the style of a hotel menu, most meals consisted of soup and potatoes; the only meat was beef on Sundays, and breakfast was merely 'Kaffee'.

Washing facilities were as depicted on the attached notice; 7.30am to 9am on Mondays, Wednesdays and Fridays!

Finally, the album contains a postcard:

Clausthal 11/12/18
My dear Ma, Pa and all
This is really the last, as we leave today at 2.30pm.
Trust therefore to see you in a few days.
Pip-pip
Your loving Son
  Harry

The album caption notes that this card arrived on 15 January 1919. Happily, Harry Potter arrived home earlier, and in time for Christmas 1918, as his Leave or Duty Ration Book was issued at the PoW Reception Camp at Ripon on 20 December 1918, allowing him two months furlough.

Bathroom opening hours at Clausthal POW Camp (from Lt Harry Potter's album)

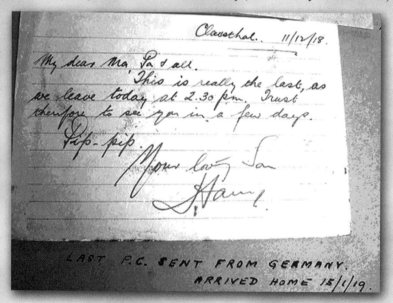

Last postcard from Lt Harry Potter at Clausthal POW Camp - sent 11 December 1918 and arrived home on 15 January 1919

Figure 25 - POW Camp at Clausthal, Germany, notice and letter from Lt Harry Potter, 1918

Disability and other Pensions

Pensions to disabled or invalid officers and men may be noted at TNA in registers in PMG 4, PMG 9, and PMG 42. A sample of pension case files are contained in PIN 26 and PIN 76. Although there are over twenty-two thousand files (for all services), this represents only about two per cent of pensions awarded. The latter series may be searched by name using the website for TNA.

The Veterans Agency, formerly the War Pensions Agency, forms part of the Ministry of Defence and administers soldiers' pension entitlement. Website: www.veterans-uk.info

'Local' Newspapers and Books

There has always been much local interest throughout the UK in the activities of servicemen of that particular area. All researchers are well advised to contact the local history section or reference department of main libraries, who will usually be aware of material published for their locality.

Newspapers are a vital source of WWI information, often printing photographs, as well as recording tributes to those killed in action. For example, the Oldham Weekly Chronicle contained a series of articles about 'Soldiers of the Oldham District', which included photographs and personal details. The British Library Newspaper Library online catalogue can provide a useful listing of local newspapers.

Website: www.bl.uk/collections/newspapers.html

Locally produced books are also of great importance to the WWI researcher. For example the Manchester City Battalions Book of Honour contains lists of soldiers in those battalions of the Manchester Regiment, as well as platoon or company photographs. There is also a section giving lists of employees of Manchester commercial companies serving in both the City Battalions and in other regiments. A fully searchable CD of this book has now been produced by the Manchester and Lancashire Family History Society.

The Pals Series of books is very much based on local information and sources, and usually includes nominal rolls and medal lists of volunteer battalions. 'Pals' volumes are either in print or reprinted for the following cities and towns: Accrington, Barnsley, Birmingham, Bradford (16th, 18th and 20th (Service)

Battalions of the Prince of Wales Own West Yorkshire Regiment), Hull, Leeds, Liverpool, Manchester, Sheffield City (12th York and Lancaster) and Swansea. These are all published by Pen and Sword Books, Barnsley. Website www.pen-and-sword.co.uk

Two examples of books available for the county of Cheshire are given as typical of what may be discovered throughout the United Kingdom:

Subalterns of the Foot - Three World War I Diaries of Officers of the Cheshire Regiment, Anne Wolff 1992, Square One Publications, Worcester. This excellent book contains a commentary and extracts from the diaries of Thomas Lane Claypole Heald (1889-1980), Adrian Eliot Hodgkin (1890-1972) and George McGowan (born 1892 - still making cider in Victoria, Australia, in 1982).

34 Men of Moulton - A Study of the men of Moulton village who died serving humanity in the Great War 1914-1918, Geoffrey A Crompton, 2001, IMCC Ltd, Riverdream, Taggs Island, Hampton.

'National Roll of the Great War'

This was a commercial publication, originally intended to record the names of all the soldiers, as well as many in other services or those who helped the war effort at home, during WWI. However, only fourteen volumes were published, covering major parts of Bedfordshire, Birmingham, Bradford, Leeds, London, Luton, Manchester, Northampton, Portsmouth, Salford and Southampton.

The publication appears to include predominantly other ranks, and also survivors of the conflict. All volumes are available at the SoG Library in London, while a full set is kept at the Imperial War Museum.

The set has been republished with an index by Naval and Military Press. It is also available on-line by subscription to www.findmypast.com , including an initial free index check.

From Section XIV for Salford, the following example is taken:

ACTON, J., Private, 2nd Lancashire Fusiliers
Volunteering in January 1915, he proceeded to the Dardanelles two months later. In
this seat of operations he took part in the landing at Suvla Bay, and after the
Evacuation of the Peninsula saw fighting at Katia in Egypt. In February 1917 he was

transferred to France, where he was in action in the Ypres, the Somme, Arras, Nieuport and Givenchy sectors. He was demobilized in February 1919, and holds the 1914-15 Star, and the General Service and Victory Medals.

23, Booth Street, Pendleton

A **Roll of Honour** may also be found in local archives or libraries. For example the County Borough of Huddersfield, Yorkshire, collected information from individuals or from their families. The completed manuscript forms are available in the Central Library there. An example is given below:

The Great War, County Borough of Huddersfield, Roll of Honour
General List – The Central Public Library Huddersfield

Please give FULL particulars. The greatest accuracy is necessary. Only well authenticated facts should be given. Fuller or corrected information will be gladly received at any time after this Schedule has been returned. (Next sentence was deleted: portraits may be sent; in uniform if possible.)

Full Name: Lewis Ellam
Place and date of birth: 12 Oct 1887 7 St Johns Square Newtown Huddersfield
Where educated: Beaumont St Board School
Where living at time of joining the forces: 17 William St Huddersfield
Profession or occupation: Hoist man
Married   or single: Widower
R Navy, Regiment or Corps: 1/7 West Yorkshire Regiment
Date of joining and Rank: Private 268692
If dead
Date of Death and Rank: October 24 1918 – Private
If killed in action, where:
If died of wounds, where received and date:
Where death occurred: Jeumont Hospital Belgium
Other causes of death: Influenza (while Prisoner of War)
If wounded
Where were wounds received and date: May 2nd 1917 Beaumont Hammel
(No entries in section on Honours or place of residence of parents)
Signature and address of person giving above information:
Joe Ellam 19 William Street Huddersfield

Memorial Plaque and Scroll

About 1,150,000 plaques and scrolls were issued, from 1919 onwards, to commemorate those who fell in all theatres of war from 4th August 1914 up to early 1920. Many will have been preserved in families as a memento of a fallen relative.

The bronze plaque was circular, slim and just under five inches diameter, and made as a precision casting. A competition in 1917 for the design resulted in submission of more than eight hundred entries from artists world-wide. The winning design, 'Pyramus', had been entered by Mr E Carter Preston of the Sandon Studies Society in Liverpool. His design included a figure of Britannia, with trident and laurel wreath, centered round a blank tablet, on which the name of the fallen would be inscribed.

The scroll, on good quality paper, sized eleven by seven inches, had the wording:

> *He whom this scroll commemorates was numbered among those who, at the call of King and Country, left all that was dear to them, endured hardness, faced danger, and finally passed out of the sight of men by the path of duty and self-sacrifice, giving up their lives that others might live in freedom.*

> *Let those who come after see to it that his name be not forgotten.*

> *Rank, Name, Regiment*

A printed covering letter, bearing a facsimile of the King's signature, was despatched with the scroll.

> *Buckingham Palace*
> *I join my grateful people in sending you this memorial of a brave life given for others in the Great War.*
> *George R. I.*

Courts Martial

From the start of WWI to 1924, death sentences were passed by the British army on over 3 000 British soldiers, mainly for the offence of desertion, but also for cowardice, murder, mutiny, treason or sleeping on duty. Over 90% of these sentences were later commuted to other punishments, such as hard labour or imprisonment.

A full list of those who received death sentences, for all offences except mutiny, is contained in 'Death Sentences passed by Military Courts of the British Army, 1914-1924' by G Oram and J Putkowski. The book includes a reference number from which access may be gained to the original documents at TNA, mostly in WO 213, WO 92 and WO 90.

An earlier book, 'For the Sake of Example, Capital Courts Martial, 1914-1918', by Judge Anthony Babington, gives many further details and insights into this contentious subject. Lyn Macdonald's 'Voices and Images of the Great War' includes a copy death certificate for a Private Albert Ingham, age 24. Cause of death is given as 'Shot by sentence of FGCM (Field General Court Martial)' for 'Desertion'. Babington's book features a picture of his epitaph on the grave at Bailleulmont Communal cemetery in France which reads:

10495 Private A Ingham, Manchester Regiment
1st December 1916
Shot at Dawn, One of the First to Enlist
A Worthy Son of his Father

For the offence of mutiny, a list of over 2 000 men charged is given in 'British Army Mutineers 1914-1922' by J Putkowski. The relevant TNA reference is again given, and most records will be found in WO 86, WO 90, WO 92 or WO 213.

More details, including sources at TNA for lesser offences, are contained in two Research Guides issued by TNA. These are British Army: Courts Martial, 17th – 20th Centuries and British Army: Courts Martial, 1914-1918, First World War.

In August 2006, the Government announced that it would be seeking parliamentary approval to pardon all 306 soldiers executed during the First World War. This followed a successful 14-year battle by the daughter and family of Private Harry Farr, 2nd Battalion West Yorkshire Regiment, to clear his name.
The Secretary of State for Defence, Des Browne, said: 'Although this is an historical matter, I am conscious of how the families of these men feel today. They have had to endure a stigma for decades. I believe a group pardon, approved by Parliament, is the best way to deal with this. After 90 years, the evidence just doesn't exist to assess all the cases individually.' (Times, 16 August 2006.)

The full list of the 306 British soldiers executed may now be found at http://www.janpieterchielens.be/shotatdawn/page59.html

Commonwealth Forces in WWI

Although strictly not within the remit of this booklet, it is very important to refer to the forces from Commonwealth countries who made such a vital contribution to the British side during WWI. Many family historians will find family members who have emigrated and then served in the armed forces of their adopted country. Similarly many from Commonwealth countries served in the British army.

Australia

'The **Australian War Memorial** is the nation's tribute to the sacrifice made by Australians who died serving their country in time of war, and to those who served with them. The Memorial is the site for the nation's major commemorative ceremonies on Anzac Day and Remembrance Day. It is also a museum and art gallery housing relics of wars in which Australians were involved and an extensive art collection. It has important holdings of archival, printed and audio-visual material which help make it a significant centre of research into Australian military history and the impact of war on Australian society.' The above forms part of the introduction to 'Roll Call! A guide to genealogical sources in the Australian War Memorial', located at Canberra, ACT.

Their website may be found at www.awm.gov.au/database/biographical.asp and provides a particularly well organised series of databases which may be searched by name. These include:

First World War Nominal Roll
First World War Embarkation Roll
Honours and Awards
Roll of Honour
Unit War Diaries

The **National Archives of Australia** have made a whole range of military records, including those for WWI, freely available on-line. These include service dossiers (B2455) for the Australian Imperial Force. Applications to enlist (MT 1486/1) are also listed on-line. Website: www.naa.gov.au

An example is given of the first page from the Service Record of Joseph Harvey, born in England, who emigrated to Australia and served in the AIF.

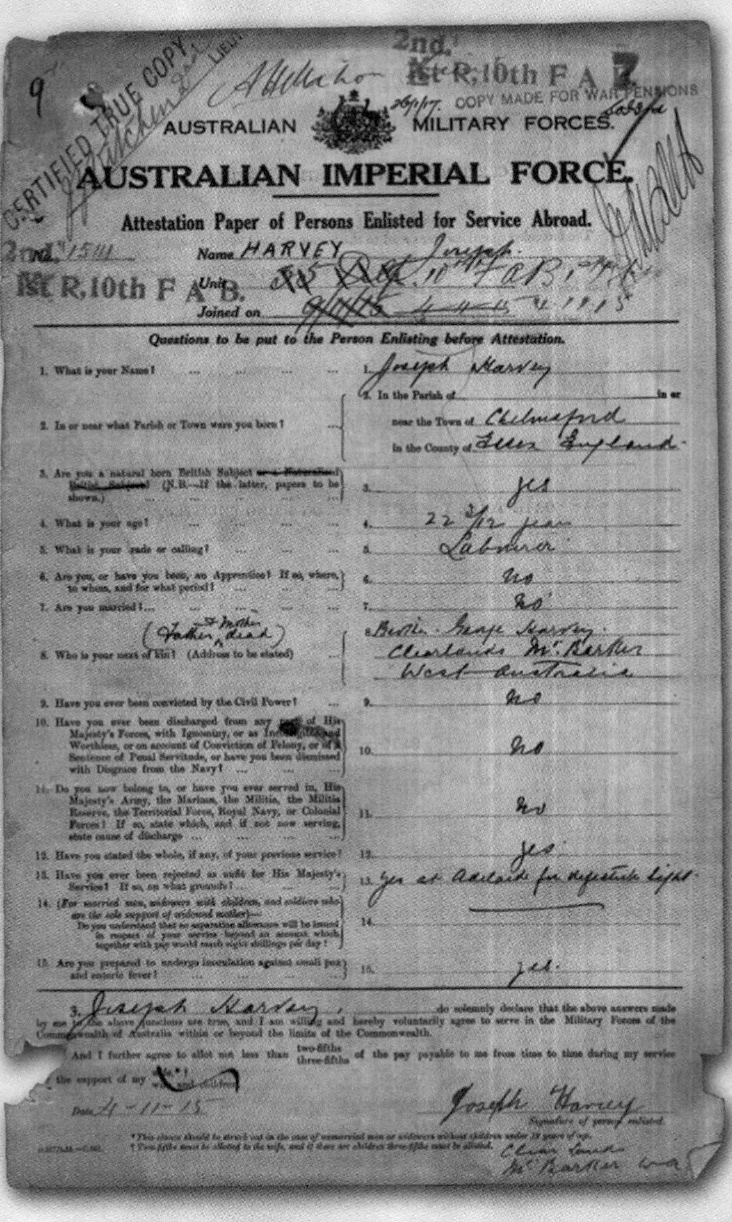

9

CERTIFIED TRUE COPY

2nd.

1st R,10th F A B

COPY MADE FOR WAR PENSIONS

AUSTRALIAN MILITARY FORCES.

AUSTRALIAN IMPERIAL FORCE.

Attestation Paper of Persons Enlisted for Service Abroad.

2nd No. 1511 Name HARVEY Joseph

1st R,10th F A B. Unit 10th F.A.B.

Joined on 4.11.1915

Questions to be put to the Person Enlisting before Attestation.

1. What is your Name? ... 1. Joseph Harvey
2. In or near what Parish or Town were you born? ... 2. In the Parish of ____ in or near the Town of Chelmsford in the County of Essex England
3. Are you a natural born British Subject ~~or a Naturalized British Subject~~ (N.B.—If the latter, papers to be shown.) ... 3. yes
4. What is your age? ... 4. 22 3/12 years
5. What is your trade or calling? ... 5. Labourer
6. Are you, or have you been, an Apprentice? If so, where, to whom, and for what period? ... 6. no
7. Are you married? ... 7. no
8. Who is your next of kin? (Address to be stated) (Father & Mother dead) ... 8. Brother George Harvey Clearlands Mt Barker West Australia
9. Have you ever been convicted by the Civil Power? ... 9. no
10. Have you ever been discharged from any part of His Majesty's Forces, with Ignominy, or as Incorrigible and Worthless, or on account of Conviction of Felony, or of a Sentence of Penal Servitude, or have you been dismissed with Disgrace from the Navy? ... 10. no
11. Do you now belong to, or have you ever served in, His Majesty's Army, the Marines, the Militia, the Militia Reserve, the Territorial Force, Royal Navy, or Colonial Forces? If so, state which, and if not now serving, state cause of discharge ... 11. no
12. Have you stated the whole, if any, of your previous service? 12. yes
13. Have you ever been rejected as unfit for His Majesty's Service? If so, on what grounds? ... 13. yes at Adelaide for defective sight
14. (For married men, widowers with children, and soldiers who are the sole support of widowed mother)— Do you understand that no separation allowance will be issued in respect of your service beyond an amount which, together with pay would reach eight shillings per day? 14. ____
15. Are you prepared to undergo inoculation against small pox and enteric fever? ... 15. yes

I, Joseph Harvey, do solemnly declare that the above answers made by me to the above questions are true, and I am willing and hereby voluntarily agree to serve in the Military Forces of the Commonwealth of Australia within or beyond the limits of the Commonwealth.

And I further agree to allot not less than two-fifths / three-fifths of the pay payable to me from time to time during my service for the support of my wife and children.

Date 4-11-15

Joseph Harvey
Signature of person enlisted.

* This clause should be struck out in the case of unmarried men or widowers without children under 18 years of age.
† Two-fifths must be allotted to the wife, and if there are children three-fifths must be allotted.

Clear Lands Mt Barker WA

Reproduced by permission of the National Archives of Australia

Figure 26 - Army Service Record for Gunner Joseph Harvey, 10th FAB, Australian Imperial Force, 1915

Canada

Over 600 000 Canadians enlisted in the **Canadian Expeditionary Force** (CEF) during WWI. The CEF database is an index to those personnel files which are held at Library and Archives Canada, Ottawa, Ontario. Since 1996 a programme of digitization of CEF Attestation papers has put on-line over 800 000 images (by 2005). Website: www.collectionscanada.gc.ca/databases/cef

ArchiviaNet is an online research tool, which permits access to a wide range of Canadian archives, including military material. Of particular interest are the sections relating to Soldiers of the South African War (1899-1902), Soldiers of the First World War (1914-1918) and War Diaries of the First World War. Website: www.collectionscanada.gc.ca/archivianet

An example may be taken from the database of Soldiers of the First World War (1914-1918). Here it is possible to make a search of a name index, and then to download (both free of charge) a copy of an Attestation Paper, which included the following details:

Canadian Over-Seas Expeditionary Force (CEF) – 9th Battalion 3rd Brigade

Name:	*John Watts (indexed as John Robert Watts)*
Birthplace:	*Buxton, Lamas, Norfolk, England*
Next-of-kin:	*(Father) Thomas Watts*
Address of next-of-kin:	*Buxton, Lamas, Norfolk, England*
Date of birth:	*5th June 1888*
Trade or Calling:	*Railroads*
Married:	*No*
Willing to be (re-)vaccinated?	*Yes*
Belong to Active Militia?	*No*
Served in any Military Force?	*No*
Understand terms of engagement?	*Yes*
Willing to serve in the CEF?	*Yes*

The above questions were put before attestation, and were followed by a signed and witnessed declaration and oath, dated 16th September 1914 at Val Cartier, P.Q. A description form was then filled out prior to a medical examination, so that the formalities could be completed on 23rd September with certificates from a magistrate and the officer commanding unit.

Veterans Affairs Canada (VAC) has created a database entitled the Canadian Virtual War Memorial 'to recognize and keep alive the memory of the achievements and sacrifices made by those who served Canada in the defence of freedom and so have contributed to the development of Canada as a nation'. This gives information about the graves and memorials of more than 116 000 Canadians and Newfoundlanders, who gave their lives for their country. On the website www.vac-acc.gc.ca one should follow links to Canada Remembers and then to Virtual War Memorial.

War Diaries have been mentioned above in a separate section. However, Library and Archives Canada has posted on its website extensive material relating to the Canadian Expeditionary Force, including many pages from the War Diaries of units of the British army, if these forces had been under Canadian command.

2389 Private Thomas B Watts had enlisted with the Northumberland Fusiliers but his service papers are now missing. His date of disembarkation is noted in the Medal Rolls (WO 329/2602 and WO 329/590) as 19th April 1915. He served in France and Belgium in the Northumbrian Division Cyclists Company (in A Cyclists Corps), then attached to the 7th Battalion of the Northumberland Fusiliers, according to the medal index cards (WO 372).

The War Diaries for the 7th Battalion of the Northumberland Fusiliers, for April 1915 to January 1918, are kept at TNA in WO 95/2830. However, copies of these War Diaries have been made by the Canadian Archives and are held in Ottawa under RG 9 III D 3. They have now been digitized and may be viewed on-line using their database of War Diaries of WWI.

www.collectionscanada.gc.ca/archivianet/020152_e.html

The reason for the association of the Northumberland and Canadian Forces is given in a Report on the Action at St Julien on Monday 26th April 1915, contained in Appendix V of the War Diary for the 50th Division, 149th Infantry Brigade.

On the morning of the 26th April 1915, the Northumberland Infantry Brigade (4th, 5th, 6th and 7th Battalions Northumberland Fusiliers), were concentrated at Wieltje and placed under the orders of the 1st Canadian Division as Reserve.

(See War Diaries, April 1915, 149th Infantry Brigade, p10, page e001583716 on the Canadian website).

It was also possible to discover the location of the various units of the Northumbrian Division, from a General Staff War Diary for 19th-30th April 1915. The 7th Bn Northumberland Fusiliers were then based at Wieltje, while the Divisional Cyclist Company was with Divisional Headquarters at Steenvorde.

The new **Canadian War Museum** (CWM) is a major national museum of military history, covering Canada's military past. It is located centrally at 1 Vimy Place, Ottawa, Ontario K1R 1C2.

Library and Archives Canada may be contacted using their website
http://www.collectionscanada.gc.ca

Other useful details and links may be found from the website of the Canadian genealogy centre:
http://www.genealogy.gc.ca

India

During the First World War, the Indian Army increased by a factor of six to 1,400,000 men. They first saw action against German colonies in China in August 1914, and by October 1914 the Indian Expeditionary Force was fighting on the Western Front. As a single force the Indian Corps' first major action was at Neuve-Chapelle in March 1915; nearly 5 000 Indian troops are commemorated on the memorial there. About 130 000 Indian troops served in France and Belgium, and almost 9 000 of them died.

A force of about 150 000 Indians were involved in the defence of the Suez Canal in 1915-1916 and then in the Palestine campaign late in 1918. Of these, almost 7 000 Indian lives were lost. During 1915, more than 1 500 Indians were killed in the Gallipoli campaign.

Indian forces suffered their most severe losses in Mesopotamia. Nearly 500 000 Indian troops fought in a long campaign against the Turks, and lost almost 45 000 men, many due to climate and disease.

By the end of WWI, over a million Indians had served overseas, at a cost of 60 000 dead. They earned over 9 000 decorations, including eleven VCs. The GRO holds registers of Indian Services War Deaths, 1914-1921.

Jack Straw, MP for Blackburn (and Foreign Secretary from 2001 to 2006), wrote movingly of their contribution in his article, 'Wear a poppy, too, for these forgotten legions of Asia'. (Times, 10 November 2003.) An extract is quoted below:

> *'Blackburn is twinned with Peronne, a small town in northern France, which saw some of the worst fighting in the First World War. When Sir Bill Taylor, our council leader was visiting the Commonwealth War Graves Commission cemetery there not long ago he noticed that a lot of the graves were of soldiers with Asian-sounding names. The Commission's records are impeccable. And reveal that, in fact, more than half the British dead were Asian. Of a total of 577 Commonwealth soldiers buried there, 320 are of Asian origin.*
>
> *'There lie 'Ainsworth, Private Harry, 20063 1st/4th Bn East Lancashire Regiment, 1st June 1917' and 'Barnes, Private WH, 240877 1st/5th Bn East Lancashire Regiment, died of wounds 8th June 1917, age 19, son of James William and Clara Barnes of 5 Hinton Street Burnley' – both old familiar East Lancashire names. But, in the same cemetery, falling in battle on the same side – ours – are some of the newer East Lancashire names: 'Khan, Muhammed Khan, Sowar 2610 18th King George's Own Lancers 2nd December'; Sheik Muhammed, Labourer, 56 3rd Labour Corps, 11th August 1917'. And so it goes on'.*

The British Library now holds the records of the **India Office** in its Oriental and India Office Collections. The Records of the Military Department include many personal files of British officers and Warrant officers in the Indian Army. The 75 year rule applies whereby files are opened, on an annual basis, 75 years from the date of entry of the serviceman/woman into the service. The records of service cover mainly European personnel. More detailed information may be found through the Access to Archives website – www.a2a.org.uk., by looking for the British Library and then under IOR. See also the section on 'Indian Armies' in Chapter 5.

The website www.firstworldwar.com gives an interesting summary of the contribution of up to 100,000 Sikhs to the British war effort, in a feature article on 'Lions of the Great War'.

New Zealand

The following note appears on a New Zealand government website, www.archives.govt.nz/doingresearch/nzdfpersonnelfiles.php giving information about the personnel records of soldiers who served in the Boer or South African War and also World War I.

Defence Service personnel files transferred to Archives New Zealand (World War I)

The military personnel files of those who served in our Defence Services during the South African War and the First World War have been transferred to Archives New Zealand from the New Zealand Defence Force, Personnel Archives. The records transferred are for personnel whose service ended prior to 31 December 1920. Archives New Zealand will keep and care for the records in perpetuity. They will undergo conservation treatment as required, and be located in a special temperature and humidity controlled environment. The records have open access and can be accessed by families, researchers and the general public.

Archives New Zealand now holds 122 357 files for people who served in the First World War. Approximately 6 000 personnel files of servicemen and women who were still serving in New Zealand's military forces after 31 December 1920 have in most cases been retained by NZDF Personnel Archives at Trentham. The exceptions to this are files that have been split into multiple parts. In this instance the earlier file parts, that pre-date 1920, have been transferred to Archives New Zealand, but later file parts for the same individual will be retained by NZDF Personnel Archives until further notice.

A search was made on the New Zealand government website, www.archives.govt.nz, for a distant relative who had emigrated to New Zealand, and reference was found to him in the WWI listings.

Cater, Harry Robert - WWI 3/2834 - Army 1914-1918

Agency	series	accession	box/item	record
AABK	18805	W5530	52	0023657

Records may be viewed free at Archives New Zealand, Head Office, Wellington, PO Box 12-050, 10 Mulgrave Street, Wellington. There is also a research and photocopying service, available from Access Services at the above address, or via email at reference@archives.govt.nz.

All queries regarding medals are handled by the Medals Office, HQ NZDF, Private Bag 905, Upper Hutt 5140, New Zealand. Website: http://medals.nzdf.mil.nz/

Official war graves information is held by the Heritage Operations Unit, Ministry for Culture and Heritage, PO Box 5364, Wellington. Website: www.mch.govt.nz/emblems/monuments/index.html

Further information may be obtained from the following websites:
www.archives.govt.nz   or
www.archives.govt.nz/doingresearch/nzdfpersonnelfiles.php

South Africa

The National Archives of South Africa maintain a website at
www.national.archives.gov.za This includes a database of gravestones from the
Genealogical Society of South Africa. Of 18 events relating to the surname Watts,
three were private soldiers of the British army:

Name	Regiment	Date of Death	Cemetery
Watts, -	60th Royal Rifles, 3rd Bn	03-02-1881	Schuins Hoogte, Ingogo, Newcastle, KwaZulu-Natal
Watts, -	6th Dragoon Guards	26-10-1900	Kloof Cemetery, Heidelberg, Transvaal
Watts, F	13th Hussars	31-01-1901	Kloof Cemetery, Heidelberg, Transvaal

Books about World War I - Odds and Ends or Lucky Dip

There have been so many publications about both World Wars that it has become
almost impossible to categorise them. The authors have therefore collected together
here material about some recent books and events which would seem to be of
interest to the family historian.

The now classic series of booklets originated by **Norman Holding** form essential
reading for all researchers wishing to understand army organisation, as well as to
locate personal material about soldiers. These are: World War I Army Ancestry,
More Sources of World War I Army Ancestry and The Location of British Army
Records 1914-1918. Two of the above are now in more recent editions, co-authored
by **Iain Swinnerton**, who has also written Identifying your World War I Soldier
from Badges and Photographs. All these booklets are published by the Federation
of Family History Societies.

For those wishing to read personal accounts, from diaries and letters of WWI
officers and soldiers, combined with a lucid historical thread, the series of books by
Lyn Macdonald must be read. These now include: 1914-1918 Voices and Images
of the Great War, 1914 The Days of Hope, 1915 The Death of Innocence, To the
Last Man Spring 1918, They Called it Passchendaele, The Roses of No Man's Land
and Somme.

Tommy, The British Soldier on the Western Front, 1914-1918, **Richard Holmes**, 2004, Harper Perennial, has been praised by both critics and scholars.

The campaign at Gallipoli has been fully described in the outstanding book by **Les Carlyon**.

The conflict between Britain and Germany in Africa is very little recorded or studied in comparison with the activities in Europe. The Forgotten Front: the East African campaign 1914-1918 by **Ross Anderson** should rectify this for interested readers. A personal account of the service in East Africa of her father, Ernest Clarke, has been given by Brenda Flynn. (Manchester Genealogist, Volume 41, No 1, 2005.)

World War I in Postcards, by **John Laffin**, features a whole range of pictorial work, reflecting the mood of the time. Captain **Bruce Bairnsfather** (1887-1959) was probably the most famous cartoonist of the Great War and his character, Old Bill, was popular long after the conflict. (Joe Bristow's website is devoted to Bairnsfather information and memorabilia: www.olebill.zoomshare.com)

There are now hundreds of individual accounts and each student of the period will have their own favourites. They should certainly include a recent compilation of letters, many from the front lines in France and Belgium, from March 1915 right through to December 1918**: Laurence Attwell's Letters from the Front**, edited by William A Attwell, 2005, Pen and Sword Military, Barnsley. He served in B (HQ) Company of 1/15 (County of London) Battalion of the Prince of Wales's Own, Civil Service Rifles. The editor has interspersed the fluent letters with well researched extracts from the War Diaries of this battalion.

The history of **troopships** throughout the ages is well covered in Soldiers Lost at Sea, a Chronicle of Troopship Disasters, **James E Wise Jr and Scott Baron**, 2004, Naval Institute Press, Annapolis, Maryland. Apart from providing detailed accounts of a few incidents, the authors give a table listing lost troopships of all nations, for both World Wars.

Through German Eyes: The British and the Somme 1916, **Christopher Duffy**, 2005, Weidenfeld & Nicolson is a most unusual book. It presents accounts of the interrogations of some of 4 000 British Empire soldiers taken prisoner on the Somme. The records are now held in German archives, namely in the Kriegsarchiv

(Abteilung IV) of the Bayerisches Hauptstaatsarchiv, Munich. Duffy also compares the German accounts with the statements of former British officer prisoners, held in personal files of the investigating committee after the war, now in WO 339 at the National Archives, Kew.

Voices from the past?

A German academic interested in dialect and pronunciation made recordings of British prisoners of war. They were asked to read the parable of the prodigal son and these old shellac recordings have now been transferred to digital form at the Humboldt University in Berlin. Although soldiers are not named, they gave their county and locality, and efforts are now being made to identify the individuals concerned. (See The Guardian, 6 July 2006)

A BBC 4 documentary, 'How the Edwardians spoke', was also made on the above subject in April 2007:

'Hundreds of recordings have come to light which reveal the accents and dialects of British prisoners-of-war held in German camps and recorded during the First World War. This archive presents a unique glimpse into the way ordinary men spoke at the time.

As the war raged Wilhelm Doegen, an expert in technical sound recording, realised that on his doorstep was a captive resource of prisoners whose speech and music would be fascinating for his research. Along with Alois Brandl, an Austrian academic specialising in British accent and dialect, he set out to record the voices of prisoners-of-war in more than 70 camps. Brandl's work before the war had also brought him into contact with Thomas Hardy, himself fascinated by rural dialect, and Henry Sweet, a leading phonetician thought to be one of the models for Henry Higgins in Pygmalion.

The recordings were meticulously catalogued, and miraculously survived the devastation of Berlin during the Second World War. By chance an author researching local dialect recently stumbled across them. One of the texts often read by the prisoners was The Prodigal Son. This story of a man returning home to his family was particularly poignant given the loss of life during the First World War. For the lucky ones who did come home, the horrors of the war often overshadowed the rest of their lives.

Following their recording, for the best part of a century the voices of the prisoners-of-war fell silent. But now some have been heard by their relatives and can shed light on a world of changing voices through the 20th century.'

"WELL, IF YOU KNOWS OF A BETTER 'OLE, GO TO IT!"

CHAPTER SEVEN
World War Two Records

As for World War One, the Second World War (WWII below) remains a subject of constant interest for professional and amateur historians alike. Yet again, most family historians discover that family members were involved. Beside the oral traditions, there are many examples of family mementoes kept by relatives, such as letters, post cards, photographs and medals.

Service records are only available for soldiers who participated in WWII, at present, on personal application to the Ministry of Defence. Fortunately most service records from WWII have survived, unlike those for WWI, which were bombed and partially destroyed during WWII. The first three sections below deal with service records for **other ranks, officers and women.**

For soldiers who were killed in World War II, there are three sources which may be searched for further details. Foremost are the indexes and website provided by the **Commonwealth War Graves Commission**. The separate **indexes to war deaths compiled by the General Register Office** can lead the researcher to an official certificate, which may be purchased from them. Finally, **an Army Roll of Honour, 1939-1945, Soldiers Died in World War II**, has been prepared in a fully searchable form on a CD-ROM by Naval and Military Press.

There are many other lesser sources of information for soldiers of WWII. Although none is likely to give a very complete picture of his service, it is well worthwhile following up every small lead for clues to a soldier's experiences.

Army Service Records for Other Ranks

Army service records for those who served after 1920 are still held by the Ministry of Defence. Copies of these may be requested by veterans or by their next of kin from the Army Personnel Centre now located in Glasgow.

For **ex-soldiers** wishing to access their service records, it is first necessary to obtain from them a Subject Access Request Form. This may be found online at www.veterans-uk.info/service_records/sar.doc. As army service records are held by service number, rank, full name and date of birth, it is important to provide as much of this information as possible, to assist in locating the correct record.

The completed Subject Access Request Form is then to be sent to the Army Personnel Centre, Disclosure 2, Mail Point 515, Kentigern House, 65 Brown Street, Glasgow G2 8EX.

For **deceased ex-servicemen or women**, information can only be released with the consent of the next of kin. Forms for the 'Request for service details' and a 'Certificate of Kinship' may be found online at
http://www.veterans-uk.info/service_records/service_records.html The next of kin is regarded as the first living relative on the following list: widow/widower, son/daughter, grandchild, father/mother, brother/sister, nephew/niece, grandparent, 'other'. There is no charge to a widow or widower, but a fee of £30 is otherwise currently (2008) required.

The completed Certificate of Kinship and Search Document are then to be sent to Army Personnel Centre, Historical Disclosures, Mail Point 555, Kentigern House, 65 Brown Street, Glasgow G2 8EX.

A request was made for his **service papers** by **Mr Graham W Roe**. At the age of 18 he had enlisted in March 1943, under the National Service Acts 1939 to 1941 which required conscription of all males aged 18 to 41 (and later to the age of 51). He served firstly in the Green Howards and then in the Hallamshire Battalion of the York and Lancaster Regiment. With the latter he landed on the Normandy beaches on the third day of the invasion in June 1944 and reached Berlin in 1945 having carried heavy signalling equipment, and a rifle, most of the way. In September 1946 he was transferred to the Royal Army Service Corps but was not 'demobbed' until June 1947.

A personal account of his army experiences, written by **S/14562445 W/Sgt G. W. Roe** primarily at the request of his grandchildren who were undertaking a school project, makes fascinating reading. One can also find reference to him and the Hallamshire Battalion in regimental histories and diaries. As always service records merely give the bare facts of names, dates and places.

The main form received on request from the MoD was:

Army Form B 200D Territorial Army - Record of Service Paper

The first section features 'questions to be put to the man on joining the Unit to which he is posted' - initially to No 55 P. T. Wing, General Service Corps. This records name, address, date of birth, nationality and also that of parents, marital status, previous service and whether insured under the National Health or Unemployment Insurance Acts.

The next sections are: Identification of (soldier) on Joining, Military History Sheet and Statement of Services; finally there are sections for Name, Address and Relationship of Next-of-Kin (with the advice that 'This entry has no effect as a Will') and Particulars of Marriage, Particulars of Children.

Some details of interest are given below:

Joined No 55 P.T. Wing	*P(riva)te*	*18.03.43*
Transferred to Green Howards Pte		*29.04.43*
Transferred to York and Lanc. R Pte		*18.08.43*

Total reckonable Service for War Gratuity	*18.3.43 to 15.8.46*	*3 years 151 days*

BAOR - Transferred to RASC	*W/Cpl*	*05.09.46*

Proceeded on release leave	*Sgt*	*12.06.47*

Release Leave	*56 days*	*from 13.06.47 to 07.08.47*
O/S Leave admissible	*36 days*	*from 08.08.47 to 12.09.47*
Rank for pay during Release	*Sgt*	
Rank for War Gratuity	*Cpl*	
Discharged on completion of engagement, allocated		*17.06.47*
to ... General Reserve Group P, and subject to recall		
to age 45, Navy, Army and Air Force Reserves Act 1954		

Released to Class 'Z' (T), Royal Army Reserve, Sgt   *12.09.47*
(Class 'A' Release)

Discharged from Reserve Liability, Navy, Army   *30.06.59*
and Air Force Reserve Act 1959

Service and Casualty Form B 103-1 and Continuation Sheet B 103-2

These forms give full details of all movements, amplifying the summary contained in the Record of Service Paper (B 200D) - see extracts from that above. Receipt of medals is also noted here. The 1939/45 Star and the France and Germany Star were awarded in November 1945, and the War Medal 1939/45 in 1947. A single index card (B 102), completed on both sides, reproduces most of the material on these forms.

S.P. Sheet 200A (Nov. 44) Qualification Form (25/01/1947)

This form gave very full details under the following categories: Education, Civilian Employment, Military Employment, Other Experience, MO's Report and Test Results. The latter were in six categories: S.G., Matrix, Bennet, Arith., Verbal and Instr.

Finally the PSO gave his Remarks and Training Recommendations:

> *Recommended for clerical duty. Tallish fit man of smart appearance and high standard of intelligence. Keen to continue clerical work for a few months.*

Notification of Impending Release (08/06/1947)

This provided a brief report and testimonial, to be given to the OC at the Military Disembarkation Camp in the UK, from W/Sgt Roe's immediate superior officer at 85 Graves Concentration Unit, Kleingemünd, then a small village on the opposite bank of the river Neckar from Neckargemünd in Germany.

Army Service Records for Officers

As for previous generations of officers, a good starting point for their service is Army Lists, which may be found in large reference libraries and on open shelves at the National Archives, Kew.

A request for an army officer's Service Record was made to the Army Personnel Centre at the Ministry of Defence, using the method noted above for W/Sgt Graham Roe (see under Army Service Records for Other Ranks).

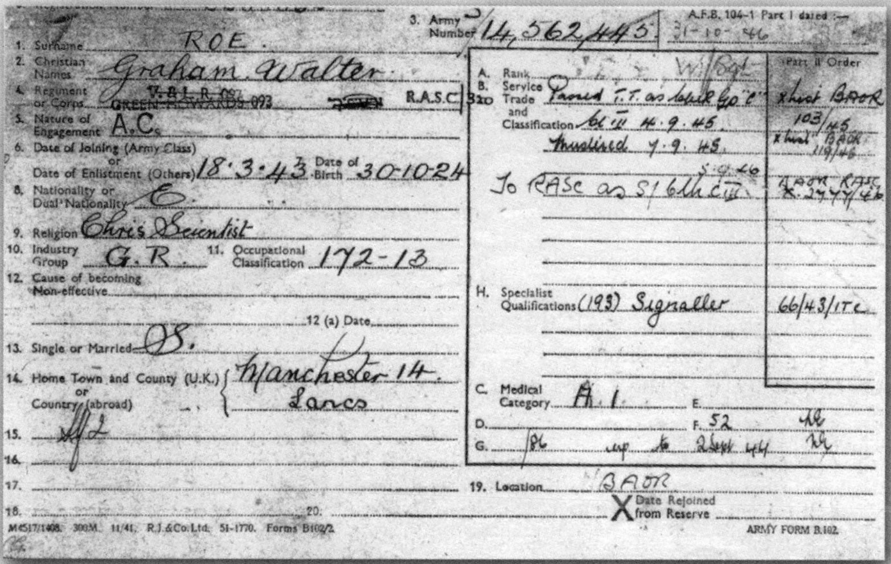

1. Surname ROE.
2. Christian Names Graham Walter
3. Army Number 14,562,445
A.F.B. 104-1 Part I dated 31-10-46
4. Regiment or Corps Y.& L.R. 092 GREEN HOWARDS 093 R.A.S.C. 320
5. Nature of Engagement A.C.
6. Date of Joining (Army Class) or Date of Enlistment (Others) 18·3·43
7. Date of Birth 30·10·24
8. Nationality or Dual Nationality E.
9. Religion Chris Scientist
10. Industry Group G.R.
11. Occupational Classification 172-13
12. Cause of becoming Non-effective
12 (a) Date
13. Single or Married S.
14. Home Town and County (U.K.) or Country (abroad) Manchester 14. Lancs
15. Sfd
16.
17.
18.
19. Location BAOR
20.
X Date Rejoined from Reserve

A. Rank W/Sgt
B. Service Trade and Classification Passed T.T. as Clerk Gp "C" Cl III 4.9.45. Mustered 7.9.45. To RASC as S/Clk C III 5.9.46
Part II Order: x list BAOR 103/45; x list BAOR 119/46; BAOR RASC X 2477/46
H. Specialist Qualifications (193) Signaller 66/43/ITC
C. Medical Category A.1
D.
E.
F. 52
G. /86 up to 2 Sept 44

M4517/1408. 300M. 11/41. R.J.&Co.Ltd. 51-1770. Forms B102/2.
ARMY FORM B.102.

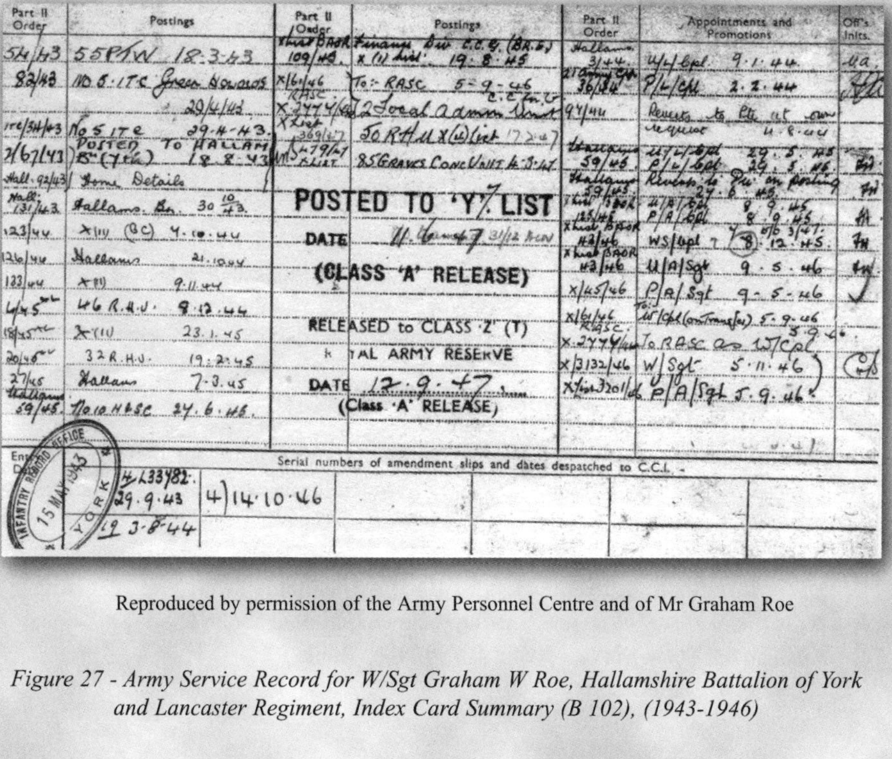

Part II Order	Postings	Part II Order	Postings	Part II Order	Appointments and Promotions	Off's Inits.
54/43	55 PTW 18·3·43	x list BAOR 109/45	Finance Div C.C.G. (Br. E.) x (i) list 19·8·45	Hallams 3/44	L/Cpl 9.1.44	
82/43	No 5 ITC Green Howards 29/4/43	x/61/46	To:- RASC 5-9-46	2 Army Gp 36/44	P/L/Cpl 2.2.44	
ITC/34/43	No 5 ITC 29·4·43	x 2477/46 RASC	2 Local admin Unit C.C.G.	97/44	Reverts to Pte at own request 4.8.44	
2/67/43	Posted to Hallam Bn (7th) 18·8·43	x list 369/47	JORAU x (ii) list 17.2.47	Hallams 59/45	U/L/Cpl 29.5.45	
Hall. 92/43	Home Details	479/47 x list	85 Graves Conc Unit 4·3·47	Hallams 59/45	P/L/Cpl 29.5.45	
Hall. 131/43	Hallams Bn. 30·10·43				Reverts to Pte on posting 27.6.45	
123/44	x (ii) (BC) 4·10·44			x list BAOR 125/45	U/A/Cpl 8.9.45	
126/44	Hallams 21.10.44			x list BAOR 43/46	P/A/Cpl 8.9.45	
133/44	x (i) 9.11.44			x list BAOR 43/46	WS/Cpl 12.9.45	
4/45	46 R.H.U. 8.12.44			x/45/46	U/A/Sgt 9.5.46	
18/45	x (ii) 23.1.45			x/61/46	P/A/Sgt 9-5-46	
20/45	32 R.H.U. 19.2.45			x 2477/46 RASC	W/Cpl (on Trans(s)) 5.9.46	
27/45	Hallams 7.3.45			x/3132/46	To RASC as W/Cpl 5.9.46	
Hallams 59/45	T/O 10 HRSC 24.6.45			x list 3201/46	W/Sgt 5.11.46	
					P/A/Sgt 5.9.46	

POSTED TO 'Y' LIST
DATE 31/12 ...
(CLASS 'A' RELEASE)
RELEASED to CLASS 'Z' (T)
ROYAL ARMY RESERVE
DATE 12.9.47
(Class 'A' RELEASE)

INFANTRY RECORD OFFICE 15 MAY 1943 YORK

Serial numbers of amendment slips and dates despatched to C.C.I.

4/L33482. 29.9.43	4) 14.10.46					
/19 3-8-44						

Reproduced by permission of the Army Personnel Centre and of Mr Graham Roe

Figure 27 - Army Service Record for W/Sgt Graham W Roe, Hallamshire Battalion of York and Lancaster Regiment, Index Card Summary (B 102), (1943-1946)

However, it is important to note that officers' files for this period may be very sparse, such that the most that would be supplied is Army Form B 199. Historical Disclosures Section also advised that 'in a significant proportion of files there is no Army Form B 199 and … little that can contribute to a chronological record of service. Pre World War 2 officers' files, including those of regular officers with long careers, can be extremely disappointing because administration was largely carried out by Regiments and there does not seem to have been uniformity of record keeping'.

Our application was fortunate and did in fact lead to the receipt of copies of several typical forms. The main form, however, was:

Army Form B 200d Territorial Army - Record of Service Paper

The first section features 'questions to be put to the man on joining the Unit to which he is posted' - initially to the Royal Norfolk Regiment. This records name, address, date of birth, nationality and also that of parents, marital status, previous service and whether insured under the National Health or Unemployment Insurance Acts.

The next section summarises 'Particulars of Service, Record of Movements, Appointments etc'. These included the following:

Late cadet from OCTU to be 2nd Lieutenant South Lancashire Regiment	*Warrington*	*28.2.41*
C.T.B.A. to H.C. P.T School	*W.E.F*	*24.3.41*
Attached Transit Camp Glasgow for attachment to Indian Infantry	*Glasgow*	*8.4.42*
Embarked from Glasgow for India		*13.4.42*
Struck off strength 9 Bn S Lan R on embarkation		*13.4.42*
Intelligence Corps (India) Attached 13.F.F.Rif		*1.11.42*
Apptd G.S.O.3 (ALO) No 6 Liaison Sect		*16.4.44*
Entered Concessional area		*9.12.44*
Date Struck off Unit Strength		*19.5.46*

Final sections of B 200d refer to Medical Fitness (Category A) and Promotions:	
2nd Lieutenant	*22.2.41*
W/S Lieut	*22.8.42*
T/Maj Relinq'd	*28.2.46*
Registered member of the Army Officer Emergency Reserve	*14.2.49*
Relinquished Commission	*1.7.59*
Ceases to belong to AOER	*2.12.74*

I. A. F. Z-2041 Record of Services Officers, Indian Services
This form also provides a summary of this officer's career, in particular giving details of his service in India from November 1942 to May 1946.

Subsidiary forms are listed in chronological order.

A.F. B2617 (Inset) Candidate for Admission to an Officer Cadet Training Unit -
Certificate of Moral Character for the Last Four Years (This form to be attached to Army Form B.2617 at Part III) (19/9/1940)

B.2617 Recommendation Form for Candidates for Office Cadet Training Units (22/10/1940)

B2091 Recruit's Depot Training Report (Infantry) (at Norwich 7/11/1940)

B.2616 Cadet Record Sheet (21/02/1941)

B199A
This form records personal details of officer and next of kin, together with educational qualifications and army courses attended, up to 13/9/1941.

G.1033 Issue and Receipt Voucher
   - Issue of Pistol Revolver No 2 .350 at Kirkwall (Not dated)

W-5138 (Modified for India) Document of Authority for Personnel Proceeding to the U.K. (07/11/1945)

   - Authority for the Move - Reason for return to the U.K.:
     Reversion to Home Estab. on Long Service Grounds
     Date of Arrival Overseas (present tour): 10 June 1942
   - For Use of Movement Control Staff at Port of Disembarkation:
     Stamped at Southampton on 29 December 1945

W3149 Report of Medical Examination - Officers and other ranks of the Military Forces, Nursing and Auxiliary Services who are relegated to unemployment or transferred to the Army Reserve, or retired or discharged for any other reason than invaliding. (09/05/1946)

   - Service in India and Burma   3 years 9 months
   - Service in U.K.   2 years 2 months

X212 (Duplicate) Release Certificate
Emergency Commissioned Officers - Regular Army (Class 'A' Release in U.K.)
-   Grant of 100 days' leave commencing 20 May 1946, and released from
    military duty with effect from 28 August 1946 under Regulations for
    Release from the Army, 1945 (01/07/1946)

X.304 War Gratuity Assessment Form (Officers) (28/8/46)

Office Form No.163
-   Letter from Officer in Charge, Army Pay Office to The War Office A.G.I
    (Officers) D amending rank from Captain to Major (24/01/1947)

*OFFR-FFS/1 (??) Application by Released Officers etc., to join the Regular Army
Reserve of Officers or the Army Officers Emergency Reserve* (06/02/1949)
-   Summary of Service refers to commission on 26 February 1941
    Intelligence School Karachi 1942-3
    Air Liaison Course Peshawar 1944
    Brigade Intelligence Officer N.W.F.P. 1942-1944
    Interpreter Standard in Urdu and Pushto

Letter from War Office noting acceptance of application for registration in the Army
Officers Emergency Reserve (14/02/1949)

Army Service Records for Women

Women served during WWII, apart from much civilian work on the 'Home Front'
and in munitions factories, in the Auxiliary Territorial Service (ATS), First Aid
Nursing Yeomanry (FANY) and in Queen Alexandra's Imperial Military Nursing
Service (QAIMNS). Nursing support was also provided by Voluntary Aid
Detachments (VADs) of the Red Cross and the Order of St John.

The ATS was formed in 1938, but was absorbed into the Women's Royal Army
Corps (WRAC) in 1949. Their duties were initially clerical, cooking and
storekeeping, and then later included many other functions, such as driving, post
and telephony. They numbered over 200 000 in 1943. Service Records are still with
the MoD, see above as for men's service papers.

The FANYs were a varied and perhaps eccentric group of individualists. Over a
thousand acted as wireless operators within the Special Operations Executive.
Some were parachuted into occupied Europe and twelve of them died in
concentration camps. In 1999 they became Princess Royal's Volunteer Corps. Their

records are held at their HQ, FANY(PRVC), TA Centre, 95 Horseferry Road, London SW1P 2DY

QAIMNS was renamed Queen Alexandra's Royal Army Nursing Corps (QARANC) in 1950. They were soldiers and nursed soldiers, as the authors' aunt would always remind them. A request for the service papers for **Major Phyllis Heymann**, **MBE** was made to the Army Personnel Centre at the Ministry of Defence, using the method noted above for W/Sgt Graham Roe (see under Army Service Records for Other Ranks). Moreover, the provisos under Army Service Records for Officers should be carefully noted.

Examples are given below from the papers received for Major Heymann. The primary source is her record of service.

Army Form B 199A - Record of Service -Officers

MoD in fact provided photocopies of two versions of this form, headed Original and Duplicate, although both were countersigned by the officer on 27 March 1950. Some typical entries from a very detailed record are quoted here.

Personal Number	*206217*
Present Rank and Type	*Major (in 1959; Sub in 1949)*
Surname	*HEYMANN*
First Name(s)	*Phyllis Cater*
Commission Type	*Reg (at 1.2.49) RAROII (at 17.9.59)*
Seniority Date	*28.4.36*
Regiment/Corps	*Queen Alexandra's Royal Army Nursing Corps*
Address	*The Cave House, Tjiklos, PO Box 53, Kyrenia, Cyprus*
Date of Birth	*29 May 1908*
Place of Birth	*Menston-in-Wharfedale Yorkshire*
Nationality at Birth of	
Officer	*English*
Father	*English*
Mother	*English*
Emergency Addressee	*Mrs T B Watts 12 Rothesay Drive Highcliffe Hants*
	(at 20.4.59)
Relationship	*Sister*

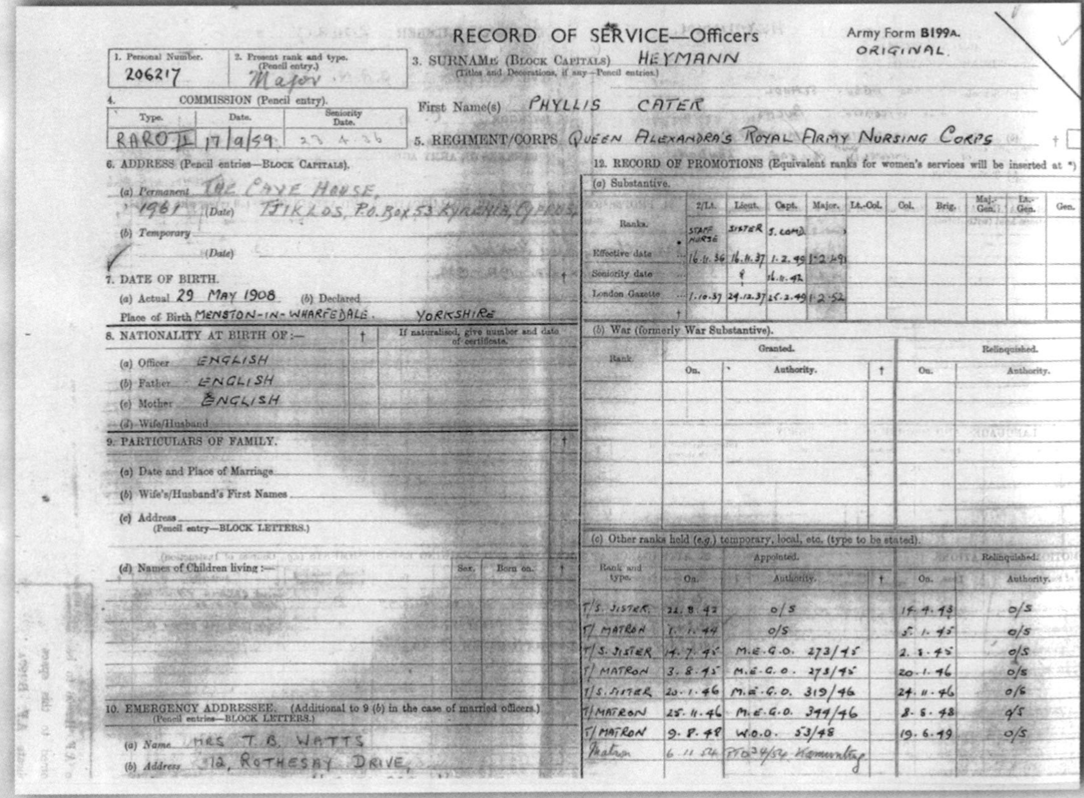

RECORD OF SERVICE—Officers

Army Form B199A.
ORIGINAL.

1. Personal Number. 206217

2. Present rank and type. (Pencil entry.) Major

3. SURNAME (BLOCK CAPITALS) HEYMANN
(Titles and Decorations, if any—Pencil entries.)

First Name(s) PHYLLIS CATER

4. COMMISSION (Pencil entry).

Type.	Date.	Seniority Date.
RARO II	17/9/59	23 4 36

5. REGIMENT/CORPS QUEEN ALEXANDRA'S ROYAL ARMY NURSING CORPS

6. ADDRESS (Pencil entries—BLOCK CAPITALS).

(a) Permanent THE CAYE HOUSE, TSIKLOS, P.O. BOX 53 KYRENIA, CYPRUS
1961 (Date)

(b) Temporary
(Date)

7. DATE OF BIRTH.

(a) Actual 29 MAY 1908 (b) Declared

Place of Birth MENSTON-IN-WHARFEDALE. YORKSHIRE

8. NATIONALITY AT BIRTH OF :— If naturalised, give number and date of certificate.

(a) Officer ENGLISH
(b) Father ENGLISH
(c) Mother ENGLISH
(d) Wife/Husband

9. PARTICULARS OF FAMILY.

(a) Date and Place of Marriage
(b) Wife's/Husband's First Names
(c) Address
(Pencil entry—BLOCK LETTERS.)
(d) Names of Children living :— Sex. Born on.

10. EMERGENCY ADDRESSEE. (Additional to 9 (b) in the case of married officers.)
(Pencil entries—BLOCK LETTERS.)

(a) Name MRS T.B. WATTS
(b) Address 12, ROTHESAY DRIVE,

12. RECORD OF PROMOTIONS (Equivalent ranks for women's services will be inserted at *)

(a) Substantive.

	2/Lt.	Lieut.	Capt.	Major.	Lt.-Col.	Col.	Brig.	Maj.-Gen.	Lt.-Gen.	Gen.
Ranks.	STAFF NURSE	SISTER	S. COMD.							
Effective date	16.1.36	16.4.37	1.2.45	1.2.49						
Seniority date		"	16.1.42							
London Gazette	1.10.37	24.12.37	15.2.49	1.2.52						

(b) War (formerly War Substantive).

Rank.	Granted. On.	Granted. Authority.	Relinquished. On.	Relinquished. Authority.

(c) Other ranks held (e.g.) temporary, local, etc. (type to be stated).

Rank and type.	Appointed. On.	Appointed. Authority.	Relinquished. On.	Relinquished. Authority.
T/S. SISTER	21.8.42	O/S	14.4.43	O/S
T/ MATRON	1.1.44	O/S	5.1.45	O/S
T/S. SISTER	14.7.45	M.E.G.O. 273/45	2.8.45	O/S
T/ MATRON	3.8.45	M.E.G.O. 273/45	20.1.46	O/S
T/S. SISTER	20.1.46	M.E.G.O. 319/46	24.11.46	O/S
T/ MATRON	25.11.46	M.E.G.O. 344/46	8.8.48	O/S
T/ MATRON	9.8.48	W.O.O. 53/48	19.6.49	O/S
Matron	6.11.54	PTO 34/54 Komunting		

Figure 28 - Army Service Record for Major Phyllis C Heymann, Queen Alexandra's Royal Army Nursing Corps, front page of Army Form B 199A, (1936-1954)

Reproduced by permission of the Army Personnel Centre

Record of Promotions

(a) Substantive	2/Lt Staff Nurse	Lieut Sister	Capt J Comd	Major
Effective Date	16.11.36	16.11.37	1.2.49	28.4.50
Seniority Date	28.4.36	16.11.42	28.4.50	
London Gazette	1.10.37	24.12.37	25.2.49	9 May 50

(b) War (formerly War Substantive) - this section was not filled in

(c) Other Ranks held - this section gave periods of appointment as Sister and Matron, from August 1942 to November 1954.

National Insurance Number and Medical Data, in a tabular abbreviated format, were given here.

Where Educated	Wycombe Abbey School, High Wycombe, Bucks
	Manchester University
	University College London
Civil Occupation	S.R.N.
Religion	C of E
Professional and Academic	SRN Charing Cross Hospital London WC2 1932-1936
Qualifications and Attainments	ATC India No 159 11.1.39

Appointments and Movements - this section gives about sixty 'occurrences' with their date, her rank and the corresponding UK or Command Overseas. They commence in November 1936 with appointment as Staff Nurse at QA Military Hospital, Millbank, London and end in September 1959 as Major at the British Military Hospital, BAOR, Rinteln. Selected items are reproduced here, to provide an interesting summary of her war service and other foreign postings.

Occurrence	Rank	UK/Command Overseas	Effective Date
Posted to QA Mil Hosp Millbank	Staff Nurse	UK	16.11.36
Embarked for India	Sister		6.9.38
Disembarked India, posted to Lahore	Sister	India	30.9.38
Posted to Ferozepore	Sister	India	14.3.39

Posted to Lahore	Sister	India	14.8.39
Posted to Karachi	Sister	India	12.7.40
Posted to Sialkot	Sister	India	3.10.40
Posted to Dalhousie	Sister	India	9.7.41
Posted to Sialkot	Sister	India	1.8.41
Posted to Lahore	Matron	India	28.5.44
Embarked for UK	Matron	India	31.10.44
Disembarked UK	Matron	UK	8.12.44
Embarked for MELF	Sister	UK	27.6.45
Disembarked for MELF	Sister	MELF	7.7.45
Posted to No 3 GH	Ass Matron	MELF	12.7.45
Posted to No 27 GH	S Sister	MELF	20.1.46
Posted to No 43 GH	S Sister	MELF	18.6.46
Posted to GHQ (Med) MELF	Matron	MELF	25.11.46
Embarked for UK	Matron	MELF	30.6.48
SOAS Depot and embarked for MELF	Major	UK	4.4.52
Disembarked ME	Major	MELF	16.4.52
TOS BMH Cyprus (in Cyprus until 8.5.53)	Major	MELF	17.4.52
SOAS Depot Hindhead emplaned for FARELF	(Major)	UK	30.10.54
TOS BMH Kamunting (as Matron). (In Malaya until 1.10.57)	Major	FARELF	6.11.54
Honours and Awards	War Medal		1939-45
	Defence Medal		
	GS Medal (Palestine)		(1948)
	Clasp 'Malaya'		(1954)

Further papers generally duplicate much of the above information. They include the following:

Application Form (23/3/1936) for, and Record of Service in, Queen Alexandra's Imperial Military Nursing Service - this covered the period from the date of her first appointment in November 1936 to 1949/1950 when the Service was renamed as QARANC. Presumably the Record of Service, Form 199A as quoted above, was completed at the time of this transfer.

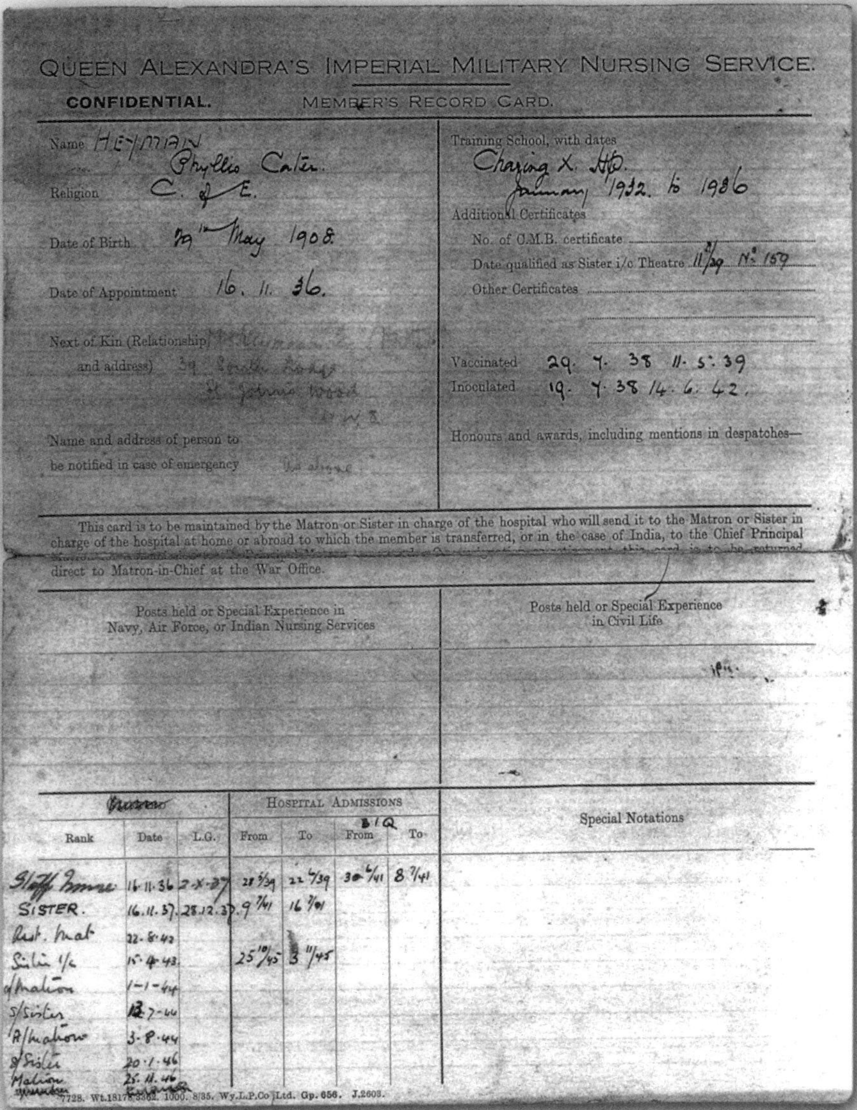

QUEEN ALEXANDRA'S IMPERIAL MILITARY NURSING SERVICE.

CONFIDENTIAL.   MEMBER'S RECORD CARD.

Name HEYMAN
         Phyllis Cater.

Religion   C. of E.

Date of Birth   29th May 1908

Date of Appointment   16. 11. 36.

Next of Kin (Relationship)
   and address)   39 South Bank
                  St. Johns Wood
                  N.W.8

Name and address of person to
be notified in case of emergency   As above

Training School, with dates
   Charing X. Hp.
   January 1932. to 1936

Additional Certificates
   No. of C.M.B. certificate
   Date qualified as Sister i/c Theatre 11/29 No 159
   Other Certificates

Vaccinated   29. 7. 38 11. 5. 39
Inoculated   19. 7. 38 14. 6. 42.

Honours and awards, including mentions in despatches—

This card is to be maintained by the Matron or Sister in charge of the hospital who will send it to the Matron or Sister in charge of the hospital at home or abroad to which the member is transferred, or in the case of India, to the Chief Principal Matron ... this card is to be returned direct to Matron-in-Chief at the War Office.

Posts held or Special Experience in Navy, Air Force, or Indian Nursing Services	Posts held or Special Experience in Civil Life

			Hospital Admissions				Special Notations
Rank	Date	L.G.	From	To	B/Q From	To	
Staff Nurse	16.11.36	2.X.37	28 5/39	22 7/39	30 4/41	8 7/41	
SISTER.	16.11.37.	28.12.37.	9 7/41	16 7/41			
Act. Mat.	22-8-42						
Sister i/c	15.4.43		25 10/45	3 11/45			
A/Matron	1-1-44						
S/Sister	13.7-44						
A/Matron	3-8-44						
S/Sister	20.1.46						
Matron	25.11.46						

7728. WL1817 ... 1000. 8/35. Wy.L.P.Co Ltd. Gp. 656. J.2803.

Reproduced by permission of the Army Personnel Centre

Figure 29 - Queen Alexandra's Imperial Military Nursing Service Member's Record Card from 1936

Arrival Report - Secret (Army Form B174A) - Travelling by ship, one of these forms was to be completed by every officer prior to the ship's arrival. On arrival, the form was to be collected by the embarkation staff to be forwarded to the War Office in London. In summary, this form recorded that Sister (A/Matron) P C Heymann left the British Military Hospital in Lahore on 20 October 1944, embarked from India at Bombay on 31 October 1944 and disembarked at Liverpool from the Athlone Castle on 8 December 1944. The 'cause of journey to Europe' was repatriation to the UK. This must have been a welcome arrival, after six years in India, mostly wartime, and she was granted leave until 4 January 1945.

Among all the official army forms, despite their wealth of detail, it is particularly pleasing to find personal statements from two commanding officers. The reference given by the first of these provides a good idea of the challenges she faced on arrival in Sialkot and how well she dealt with them.

(to) ADMS, Lordist, LRC   (from) Indian Military Hospital, Sialkot, dated 14-3-1944

On handing over command of the Indian Military Hospital Sialkot, I desire to place on record my appreciation of the services rendered by Sister i/c Miss P C Heymann, QAIMNS.

As the first lady nurse posted in April 1942, she had to arrange for the accommodation, furnishing of quarters and make arrangements for the nursing staff to be posted , while carrying out the ordinary duties of a Sister on the wards. I cannot speak too highly of the immense assistance she gave to the Area Commander and to me in the selection of bungalows, and of the practical and expeditious way in which she furnished with good taste the mess and rooms for Sisters and Auxiliary Nursing staff - equipped kitchens, and engaged Mess servants. I think it is necessary to point out the heavy administrative labour which all this entailed - menus - house management - Mess wages and maintaining accounts etc.

At the same time she had to organize, ab initio, the scheme of Hospital nursing duties, and to help in the training of batches of newly recruited IAMC orderlies for service overseas. It cannot be said that all these ends were obtained without friction or with cooperation, or that the situation was not trying at times, yet on no occasion have I seen Miss Heymann lose control or dignity.

Not the lightest part of Miss Heymann's duties was the command of European and Indian Sisters and Auxiliary Nurses - of the former, some with Indian experience and some fresh from the UK. The highest tribute to Miss Heymann's tact, human understanding, courtesy and efficiency is that during my command I have never heard a complaint, direct or indirect from the lady nursing services as regards accommodation, messing, hours of duty, freedom for recreation or the entertainment of their friends. Throughout a high standard of discipline has been maintained - firm but kind and without discrimination.

The nursing services of the Hospital have alleviated pain and given comfort to seriously ill patients, and to them some owe their lives. To Miss Heymann and her staff I attribute in no negligible part the good reports the Hospital has maintained.

Lieut. Colonel, IAMC
Comdg, Ind. Mily. Hospl, Sialkot

The above letter, together with a testimonial from the succeeding CO, was forwarded on 12 May 1944 from the Commander-in-Chief in India, at General Headquarters New Delhi, to the War Office in London. These provided the basis for her promotion from Sister to Acting Matron.

VADs supported with general nursing duties at auxiliary hospitals (and some military ones too) and at convalescent homes in Britain, besides work in civil defence and welfare, and as drivers. Some records for VADs are held at the British Red Cross Museum and Archives, 44 Moorfields, London EC2Y 9AL.

A history of nurses in WWII, Sisters in Arms, has been written by Nicola Tyrer, also the author of The Women's Land Army.

More details are given in TNA Research Guide: Nurses and Nursing Service, British Army

Commonwealth War Graves Commission

The fine work of the Commonwealth War Graves Commission is described above in the corresponding section of Chapter Six - World War One.

Their Debt of Honour Register now forms an invaluable finding aid on their website www.cwgc.com. Civilian deaths are also included for WWII.

Other War Memorial Projects

See the corresponding section in Chapter Six - World War I.

Index to War Deaths at General Register Office

The Index to War Deaths for the whole period 1939-1945 is held by the General Register Office, but is now accessible to researchers world-wide on microfiche and on-line.

Entries relating to Scottish and Irish soldiers were sent to the GROs in Edinburgh and Dublin, where separate indexes have been made.
TNA Research Guide: War Dead, First and Second World Wars

Army Roll of Honour, 1939-1945, Soldiers Died in World War II

The Army 'Roll of Honour' for soldiers who died in World War II is preserved at the National Archives in WO 304. It includes all who died between 1 September 1939 and 31 December 1946. Many categories are covered for deaths in service: those killed in action, those who died of wounds or disease as well as deaths which were non-attributable, for example from natural causes.

The information, which was partially in a coded form, has been issued in a fully searchable database on CD-ROM by the Naval and Military Press Ltd, Unit 10, Ridgewood Industrial Park, Uckfield, East Sussex TN22 5QE. The same database is now on-line at www.military-genealogy.com .

The index may be searched free, following free registration, and enables one to find a required soldier. One 'credit' is then paid to see each soldier's details. An example is given below.

Branch at Death	*Infantry*
Regiment, Corps etc	*The Loyal Regt (North Lancashire)*
Branch at 1/9/39	*Yeomanry*
Regiment, Corps etc	*The Duke of Lancaster's Own Yeomanry*
Surname	*Clapperton*
Christian Name(s)	*Harold*
Initials etc	*H K*
Rank	*Lieutenant*
Number	*219888*
Born	*Bolton*
Residence	*Bolton*
Died Date	*25/04/43*
Theatre of War	*North Africa*

Campaign Medals

The 1939-1945 Star was the primary service medal, generally issued to those who completed six months' active service overseas. Soldiers might also have received the following: the Africa Star, the Burma Star, the Italy Star, the Pacific Star, the Defence Medal and the War Service Medal - and even the Atlantic Star, if attached to the RN or Merchant Navy.

The MoD Medal Office is the sole authority for the issue of medals authorised by Her Majesty to British service personnel and veterans. It was formed in February 2005 from the previous separate service Medal Offices and is based at RAF Innsworth.

'Significant investment in personnel and technology, especially two brand new laser-engraving machines, has led to a substantial reduction in the historic backlog of medals and underlines the priority the MoD attaches to the prompt delivery of medals to veterans, their relatives and serving personnel. Over the past 18 months the MoD Medal Office has engraved and despatched more than 160 000 medals to service personnel and veterans.

Applications for medals for currently serving personnel are co-ordinated and sent by the RN, RM, Army and RAF units and the MoD Medal Office despatches medals to the units for presentation to the recipients. Serving personnel should therefore always apply for medals through their units and consult their admin staff with any medals queries.

Many applications are still received from service veterans who did not claim their medals at the time, particularly from World War II. The next of kin of veterans now deceased are also entitled to claim any medals that had not been awarded. Claims for medals for service in the Home Guard are also dealt with by the MoD Medal Office.'

MoD Medal Office, Service Personnel and Veterans Agency, Building 250, RAF Innsworth, Gloucester GL3 1HW.

Website: www.mod.uk/DefenceInternet/DefenceFor/Veterans/Medals

More details are given in TNA Research Guide: Medals, British Armed Services, Campaign and other Service Medals.

Gallantry Medals

Gallantry medals, such as VC, DSO, MC, DCM and MM may be located initially in the London Gazette. At TNA, the recommendations for these medals may be found in WO 373, while a chronological listing from the London Gazette is in WO 390/9-13.

For officers and soldiers who were awarded a gallantry medal and served in the North West Europe theatre of war, after D Day in 1944, one may search the TNA Catalogue under the name of the recipient, limiting the search to WO 373. Website: www.nationalarchives.gov.uk/catalogue/search.asp

More details are given in TNA Research Guide: Medals, British Armed Services, Gallantry, and Further Information.

War Diaries

War diaries can give very useful background information on the activities of units on active service. At TNA they are preserved in series WO 165 to WO 179, and in WO 215 to WO 218. These are listed in Appendix Four, where it will be seen that war diaries are arranged by the theatre of operation. Hence a researcher needs to know where a soldier served. Orders of Battle will be helpful in determining which units were serving in which theatre of war. These are to be found in WO 212, while a printed version, Col H F Joslen's Orders of Battle in the Second World War (2 vols, HMSO, 1960), is available in the Reading Rooms at TNA.

More details are given in TNA Research Guide: British Army: Campaign Records, 1939-1945, Second World War.

Prisoners of War

At TNA there are comprehensive lists of both British and Commonwealth PoWs, in WO 392/1-26. These relate to all those held by German authorities. HMSO published lists of about 170 000 PoWs in 1945, and these volumes were reprinted in 1990 by the Imperial War Museum.

Information on prisoners of the Japanese may be located at TNA using index cards in WO 345. Also prisoners held at Singapore are noted in WO 367.

More details are given in TNA Research Guide: Prisoners of War, British, 1939-1953.

Home Front

War time air raids, blackout and civil defence duties are all well known to the British population, especially those whose families lived in the large conurbations. There was also the formation of the Local Defence Volunteers, better known as the Home Guard, which was active from May 1940 until the end of 1944.

Enquiries about Home Guard records should be addressed to the Army Personnel Centre in exactly the same way as those about Army records - see above under Army Service Records for Other Ranks. Historical Disclosures Section also advised that 'the information held on Home Guards is very limited - it normally consists of one double sided A4 sheet of paper, Army Form W3066, containing personal details on enlistment and very little else. No details are held of the duties performed by an individual during his service.' An information leaflet, 'Home Guard Records and Family Interest Enquiries' may be obtained from the Army Personnel Centre.

The Reading Rooms at TNA hold a set of Home Guard lists, including details of officers. Home Forces War Diaries are also held at TNA in over 17 000 pieces of WO 166.

A website for the Home Guard may be found at www.home-guard.org.uk

More details are given in TNA Research Guide: Home Front: Second World War, 1939-1945.

For the following topics, the reader is referred to the corresponding sections in Chapter Six - World War One:

Imperial War Museum
Regimental Museums
London Gazette
Red Cross
Disability and other Pensions
'Local' Newspapers and Books,
Commonwealth Forces: Australia, Canada, India, New Zealand and South Africa

Following World War Two

The Armed Forces Memorial is the first national memorial dedicated to the men and women of the United Kingdom Armed Forces (Regular and Reserve) killed on duty or as a result of terrorist action since the Second World War.

The start date is 1 January 1948, which follows on directly from the Commonwealth War Graves Commission which commemorates those who died up to 31 December 1947. The one exception is for those killed in Palestine who are included on the Memorial.

A Roll of Honour may be searched on-line for full details of those commemorated. Website: www.forcesmemorial.org.uk

The National Memorial Arboretum is located on Croxall Road, Alrewas, near Lichfield in Staffordshire; postcode DE13 7AR. Website: www.nationalmemorialarboretum.org.uk

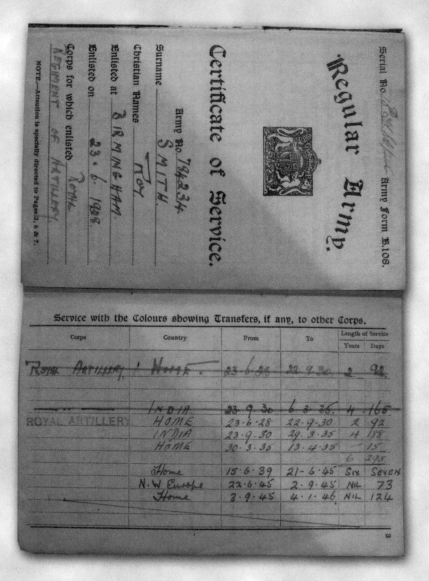

Certificate of Service issued to soldier - page showing transfers from 1928 to 1946 for Roy Smith, Royal Regiment of Artillery. (Note: this small book would normally be retained by the soldier or his family.)

Figure 30 - Certificate of Service, Roy Smith, 1928-1946

REFERENCES & BIBLIOGRAPHY

This section includes both publications mentioned in the text of the book and also suggestions by the authors for general reading. Reference numbers in the text have been avoided, whereas authors' names have been given there. Hence references are given here in alphabetical sequence of author's surname. This section has hopefully been arranged in such a way that topics may be easily located and hence it may be studied on its own account. References for books held in the library at the Society of Genealogists are shown in square brackets.

Chapter One - Introduction and General - Army

Beckett, Ian F W, Discovering English County Regiments, A Shire Book (number 294), 2003 (enlarged and rewritten edition of Arthur Taylor's work, 1970/1987) [ARM/G58].

Brereton J M, A guide to the regiments and corps of the British army on the regular establishment, Bodley Head 1985.

Brereton J M, The British soldier, a social history from 1661 to the present day, Bodley Head 1986.

Fortescue, Sir J W, A history of the British army, Macmillan, 13 volumes, 1899-1930 (Reprinted in 19 facsimile volumes, including maps, by Naval and Military Press 2004.)

Hamilton-Edwards, Gerald, In search of army ancestry, Phillimore 1977 [ARM/G15&G48].

Neuburg, Victor, Gone for a soldier - a history of life in the British Ranks from 1842, Cassell 1989 [ARM/G46].

Palmer, Roy, The Rambling Soldier - life in the lower ranks, 1750-1900, through soldiers' songs and writings, Penguin/Peacock Books 1977 and 1986 [ARM/G49].

Scotland before 1707

Dalton, Charles, The Scots army, 1661-1688, Eyre & Spottiswoode, London; William Brown, Edinburgh, 1909; reprint Greenhill Books 1989 [SG/G3].

Terry C S, (ed), Papers relating to the Army of the Solemn League and Covenant, 1743-1647, two volumes, Scottish Historical Society, 1917 [SC/PER].

Further Reading - Army

Bruce, Anthony P C (ed), A bibliography of British military history from the Roman invasion to the Restoration, Munich, 1981.

Bruce, Anthony P C (ed), An annotated bibliography of the British army, 1660-1914, New York, 1975 [ARM/G94].

Fowler, Simon, Tracing your army ancestors, Pen and Sword, 2006 [ARM/G67].

Hallows, Ian S, Regiments and Corps of the British army, Arms and Armour Press, London, 1991 (includes details of regimental journals, histories, museums and associations).

Higham, Robin (ed), A guide to the sources of British military history, Routledge and Kegan Paul 1972.

Reid, Stuart, The Last Scot's Army, 1661-1714, Partizan Press, Leigh-on-Sea, 2003 (author also of other books on the Scots armies of the 17th century).

Spencer, William, Family History in the Wars, how your ancestors served their country, The National Archives, 2007.

Spencer, William, Army Records, a guide for family historians, The National Archives, 2008.

Swinnerton, Iain, The British Army: its history, tradition and records, FFHS 1996 [TB/RG113].

Urban, Mark, Generals - ten British commanders who shaped the world, Faber and Faber, 2005

Venning, Annabel, Following the drum (the lives of army wives and daughters, past and present), Headline, 2005

White, Arthur S, A bibliography of regimental histories of the British Army, (updated edition by) Naval and Military Press, 1992 [ARM/G73].

British Library Catalogue, BLC to 1975, Volumes 96 and 97, pages 891 to 1092, cover publications about the army; army lists are at page 931 et seq. This is all now searchable on-line using 'keywords'.

Chapter Two - Officers (prior to 1914)

Askwith W H, List of officers of the Royal Regiment of Artillery, 1716-1899, 1900 [ARM/RH5].

Askwith W H & Morgan F C, List of officers of the Royal Regiment of Artillery, Volume II, 1862-1914, Sheffield, 1914.

Bruce, Anthony, The purchase system in the British army, 1660-1871, Royal Historical Society 1980.

Conolly T W J & Edwards R F, Roll of Officers of the Royal Engineers, 1660-1898, Chatham, 1898 [ARM/RH21].

Dalton, Charles, English army lists and commission registers, 1661-1714, Eyre and Spottiswoode, six volumes, 1892-1904 [ARM/LST 1661]

Dalton, Charles, The Blenheim roll, 1704, Eyre and Spottiswoode, 1899 (this is also included in volume five of the previous reference) [ARM/LST 1704]

Dalton, Charles, George I's Army, 1714-1727, Eyre and Spottiswoode, 2 volumes, 1910

Dalton, Charles, Waterloo roll call, William Clowes & Son, London 1890: Eyre & Spottiswoode, London, 2nd edn 1904; 2nd edn reprinted, Arms and Armour Press, London, 1971. (NB Lists all regiments, and all officers at Waterloo) [ARM/LST 1815].

Glover, Michael, Wellington's army in the Peninsula, 1808-1814, David and Charles 1977.

Hart H G, Army List, published annually, 1840-1915 [ARM/LST].

Peterkin A, Johnston W and Drew R, Commissioned officers in the medical services of the British army, 1660-1960, Wellcome Historical Medical Library 1968 [ARM/RH100 & 100A].

Army List, official annual publication since 1754 [ARM/LST]

House of Commons Journals (see Appendix 2, Army Estimates), Vol 68 (1812-3) pp 716-9, 69 (1813-4) 560-5, 70 (1814-6) 539-548, 71 (1816-7) 587-9, 72 (1817) 528-542, 73 (1818) 469-484, 74 (1818-9) 682, 75 (1819-20) 526.

Further Reading - Officers prior to 1914

Dalton, Charles, Irish army lists, 1661-1685, London, 1907.

Dalton, Charles, The Scots army, 1661-1688, Eyre & Spottiswoode, London; William Brown, Edinburgh, 1909; reprint Greenhill Books 1989 [SC/G3].

Reid, Stuart, Officers and regiments of the royalist army, being a revised list of indigent officers, 1663, in five volumes, Partizan Press, Leigh-on-Sea, 1985/6 [ARM/LST 1663].

Chapters Three and Four - Other Ranks (prior to 1914)

(for Militia and Campaign references - see below under Chapter Five).

Barlow, Angela, War Office musters, Journal of the Manchester and Lancashire FHS, 26 (2), April 1990 [LA/PER].

Beckett, James Deuchar, The Beckett Soldiers Index, A-C, Jade Publishing Company, 5 Leefields Close, Uppermill, Oldham, Lancashire OL3 6LA, 2003.

Chambers, Barbara, Regimental Indexes, ca 1806 - a continuing series of volumes, the first being published in 1998, to cover WO 25/871-1120 - see Chapter Three for full details and contact addresses [CD-ROM].

Crowder, Norman K, British Army Pensioners Abroad, 1772-1899, Genealogical Publishing, Baltimore, 1995 (An index and summary of WO 120, pieces 35, 69 and 70, which include many Chelsea pensioners who settled in Canada) [ARM/G33].

Joslin E C, Litherland A R, Simpkin B T, Spink's standard catalogue of British and associated orders, decorations and medals with valuations, Spink, 1990.

Kitzmuller II, John M, In search of the 'forlorn hope': a comprehensive guide to locating British regiments and their records (1640-WWI), Manuscript Publishing Company, Salt Lake City, 1988 [ARM/G71A-B & G72].

Leslie N B, Battle Honours of the British and Indian armies, 1695-1914, Leo Cooper 1970.

Norman C B, Battle Honours of the British army, 1662-1901, Murray 1911; David and Charles reprints 1971.

Oliver, Rosemary M, War Office district pension returns, Genealogists' Magazine, 21 (6) pp 196-199, 1984 [PER/GEN].

Spencer, William, Medals - the researcher's guide, National Archives, 2006 [MED61].

Watts, Christopher T and Michael J, In search of a soldier ancestor, Genealogists' Magazine, 19 (4) pp 125-128, 1977 [PER/GEN].

Wyke, Terry and Rudyard, Nigel (compiled and edited), Military History in the North West, Bibliography of North West England, Manchester, 1994.

Further Reading - Other Ranks prior to 1914

Adkin, Major Mark, The Sharpe Companion - Volume 1, The Early Years - a historical and military guide to Bernard Cornwell's Sharpe novels 1777-1808, HarperCollins, 2003 (A well-presented and informative guide to many army practices of that time).

Chapter Five - Other sources prior to 1914

In this section, references and suggestions for further reading are sub-divided by category: campaigns/battles/actions, militia and auxiliary forces, honours/medals and museums.

Campaigns, Battles and Actions

Churchill, Winston S, My early life, a roving commission, Macmillan & Co Ltd, 1930, Reprint Society Ltd, London 1944
(includes personal accounts of service in cavalry units of the British Army in India; Sudan - with a cavalry charge at Omdurman; Boer War - his capture and escape, the relief of Ladysmith and the advance to Pretoria).

Cook F & A, Casualty roll for the Crimea, 1854-55, J B Hayward & Son, London, 1976 [ARM/LST 1854].

Dwelly E, Muster Roll of British NCOs and men at the battle of Waterloo: Part I Cavalry, privately published, Fleet, Hampshire, 1934 [ARM/LST 1815].

Glover, Michael, Wellington's army in the Peninsula, 1808-1814, David and Charles 1977.

Hibbard M G, List of casualties in South African Field Force, 11 Oct 1899 to 31 May 1902, 1972 (facsimile of WO 108/338) [ARM/LST 1899].

Lummis, William M and Wynn, Kenneth G, Honour the Light Brigade, J B Hayward and Son, London, 1973 [ARM/RH203] (Ts index by H N Peyton at SoG library) [ARM/G20].

Napier, Major General Sir William, The War in the Peninsula, published originally in six volumes 1826-1840, Folio Society abridgement by Brian Connell, 1973

Urban, Mark, The man who broke Napoleon's codes, the story of George Scovell, Faber and Faber, 2001.

Watt, Steve, In Memoriam: Roll of Honour - Imperial Forces - Anglo-Boer War 1899-1902, University of KwaZulu-Natal Press, 2001.

Militia and Auxiliary Forces

Arnison, Janet, A roll of Westmorland Militia (from D/LONS/L13/6/26 at Cumbria RO), Cumbria FHS Newsletter Number 41, 1986 [CH/PER].

Beckett I F W, The amateur military tradition, Manchester University Press 1991.

(The) Craven Muster Roll 1803, North Yorkshire County Record Office Publication Number 9, North Yorkshire County Council 1976 [YK/L21].

Cunningham, Hugh, The volunteer force - a social and political history, 1859-1908, Croom Helm, London, 1975.

Gibson, Jeremy and Dell, Alan, Tudor and Stuart muster rolls, a directory of holdings in the British Isles, Federation of Family History Societies (FFHS) 1989 [SoG library].

Gibson, Jeremy and Medlycott, Mervyn, Militia lists and musters, 1757-1876, a directory of holdings in the British Isles, FFHS 1989 [SoG library].

Lawes, Edward, Militia Records, Hampshire Family Historian 8 (4), 1982 [HA/PER].

Medlycott, Sir Mervyn, Some Georgian 'Censuses' - the Militia and 'Defence' Lists, Genealogists' Magazine, 23 (2) pp 55-59, 1989 [PER/GEN]

Spencer, William, Records of the militia from 1757 to 1945, PRO Readers' Guide No 3, 1997 [ARM/G70 and SP/PER].

Honours and Medals

Abbott P E, Recipients of the Distinguished Conduct Medal, 1855-1909, J B Hayward & Son, 1975 [MED 28].

Creagh, Sir O'Moore and Humphris E M, The Victoria Cross (1856-1920) and the Distinguished Service Order (1886-1923), three volumes (I VC, II and III DSO), London 1924, Hayward reprint 1978/1985 [MED 3-5, MED 38, MED 40].

Dymond, Steve, Researching British military medals, Crowood Press, Marlborough, Wiltshire, 1999/2007

Gould R W, (compiler of army section), The Army of India Medal Roll, 1799-1826, from WO 100/13, J B Hayward & Son 1974.

Joslin E C, Litherland A R, Simpkin B T, Spink's standard catalogue of British and associated orders, decorations and medals with valuations, Spink, 1990.

Leslie N B, Battle Honours of the British and Indian armies, 1695-1914, Leo Cooper 1970.

Mullen A L T, The Military General Service roll, 1793-1814, London Stamp Exchange, 1990 [MED18]

Norman C B, Battle Honours of the British army, 1662-1901, Murray 1911; David and Charles reprints 1971

South Africa, 1899-1902, officers and men mentioned in despatches, London 1902, reprinted 1971

Spencer, William, Medals - the researcher's guide, National Archives, 2006 [MED61]

Museums

Military Museums in the UK, Ogilby Trust, Third Millennium Publishing, 2007 Available direct at: www.tmiltd.com

Sibun, Colin (ed), Military Museums in the UK, Army Museum Ogilvy Trust, Third Millenium Publishing Ltd, 2007

Wise, Terence & Shirley, A guide to military museums and other places of military interest, 9th edn, published by Terence Wise, 1999 [SoG library]

Chapter Six - World War One

Soldiers died in the Great War 1914-1919 (80 parts), Imperial War Museum, HMSO 1921-2 [CD-ROM, MX601-606 and at ARM/RH]

Officers died in the Great War 1914-1919, HMSO, 1919 (also reprints by Samson, 1975 & 1979; new enlarged edition by J B Hayward, 1988; latter includes three new appendices, listing Deceased Regular Army Officers, Deceased Territorial Force Army Officers and Deceased European Officers of the Indian Army)

The History of the Great War based on official documents, Order of battle of divisions,
Part 1, The Regular British Divisions, HMSO 1935
Part 2A, The Territorial Force Mounted Divisions and the 1st Line Territorial Force Divisions (42-56), HMSO 1936
Part 2B, The 2nd Line Territorial Force Divisions (57-69) with the Home Service Divisions (71-73) and 74th and 75th Divisions, HMSO 1937
Part 3A, New Army Divisions (9-26), HMSO 1938
Part 3B, New Army Divisions (30-41) and 63rd (RN) Division, HMSO 1945
Part 4, The Army Council, GHQs, Armies and Corps 1914-1918, HMSO 1945
Compiled by AF Becke, Facsimile copy published by Ray Westlake Military Books, 1988-1990, (Copy available at TNA)

Babington, Anthony, For the sake of example, capital courts martial, 1914-1920, Secker and Warburg 1983; Paladin 1985

Enser A G S, A subject bibliography of the First World War - books in English, 1914-1978, Deutsch, London 1979

Fowler, Simon, Tracing your First World War ancestors, Countryside Books, Newbury 2003 [TB/RG97]

Holding, Norman H, World War I army ancestry, revised and updated by Iain S Swinnerton, FFHS 4th edition 2003

Holding, Norman H, Location of British army records 1914-1918, revised and updated by Iain S Swinnerton, FFHS 4th edition, 1999 [ARM/G115]

Macdonald, Lyn, 1914-1918, Voices and Images of the Great War, Michael Joseph 1988, Penguin 1991 (see below for more details of her books)

Spencer, William, Army Service Records of the First World War, PRO Readers' Guide No 19, 3rd edn 2001 [SP/PER]

Swinnerton, Iain S and Symons, Roland, Identifying your World War I soldier from badges and photographs, FFHS, 2001 [ARM/G118]

Sykes, Julian & Putkowski, Julian, Shot at Dawn, Wharncliffe Publishing, Barnsley 1989 [ARM/G93]

Pals Series - many of these include nominal rolls and medal lists - published by Leo Cooper, Pen and Sword Books:

Accrington Pals (11th East Lancs), William Turner, 1987

Barnsley Pals (13th-14th York and Lancaster), Jon Cooksey, 1986 [ARM/RH200]

Birmingham Pals (14th 15th 16th Service Bns, Royal Warwickshire Regiment), Terry Carter, 1997

Bradford Pals (16th-18th & 20th (Service) Bns Prince of Wales Own West Yorkshire Regiment), David Raw 2005/2006

Durham Pals (18th, 19th, 22nd Bns, Durham Light Infantry), John Sheen

Hull Pals (10th, 11th, 12th, 13th Bns, East Yorkshire Regiment), David Bilton,

Leeds Pals (15th Bn, Prince of Wales Own), Laurie Milner, 1991

Liverpool Pals (17th-20th Bns, The Kings), Graham Maddocks, 1991

Salford Pals (15th, 18th, 19th, 20th Bns, Lancashire Fusiliers), Michael Stedman

Sheffield City (12th York and Lancaster), Oldfield and Gibson, 1988 [ARM/RH199]

Swansea Pals (14th Service Bn, Welsh Regiment), Bernard Lewis,

Tyneside Irish (24th-27th Service Bns, Northumberland Fusiliers), John Sheen 1998 [ARM/RH222]

Wearside Battalion (20th Service Bn, Durham Light Infantry), John Sheen, 2007

Lyn Macdonald - 'the recording angel of the common soldier - all now published by Viking and/or Penguin:

1914, the days of hope, 1987

1915, the death of innocence, 1993

Somme (1916), 1983

They called it Passchendaele: the story of the Third Battle of Ypres and of the men who fought in it (1917), 1978 [ARM/G4]

To the last man, Spring 1918, 1998

1914-1918: voices and images of the Great War, 1988

The roses of no man's land, (relates to medical teams and casualties), 1980

Major and Mrs Holt's Pocket Battlefield Guides - published by Pen and Sword Books:

Gallipoli

Somme 1916/1918

Western Front-North

Western Front- South

Ypres and Passchendaele

Ypres Salient

Anderson, Ross, The Forgotten Front: the East African campaign 1914-1918, Tempus 2004

Attwell, W A (ed), Laurence Attwell's letters from the front, Pen and Sword, 2005 (a detailed account of service with the 1/15 (County of London) Battalion, Prince of Wales's Own, Civil Service Rifles, from March 1915 to December 1918)

Banks, Arthur, A military atlas of the first World War, Heinemann 1975, republished by Pen and Sword Books, 1997/2004

Carlyon, Les (L A), Gallipoli, Bantam Books, 2003

Duffy, Christopher, through German eyes: the British and the SOMME 1916, Weidenfeld and Nicolson, Orion Publishing Group, 2006

Flynn, Brenda, What did you do in the War, Daddy? - the East African campaign, 1914-1918, Manchester Genealogist, Volume 41 Number 1, 2005

Laffin, John, World War I in postcards, Alan Sutton Publishing, Gloucester, 1989

Liddell Hart, Sir Basil, History of the First World War, 1930/1934/1970, Cassell & Co, Book Club Associates [TB/HIS78]

Chapter Seven - World War Two

Bayly, Christopher and Harper, Tim, Forgotten Armies, Britain's Asian Empire and the War with Japan, Allen Lane 2004, Penguin 2005

Forty, Lt-Col George, British Army Handbook, 1939-1945, Sutton Publishing, 1998/2002

Fowler, Simon, Tracing your Second World War ancestors, Countryside Books, Newbury 2006 [TP/RG117]

Joslen, Col. Hubert F, Orders of Battle of United Kingdom and colonial formations and units in the Second World War, 1939-1945, prepared for the Historical Section of the Cabinet Office, 2 volumes, London 1960

Mills, Jon, From Scarlet to Khaki, understanding the twentieth century British army uniforms in your family album, Warden Publishing, 11 Malvern Road, Orpington, Kent BR6 9HA, 2005

Piggott, Juliet, Queen Alexandra's Royal Army Nursing Corps, Leo Cooper, London 1990 [ARM/RH151]

Terry, Roy, Women in Khaki: the Story of the British Woman Soldier, Columbus Books, London 1988. [ARM/GEN]

Tyrer, Nicola: They fought in the fields, the Women's Land Army, the story of a forgotten victory, Sinclair Stevenson, London, 1997, Tempus (paperback) 2007

Tyrer, Nicola: Sisters in Arms, British army nurses tell their story, Weidenfeld and Nicolson, London 2008

Germany and German Occupied Territories: Imperial Prisoners of War: Alphabetical Lists, HMSO, 1945, Prisoners of War: British Army 1939-1945, J B Hayward, 1990.

Further Reading - World War II

Major and Mrs Holt's Pocket Battlefield Guides, published by Pen and Sword Books: Normandy (Landing Beaches) and Operation Market Garden (Arnhem)

Troopships - Soldiers Lost at Sea, a Chronicle of Troopship Disasters, James E Wise Jr and Scott Baron, 2004, Naval Institute Press, Annapolis, Maryland. Includes a table listing lost troopships of all nations, for both World Wars.

Where did my Father-in-Law die? is a full account of recent researches by Derek Poppleton into the circumstances surrounding the **loss at sea** of Sydney Norman Bough (1913-1942). See Cheshire Ancestor Vol 33 No 3, March 2003. [CH/PER]

British Soldiers abroad and Allied Soldiers of those countries

Australia

Australian Joint Copying Project: Part I, General Introduction, 1985; Part 4, War Office, 1986

Bradley, Joyce et al, Roll Call! - a guide to genealogical sources in the Australian War Memorial, Australian War Memorial, Canberra ACT 2601, 1986

Chambers, Margaret, Finding families, the guide to the National Archives of Australia for genealogists, 1998

Donohoe, James Hugh, The British Army in Australia, 1788-1870, Index of personnel, 1996, available from the author in paperback, microfiche and disk formats, PO Box 681, Spit Junction NSW 2088

Fitzmaurice, Yvonne, Army deserters from H M Service: Volume 1, 1853-1858; Volume 2 (in Australia and New Zealand), 1853-1870; published by the author, 23 Fuller Street, Mitcham, Victoria 3132, 1988 [AHA/V/G8-9]
Montague R H, How to trace your military ancestors in Australia and New Zealand, Hale and Iremonger, GPO Box 2552, Sydney, NSW, 1989

Peake, Andrew G, Army pension records in Australia, Genealogists' Magazine, 21 (10) 368, 1985 [PER/GEN]

Sexton, Rae, The deserters - a complete record of military and naval deserters in Australia and New Zealand, 1800-65, Australasian Maritime Historical Society, Box 33, Magill S A 5072, 1989

Family Journeys, Stories in the National Archives of Australia, 2008

Canada

Quebec, Holy Trinity Anglican Registers, 1768-1800, on films C-2897 and C-2898 and Quebec Garrison Protestant Chaplaincy registers, 1797-1800, 1817-1826, on films C-2898 and C-2899 (Checklist of parish registers, Manuscript Division, Public Archives of Canada, 395 Wellington Street, Ottawa, Ontario K1A ON3, 3rd edn 1981)

Quebec, Garrison of Quebec Anglican Church registers, 1797-1871, available on films M 138/22-24; outside Canada, purchase from 'Federation des associations de familles-souches' at same address. SoG has microfilm copies of Quebec Anglican Church registers for 1797-1815 (Private communication from Archives Nationales du Quebec, 1210 avenue du Seminaire, Case Postale 10450, Sainte-Foy (Quebec) G1V 4N1)

Royal Warwickshire Regiment, 6th Regiment of Foot, in RG 8, Volumes 829-831, films C-3266 and C-3267 (Tracing your ancestors in Canada, section on Military and Naval Records, Public Archives of Canada, as above, 8th edn, 1984)

General inventory manuscripts, Vol 2 (MG11-MG16), Vol 3 (MG17-MG21), Vol 4 (MG22-MG25), Public Archives of Canada, from 1972

Tracing your Ancestors in Canada, pdf file on-line at Library and Archives Canada, www.collectionscanada.gc.ca/genealogy

Gibraltar

Burness, Lawrence R, Genealogical research in Gibraltar, Genealogists' Magazine, 21(1) 21-2, 1983 [PER/GEN]

India

Bailey, Peter A, Researching ancestors in the East India Company armies, Families in British India Society (FIBIS), 2006

Baxter I A, Baxter's Guide: biographical sources in the India Office Records, 3rd edition FIBIS/BL, 2004   [IND/ARM/GEN]

Farrington, Anthony, Guide to the records of the India Office Military Department, IOR:L/MIL and L/WS, London 1982

Fitzhugh T V H, East India Company ancestry, Genealogists' Magazine, 21(5) 150-4, 1984 [PER/GEN]

Mason, Philip, A matter of honour, Papermac 1986 (History of Indian Army)

Omissi, David, Indian voices of the Great War: Soldiers' Letters selected and introduced by the author, Macmillan, 1999

Ireland

Donaldson, Anne, British Military Graveyard, Ballincollig, Co Cork, Ireland, 1810-1922, Ballincollig Enterprise Board, 2003 [IR/M37]

New Zealand (see also under Australia)

Hughes, Hugh and Lyn, Discharged in New Zealand - soldiers of the Imperial foot regiments who took their discharge in New Zealand, 1840-1870, NZ Society of Genealogists, Box 8795, Auckland, 1988

Kendall, Shirley E, The Pensioner Gazette, PO Box 139, Penshurst, NSW 2222, 1987 onwards

Family History, Research Reference Guide, 2008, pdf file on-line at Archives New Zealand www.archives.govt.nz [NZ/G14 for an earlier version]

United States of America

Eakle, Arlene and Cerny, Jody, The source - a guidebook of American genealogy, Ancestry Publishing Company, Salt Lake City, Utah, 1984 (see chapter 8, Military Records) [CD-ROM]

Guide to genealogical research in the National Archives, National Archives and Records Administration, 700 Pennsylvania Avenue, Washington DC 20408-0001, 3rd edition, 2001   (Website: www.archives.gov/publications)

General Overseas

Yeo, Geoffrey, The British Overseas: a guide to records of their births, baptisms, marriages and deaths and burials available in the United Kingdom, Guildhall Library, London, 3rd edn 1995 [Middle Library]
Abstract of arrangements respecting registration of births, marriages and deaths in the United Kingdom and the other countries of the British Commonwealth and in the Irish Republic, HMSO, 1952 [TB/RG52]

The National Archives (TNA), Kew

General Bibliography

Bevan, Amanda, Tracing your Ancestors in the National Archives, the website and beyond, The National Archives, 7th edition, 2006 (the latest version of the handbook to the PRO holdings, first produced in 1981 by Jane Cox and Timothy Padfield) [Middle Library]

Colwell, Stella, Family Roots, Discovering the Past in the Public Record Office, Weidenfeld and Nicolson, London, 1991 [TB/FH158]

Colwell, Stella, Dictionary of Genealogical Sources in the Public Record Office, Weidenfeld and Nicolson, London, 1992 [TB/RG52, Middle & Upper Library]

Research Guides at TNA

An alphabetical list of currently available TNA Research Guides is reproduced in Appendix 4. These are also accessible on-line. The old numbered system of guides is no longer in use.

War Office Department

A numerical listing of the War Office series, from WO 1 to WO 408, is given in Appendix 3. For each series, the covering dates are given, together with the title of that series and the number of pieces it contains.

Finding aids in book form

Many of the old finding aids, published by the Public Record Office and the List and Index Society, have been rendered obsolescent by the modern catalogue system at the National Archives, Kew, and by its associated on-line counterpart. The following may occasionally be found useful still:

List of War Office records preserved in the PRO, Volume I, PRO Lists and Indexes Number XXVIII, 1908

War Office and other military records preserved in the PRO, PRO Lists and Indexes Number LIII, 1931 (an alphabetical guide)

List of War Office records, PRO Lists and Indexes, Supplementary Series, Volume VIII: 1, Kraus Reprints, 1968

List of War Office records, PRO Lists and Indexes, Supplementary Series, Volume VIII: 2, Kraus Reprints, 1968
Soldiers' Documents, 1760-1913 (WO 97), List and Index Society Volume 201, 1983

Muster Books and Pay Lists, General Series, 1760-1877 (WO 12/1-13305), List and Index Society Volume 210, 1984 (This volume lists infantry, cavalry and many other corps, not just cavalry, as incorrectly stated on the cover)

Useful addresses and websites for Publishers

Mattocks Military Books, 8 Malvern Avenue, Acomb, York, YO26 5SG/Phone 01904 786022   www.mattocksmilitarybooks.com

The Naval and Military Press Ltd, Unit 10, Ridgewood Industrial Park, Uckfield, East Sussex, TN22 5QE/ Phone 01825 749494/ Website www.naval-military-press.com
Publishers of many military CD-ROMs, including Soldiers died in the Great War, Trench Maps (1914-1918) and Army Roll of Honour 1939-1945.

Partizan Press, 818 London Road, Leigh-on-Sea, Essex, SS9 3NH/ Phone 01702 473986/716107

Pen and Sword Books Ltd, 47 Church Street, Barnsley, South Yorkshire S70 2AS/Phone 01226 734222/Website www.pen-and-sword.co.uk

Shire Publications Ltd, Cromwell House, Church Street, Princes Risborough, Buckinghamshire HP27 9AA www.shirebooks.co.uk

S&N Genealogical Supplies, West Wing, Manor Farm, Chilmark, Salisbury SP3 5AF/ Phone 01722 716121 www.genealogysupplies.com
Publisher of many military CD-ROMs, including Army Lists and Hart's Army Lists.

Internet

Books about Internet Resources

Blank, Stuart C, Researching British Military History on the Internet (The British Army and the Armies of the Commonwealth, Empire and Dominions), Alwyn Enterprises Ltd, 2007

Christian, Peter, The Genealogist's Internet, 3rd edition, TNA, 2005 (www.spub.co.uk/tgi3) [TB/COM28]

Fowler, Simon: Guide to Military History on the Internet, Pen and Sword, 2007

Websites

A selection of the most important websites for general family history research and military history research is given here. More comprehensive coverage may be found in the two books, listed above, by Stuart Blank and Simon Fowler. Other websites on more detailed topics are referred to within the text of this book.

General websites for family history research
www.nationalarchives.gov.uk
The National Archives, Kew, Richmond, Surrey, TW9 4DU.

www.nationalarchives.gov.uk/documentsonline
Documents Online gives access to databases such as World War I army campaign medal cards, WWI prisoners of war interviews, Women's Army Auxiliary Corps (WAAC), Victoria Cross Registers, Recommendations for Honours and Awards (Army), War Diaries (WO 95) - many of these have freely searchable indexes with pay-to-view documents

www.ancestry.co.uk
A commercial website, one of the first to name index the available censuses for England, Wales and Scotland, with on-line access to images for England and Wales. Their databases for World War One also include Medal Roll Index Cards, and will very soon feature all the surviving Service Records (Burnt Documents WO 363) and Pension Records (WO 364).

www.freebmd.org.uk
A very useful free website, run for many years by volunteers - it aims to provide an index from 1837 onwards of the births, marriages and deaths, for England and Wales, from the quarterly GRO indexes. A block of years may be searched, and marriage entries become cross-referenced.

www.bmdindex.co.uk
A commercial website giving access to the indexes of births, marriages and deaths in England and Wales from 1st July 1837 to 2005

www.gro.gov.uk/gro/content/certificates
The certificate ordering service for births, marriages and deaths in England and Wales from 1st July 1837

www.bmdregisters.co.uk
Access to an index and images of non-parochial registers, the originals being in RG 4, RG 5 and RG 6 at TNA

www.scotlandspeople.gov.uk
The official government source of genealogical data for Scotland

www.findmypast.com
A commercial website well-known for its index of UK passenger shipping lists from 1890 to 1960, it also has a useful military section. Free index searches are possible for 'Soldiers died in the Great War 1914-1918' and the 'National Roll of the Great War'. The 'overseas' military indexes from the GRO are also accessible on-line.

British Army - general websites

www.regiments.org
history of regiments of British, Empire and Commonwealth armies

www.army.mod.uk
the current official internet site for the British Army

Military Museums

www.iwm.org.uk
The Imperial War Museum - includes the UK National Inventory of War Memorials

www.national-army-museum.ac.uk
The National Army Museum

www.armymuseums.org.uk
Links by the Army Museums Ogilby Trust (AMOT) to regimental and corps museums of the British Army

War Graves and Memorials

www.cwgc.org
Commonwealth War Graves Commission

www.twgpp.org.uk
The War Graves Photographic Project

www.scottishwarmemorials.co.uk and www.scottishwargraves.co.uk
Scottish War Memorials and Scottish War Graves are two major new projects - see the Scottish Genealogist, Volume LV No 4, December 2008

www.roll-of-honour.org
Links to details from war memorials in many counties of the UK

www.irishwarmemorials.ie
Irish War Memorials project including names from memorials and books

Australia, Canada, India, Ireland, New Zealand, South Africa

www.naa.gov.au
National Archives of Australia

www.awm.gov.au
Australian War Memorial - nominal rolls for most wars

www.cmhg.gc.ca
a gateway to Canadian Military History (CMHG)

www.collectionscanada.gc.ca/databases/cef
Library and Archives Canada: WWI soldiers - index and images

www.bl.uk/collections/britasian/britasiasoldiers.html
Sources at the British Library for Indian soldiers in World Wars One and Two

www.irishsoldiers.com
website of the Military Heritage of Ireland Trust Ltd

www.archives.govt.nz
New Zealand Defence Force - personnel indexes for South African (Boer) War and
World War One

www.national.archives.gov.za
National Archives and Records Service of South Africa

Crimean War, Boer War, World Wars I and II

www.crimeanwar.org
Crimean war information and links

www.angloboerwar.com
includes officer biographies and VC and DSO awards

www.1914-1918.net
Many useful links and detailed information for WWI

www.westernfrontassociation.com
Western Front of WWI - major organisation with informative website, journals and discussion forum

www.gallipoli-association.org
a British based association to preserve the memory of the Gallipoli campaign

www.anzacs.net
Australian and New Zealand Army Corps, this site features names of all soldiers in cemeteries and on memorials of Gallipoli

www.leedspals.co.uk
West Yorkshire 15th Bn in WWI

www.pals.org.uk
Accrington soldiers of WWI, including absent voters and PoWs

www.fylde.demon.co.uk/welcome.htm
Great War webpages including Tom Morgan's Hellfire Corner

www.normandy-dday.com
general information about the D-Day landings, museums, cemeteries and tours

www.ddayancestors.com
a website which lists all those killed on 6 June 1944 and also offers research for casualties of the Normandy campaign

Orders and Medals

www.omrs.org.uk
Orders and Medals research society

www.victoriacross.org.uk
many details of holders of the Victoria Cross

www.gc-database.co.uk
listing of recipients of the George Cross

APPENDIX ONE
Campaigns & Medals from 1660 to 1902

Years	Campaign/Region	Honours
1662-1783	Mediterranean	Tangier (1662-1680), Gibraltar (1704 and 1779-1783)
1695-1709	Northern Europe	Namur (1695), Blenheim (1704), Ramillies (1706), Oudenarde (1708), Malplaquet (1709)
1743-1762	Northern Europe	Dettingen (1743), Minden (1759), Emsdorff (1760), Warburg (1760), Wilhelmstahl (1762)
1751-1764	India	Arcot (1751), Plassey (1757), Condore (1758), Masulipatam (1759), Badara (1759) Wandewash (1760), Buxar (1764)
1758-1759	North America	Louisburg (1758), Quebec (1759)
1759-1762	West Indies	Guadeloupe (1759), Martinique (1762), Havana (1762)
1774-1799	India	Rohilcund (1774), Guzerat (1778-1782), Sholingur (1781), Mangalore (1783), Nundy Droog (1791), Rohilcund (1794) Seedaseer (1799), Seringapatam (1799)
1778-1810	West Indies	St Lucia (1778, 1796, 1803), Martinique (1794, 1809) Surinam (1804), Dominica (1805), Guadeloupe (1810)

1793-1799	Flanders	Lincelles (1793), Nieuport (1793), Villers-en-Couche, Beaumont, Willems, Tournay (1794), Egmont-op-Zee (1799)

For campaign medals, the list below continues to give all actions for which regimental, but not necessarily individual, honours were awarded. The piece number in TNA series WO 100 is also given.

See WO 100/

1793-1814	Peninsula	Rolica, Vimiera, Sahagun (1808), Corunna, Douro, Talavera (1809) Busaco (1810), Barrosa, Fuentes d'Onor, Albuera, Almaraz, Arroyos dos Molinos, Tarifa (1811) Ciudad Rodrigo, Badajoz, Salamanca (1812), Vittoria, Pyrenees, San Sebastian, Nivelle, Nive (1813) Orthes, Toulouse (1814)	1-11 & 16
1801-1802	Egypt & Sudan	Mandora, Marabout (1801), Egypt (1802)	12
1803-1809	India	Ally Ghur (1803), Delhi (1803-4), Assaye (1803) Laswarree (1803), Deig (1803-4), Cochin (1809)	13
1806	Naples	Maida (1806)	
1806	South Africa	Cape of Good Hope (1808)	
1807	South America	Montevideo (1807)	
1812-1814	North America	Detroit (1812), Miami, Chateaugay, Chrystler's Farm, (1813), Niagara, Bladensburg (1814)	
1815	Belgium	Ligny, Quatre Bras (16 June), Waterloo (18 June)	14-15
1817-1826	India	Kirkee, Poona, Seetabuldee, Nagpoor, Maheidpoor (1817), Corygaum (1818), Nowah (1819), Bhurtpore (1826)	13
1809-1857	Minor Eastern Campaigns	Arabia - Beni Boo Alli (1809 &1821), Bourbon (1810), Java (1811), Persian Gulf (1819), Aden (1839), Persia (1856-57), Bushire,Reshire (1856), Koosh-ab (1857)	13

1824-1825	Burma	Ava, Kemmendine (1824), Arracan (1825)	
1835-1853	South Africa	South Africa (1835, 1846-47, 1851-53)	17
1839-1842	Afghanistan	Ghuznee, Khelat (1839), Kahun (1840) Jellalabad (1841-42), Kelat-i-Ghilzie, Candahar Ghuznee, Cabul (1842)	20
1840-1842	China	Canton, Chusan (1841)	
1843	India	Scinde - Meeanee, Hyderabad Gwalior - Maharajore, Punniar	
1845-1846	India (Sutlej)	Moodkee, Ferozeshah (1845), Aliwal, Sobraon (1846)	
1848-1849	India (Punjab)	Chillianwallah, Mooltan, Goojerat (1849)	13
1846-1866	New Zealand	New Zealand (1846-7, 1860-1, 1863-6)	18
1852-1853	Burma	Pegu	
1854-1855	Crimea	Alma, Balaclava, Inkerman (1854) Sevastopol (1854-55)	22-34
1857-1859	Indian Mutiny	Delhi, Lucknow (1857), Central India (1857-58)	35-39
1857-1860	China	Fatshan, Canton (1857), Taku Forts (1858 & 1860) Pekin (1860)	40-41
1867-1868	Abyssinia		43
1873-1874	Ashanti	Ashanti, Coomassie	44
1877-1879	South Africa	Zulu War - Isandhlwana, Rorke's Drift	46-50
1878-1880	Afghanistan	Ali Musjid (1878), Peiwar Kotal, Charasia, Kabul (1879), Ahmed Khel, Maiwand, Kandahar (1880)	51-53
1882-1884	Egypt	Tel-el-Kebir (1882), El-Teb, Tamaai (1884)	55-61
1884-1889	Sudan	The Nile (1884-5), Abu Klea, Kirbekan, Suakin, Tofrek (1885)	62-68
1885-1887	Burma	Burma	69-70
1895-1902	India (NW Frontier)	Chitral (1895), Malakand, Samana (1897) Tirah (1897-8), Waziristan (1901-2)	73-75 84-89
1896-1898	Egypt & Sudan	Hafir (1896), Atbara (1898), Khartoum including Omdurman (1898)	80-83
1892-1900	African Campaigns	West Africa (1892-4), Ashanti (1896), East and Central Africa / Uganda (1897-9) Ashanti / Kumassi (1900)	76-79

1900	China	Pekin (1900)	94-99
1899-1902	South Africa (Boer War)	Talana, Elandslaagte, Belmont, Modder River (1899), Tugela Heights, Kimberley, Ladysmith, Paardeburg, Driefontein, Wepener, Johannesburg, Laing's Nek, Diamond Hill, Witterburgen, Mafeking, Belfast (1900)	112-371

APPENDIX TWO
Regimental Records

Regimental titles have been taken from the books by Brereton, Leslie and from the PRO List and Index Number LIII. It is not possible, in the brief summary tables presented here, to give full details of the many changes in names of regiments, nor of renumberings.

Dates of formation of each regiment are quoted from the concordance of regiments given in the published index to the first forty volumes of the Journal of the Society for Army Historical Research. Many regiments, from the 42nd Foot onwards, were disbanded at some time, and so did not exist continuously from the earliest date of formation.

From 1881, many of the later-numbered foot regiments became second battalions of earlier named regiments, and so a cross-reference has been included under the first named. For instance, the 63rd Foot became the 1st battalion of the Manchester Regiment and 'see 96th' indicates that the 96th Foot became its 2nd battalion.

Muster Books and Pay Lists (WO 12, 1760-1877) - summary information was originally obtained from List and Index Society Volume 210 - this gives further details of piece numbers, which nowadays may be found in the (online) Catalogue at TNA.

Regimental Registers are still held by the Registrar General at the Overseas Section of the General Register Office. See corresponding section in Chapter Three.

WO 25, Registers, Various - summary information was originally obtained from PRO List and Index Number XXVIII - this gives further details of piece numbers, which nowadays may be found using the (online) Catalogue at TNA.

Soldiers' Documents (WO 97, 1760-1872) - summary information was originally obtained from List and Index Society Volume 201 - this gives further details of piece numbers, which nowadays may be found using the (online) Catalogue at TNA.

Abbreviations: Bn = Battalion. Dep = Depot. Mil = Militia. MMG's Cas. Index = Muster Master General's Index of Casualties. uos = unless otherwise stated.

CAVALRY with best-known pre-1914 titles and dates of original formation	Muster Books and Pay Lists		Regimental Registers	
	Years	WO 12/	Marriages Years	Births/Bapt Years
Household Cavalry				
1st Life Guards 1660	1759-1877	1-32	1870-1921	1870-1921
2nd Life Guards 1660	1788-1877	33-51	1870-1921	1870-1921
Royal Horse Guards - The Blues 1660	1759-1877	52-80		
Cavalry of the Line			(1794-1848)	(1800-1848)
1st (King's) Dragoon Guards 1685	1760-1878	61-137	(1885-1908)	(1885-1908)
2nd Dragoon Guards (Queen's Bays) 1685	1760-1878	138-189	For 2nd to 7th Dragoon Guards there are some Registers for ca 1877-1908	
3rd (Prince of Wales's) Dragoon.Guards 1685	1760-1878	190-240		
4th (Royal Irish) Dragoon Guards 1685	1774-1878	241-292		
5th (Princess Charlotte of Wales's) Dragoon Guards 1685	1772-1878	293-347		
6th Dragoon Guards (Carabiniers) 1685	1760-1878	348-399		
7th (Princess Royal's) Dragoon Guards 1688	1760-1878	400-452		
1st (Royal) Dragoons 1661	1760-1878	453-507	For Dragoon, Hussars and Lancers there are some Registers for ca 1840-1916	
2nd Dragoons (Royal Scots Greys) 1668	1760-1878	508-562		
3rd (King's Own) Hussars 1685	1760-1877	563-620		
4th (Queen's Own) Hussars 1685	1760-1877	621-681		
5th (Royal Irish) Lancers 1689/1858	1770-1799 1858-1878	682-684 685-703		
6th (Inniskilling) Dragoons 1689	1760-1878	704-755		
7th (Queen's Own) Hussars 1690	1760-1878	756-810		
8th (King's Royal Irish) Hussars 1693	1771-1878	811-868		
9th (Queen's Royal) Lancers 1715	1774-1877	869-921		
10th (Prince of Wales's Own Royal) Hussars	1760-1877	922-975		
11th (Prince Albert's Own) Hussars 1715	1760-1877	976-1036		
12th (Prince of Wales's Royal) Lancers	1774-1876	1037-1083		
13th Hussars 1715	1771-1877	1084-1140		
14th (King's) Hussars 1715	1772-1877	1141-1191		
15th (The King's) Hussars 1746/1759	1760-1877	1192-1244		
16th (The Queen's) Lancers 1759	1760-1878	1245-1305		
17th (Duke of Cambridge's Own) Lancers 1759	1771-1878	1306-1362		
18th (Queen Mary's Own) Hussars 1759/1858	1760-1878	1363-1398	(gap from	1822-1857)
19th (Queen Alexandra's Own Royal) Hussars 1759/1858	1779-1878	1399-1417	(gap from	1822-1861)
20th Hussars 1759/1858	1779-1878	1418-1440	(gap from	1819-1861)

Description and Succession Books		Service Returns No. 1	MMG's Casualty Index	Index to Casualty Returns	Casualty Returns		Soldiers' Documents	
Years	WO 25/	WO 25/	WO 25/	WO 25/	Years	WO 25/	1760-1854 WO 97/	1855-1872 WO 97/
		871			1823-1857	1363-1365	1-11	1272-1274
		872			1832-1851	1366-1368	1-11	1272-1274
		873		2411	1810-1851	1359-1362	1-11	1272-1274
1801-74	266-268	877	1196	2412-3	1809-1830	1369-1372		
		878	1196	2414-5	1809-1831	1373-1375		
		879	1197	2416-7	1809-1830	1376-1378	All Cavalry of the	
		880	1197	2418-9	1809-1831	1379-1381	Line arranged	
		881	1198	2420-1	1809-1830	1382-1384	alphabetically in	
		882	1198	2422-3	1810-1830	1385-1388		
1791-1829	269-272	883	1199	2424-5	1809-1830	1389-1391	WO 97/	WO 97/
		884	1200	2426-7	1809-1830	1392-1394	12-149	1275-1305
1813-75	273-274	885	1200	2428-9	1809-1830	1395-1397		
1772-1833	275-277	886	1201	2430-1	1809-1852	1398-1404		
		887	1201	2432-3	1809-1842	1405-1412		
			1202					
		888	1202	2434-5	1809-1830	1413-1415		
		889	1203	2436-7	1809-1831	1416-1418		
		890	1203	2438-9	1809-1830	1419-1422		
		891	1204	2440-1	1809-1831	1423-1425		
		892	1204	2442-3	1809-1855	1426-1431		
1813-78	278	893	1205	2444-5	1809-1837	1432-1436		
		894	1205	2446-7	1809-1830	1437-1441		
		895	1206	2448-9	1809-1830	1442-1445		
		896	1206	2450-1	1809-1830	1446-1448		
		897	1207	2452-3	1809-1854	1449-1453		
		898	1207	2454-5	1809-1846	1454-1458		
		899	1208	2456-7	1810-1830	1459-1462		
1783-1821	279-282	900	1208	2458-9	1809-1821	1463-1464		
1807-1821	283	901	1209	2460-1	18091821	1465-1466		
1795-1818	284-288	902	1209	2462-3	1809-1818	1467-1469		

CAVALRY with best-known pre-1914 titles and dates of original formation	Muster Books and Pay Lists		Regimental Registers	
	Years	WO 12/	Marriages Years	Births/Bapt Years
21st (Empress of India's) Lancers 1760/1858	1779-1878	1441-1466	(gap from	1821-1862)
22nd Dragoons 1779/1794/1802	1779-1820	1467-1478		
23rd Dragoons/Lancers 1781/1794/1803	1795-1817	1479-1488		
24th Dragoons 1794/1803	1794-1819	1489-1500		
25th Dragoons 1794/1803	1794-1819	1501-1511		
26th Dragoons 1795	1795-1802	1512-1514		
27th Dragoons 1795	1795-1802	1515		
28th Dragoons 1795	1795-1802	1516-1518		
29th Dragoons 1795	1795-1808	1519-1520	(gap from	1805-1806)
30th – 33rd Dragoons 1794	1795-1796	1521		

Description and Succession Books		Service Returns No. 1	MMG's Casualty Index	Index to Casualty Returns	Casualty Returns		Soldiers' Documents	
Years	WO 25/	WO 25/	WO 25/	WO 25/	Years	WO 25/	1760-1854 WO 97/	1855-1872 WO 97/
1806-20	289-292	903	1210	2464-5	1809-1830	1470-1471		
1796-1820	293-298	904	1210	2466-7	1810-1820	1472-1474		
1813-17	299	905		2468	1809-1817	1474		
1806-19	300-302	906		2469-70	1810-1819	1476-1478		
1806-20	303-304	907	1211	2471-2	1809-1819	1479-1480		
			1211					
1795-1815	305		1212					
			1212					
1795-1811	306-307		1213					

REGIMENTS OF FOOT GUARDS	Muster Books and Pay Lists		Regimental Registers	
	Years	WO 12/	Marriages Years	Births/Bapt Years
1st (1656) Grenadier Guards	1732, 40-1 1760-1877	1537-1538 1539-1656	See Quebec Garrison Volumes 5 & 6	
2nd (1650) Coldstream Guards	1759-1877	1657-1770	1876-1915	1876-1915
3rd (1662) Scots Guards	1762-1877	1771-1881	1796-1838 1861-1892	1804-1892
4th (1900) Irish Guards			1890-1913	1890-1913
5th (1915) Welsh Guards				

REGIMENTS OF INFANTRY
Best known pre-1914 titles given with dates of original formation and renaming

Foot	Battalion	Years	WO 12/	Marriages Years	Births/Bapt Years
1 (1633/1678)	1	1768-1877	1882-1947	1840-1903	1843-1903
Royal Regiment (1684)	2	1759-1877	1948-2009	1842-1907	1844-1907
Royal Scots (1812)	3	1804-1817	2010-2014		
Lothian (Royal Scots) (1881)	4	1805-1816	2015-2019		
	Dep			1855-1908	1862-1908
2 (1661/1684)	1	1768-1877	2020-2083	1833-1908	1854-1908
Queen's Royal (1703)	2	1857-1877	2084-2103	1845-1913	1846-1913
West Surrey (1881)				1833-1908	1834-1908
	Dep				
3 (1665/1689)	1	1760-1877	2104-2167	1849-1907	1860-1908
The Buffs (1702/1751)	2	1803-1877	2168-2193	1844-1908	1838-1908
East Kent (1881)	3			1829-1877	1841-1888
	Dep/Res			1893-1908	1893-1908
4 (1680)	1	1764-1877	2194-2259	1821-1914	1830-1914
King's Own (1715)	2	1799-1815	2260-	1839-1907	1845-1908
Royal Lancaster (1881)		1857-1877	2286		
	3	1799-1802	2287-2288	1885-1908	1885-1908
	4			1881-1912	1881-1912
5 (1674/1688)	1	1760-1877	2289-2352	1798-1914	1812-1914
Northumberland (1782)	2	1799-1815	2353-	1845-1914	1849-1914
Northumberland Fusiliers (1836)		1857-1877	-2379		
	3			1886-1912	1886-1912
	4			1879-1911	1879-1911

Description and Succession Books		Service Ret'ns No. 1	MMG's Cas. Index	Index to Cas. Ret'ns	Casualty Returns		Soldiers' Documents	
Years	WO 25/ (uos)	WO 25/	WO 25/	WO 25/	Years	WO 25/	1760-1854 WO 97/	1855-1872 WO 97/
		874		2475	1823-1850	1487-1488	150	1365-1371
		875		and	1823-1850	1489-1490	to	1372-1376
Depot: 1768-1830	WO 67/ 1-6	876		2476	1823-1850	1491-1493	218	1377-1381
1798-1832	308-311	909	1216	2477	1809-1830	1494-1498	219-239	1382-1386
1806-1831	312-313	910	1217/8		1809-1831	1499-1505		
1812-1817	314-315		1219	to	1809-1817	1506		
1798-1816	316-317	911	1219	2481	1809-1816	1507		
					1825-1831	1508		
1811-1843	318-321	912	1220	2482	1810-1845	1509-1515	240-247	1387-1389
				2483				
1804-1831	322-324	913	1221	2484	1809-1845	1516-1519	248-258	1390-1393
1807-1816	325-326	914		2485	1809-1815	1520		
1823-1833	327-328				1825-1827	1521		
		915	1222	2486	1809-1847	1522-1526	259-267	1394-1397
		916	1223	2487	1809-1815	1527		
			1224		(Depot: 1825-1828)	(1528)		
		917	1225	2488	1809-1830	1529-1533	268-276	1398-1400
		918	1226	2489	1809-1816	1535		
					(Depot: 1825-1826)	(1534)		

REGIMENTS OF INFANTRY Best known pre-1914 titles given with dates of original formation and renaming		Muster Books and Pay Lists		Regimental Registers	
Foot	Battalion	Years	WO 12/	Marriages Years	Births/Bapt Years
6 (1674/1688)	1	1760-1877	2380-2247	1835-1907	1846-1907
First Warwickshire (1782)	2	1805-1815	2448-	1842-1907	1844-1907
Royal First Warwickshire (1832)		1857-1877	-2473		
Royal Warwickshire (1881)	3			1826-1906	1826-1906
	4			1835-1907	1835-1907
	Mil			1867-1909	1867-1909
7 (1685)	1	1760-1877	2474-2565	1871-1908	1871-1908
Royal Fusiliers (1751)	2	1781-1798	2475&2541	1877-1908	1877-1908
City of London (1881)		1804-1815	2541-2545		
	Mil	1857-1877	2546-2565		
				1848-1914	1848-1914
8 (1685)	1	1760-1877	2566-2627	1824-1908	1834-1908
The King's (1751)	2	1805-1815	2628-2632	1844-1907	1848-1907
Liverpool (1881)		1857-1877	2633-2652		
	4			1867-1908	1867-1908
	Mil			1836-1899	1836-1903
9 (1685)	1	1760-1777	2653	1855-1914	1858-1914
(East) Norfolk (1782)		1781-1877	2654-2721		
Norfolk (1881)	2	1799-1815	2722-2727	1873-1914	1873-1914
		1857-1877	2728-2747		
	3	1799-1802	2748-2749		
	Mil			1825-1899	1827-1905
10 (1685)	1	1767-1877	2750-2814	1840-1909	1845-1909
(North) Lincolnshire (1782)	2	1804-1816	2815-2818	1852-1909	1852-1909
Lincolnshire (1881)		1858-1877	2819-2837		
	3			1878-1924	1878-1924
11 (1685)	1	1760-1877	2838-2909	1839-1908	1839-1908
(North) Devonshire (1782)	2	1808-1816	2910-2912		
Devonshire (1881)		1857-1858	2890		
		1858-1877	2913-2933		
	3			1825-1907	1834-1907
	Mil			1827-1908	1841-1907

Description and Succession Books		Service Ret'ns No. 1	MMG's Cas. Index	Index to Cas. Ret'ns	Casualty Returns		Soldiers' Documents	
Years	WO 25/ (uos)	WO 25/	WO 25/	WO 25/	Years	WO 25/	1760-1854 WO 97/	1855-1872 WO 97/
1804-1812	329	919 920	1227	2490 2491	1809-1842 1809-1816	1536-1542 1543	277-286	1401-1403
Depot: 1890-1908	WO 67/ 28-29							
1848-1864	330	921 922	1228	2492 2493	1809-1830 1809-1815 (1825-1830	1544-1546 1548 1547:Dep.)	287-293	1404-1408
Depot: 1806-1853	WO67/7	923 924	1229	2494 2495	1809-1830 1809-1815 (1830	1549-1553 1554 1555:Res.)	294-301	1409-1412
		925 926	1230 1231 1232	2496 2497	1809-1844 1809-1816 (1825-1826	1556-1560 1561 1562:Dep.)	302-312	1413-1415
1809-1827	331-332	927 928	1233	2498 2499	1809-1830 1809-1816 (1826-1830	1563-1566 1567 1568:Dep.)	313-321	1416-1419
1816-1829	333	929	1234	2500 2501	1809-1831 1809-1816 (1826-1830	1569-1571 1572 1573:Dep.)	322-331	1420-1423

REGIMENTS OF INFANTRY Best known pre-1914 titles given with dates of original formation and renaming		Muster Books and Pay Lists		Regimental Registers	
Foot	Battalion	Years	WO 12/	Marriages Years	Births/Bapt Years
12 (1685)	1	1760-1877	2934-3004	1802-1913	1814-1913
(East) Suffolk (1782)	2	1812-1818	3005-3006	1809-1871	1818-1870
Suffolk (1881)		1857-1877	3007-3027		
	4			1876-1913	1876-1913
	Mil/3			1821-1909	1826-1909
13 (1685)	1	1760-1877	3028-3097	1790-1914	1799-1914
1st Somersetshire (1782)	2	1857-1858	3077	1873-1906	1873-1906
Somerset Light Infantry (1822)		1858-1877	3098-3116		
Prince Albert's (1842)	Mil/3/4			1875-1922	1875-1922
14 (1685)	1	1760-1877	3117-3197	1814-1919	1818-1919
Bedfordshire (1782)	2	1804-1818	3198-3203	1873-1919	1873-1919
Buckinghamshire (1809)		1857-1858	3174		
Prince of Wales's Own (1876)		1858-1877	3204-3226		
West Yorkshire (1881)	3	1814-1816	3227		
	Mil/3/4			1884-1914	1884-1914
15 (1685)	1	1759-1876	3228-3293	1821-1913	1829-1913
Yorkshire East Riding	2	1799-1816	3294-3300	1841-1889	1844-1889
East Yorkshire (1881)		1857-1858	3275		
		1858-1877	3301-3319		
16 (1688)	1	1767-1877	3320-3385	1809-1914	1819-1914
Bedfordshire (1809)	2	1857-1877	3386-3404	1858-1876	1859-1877
17 (1688)	1	1760-1877	3405-3479	1809-1909	1809-1909
Leicestershire (1782)	2	1799-1802	3480-3481	1838-1908	1846-1908
		1858-1877	3482-3500		
	Mil/3			1832-1904	1842-1905
18 (1684)	1	1767-1877	3501-3567	1865-1897	1865-1897
Royal Irish (ca 1751)	2	1803-1814	3568-3572		
		1858-1877	3573-3591		
19 (1688)	1	1760-1877	3592-3654	1823-1906	1845-1906
Princess of Wales's Own Yorkshire (1881)	2	1858-1877	3655-3674		
Green Howards (1921)	Mil/3			1840-1902	1852-1900
20 (1688)	1	1760-1877	3675-3750	1853-1906	1858-1906
East Devonshire (1782)	2	1799-1802	3751-3753	1867-1899	1870-1901
Lancashire Fusiliers (1881)		1858-1877	3754-3777		
	Mil/3			1841-1913	1842-1913
21 (1678)	1	1760-1877	3778-3845	1826-1907	1844-1907
Royal North British Fuzileers (1751)	2	1804-1816	3846-3850	1846-1894	1852-1896
		1858-1877	3851-3870		
Royal Scots Fusiliers (1877)	Mil/3			1852-1907	1855-1908
22 (1689)	1	1760-1877	3871-3938	1798-1908	1802-1908
Cheshire (1751)	2	1814	3939	1839-1906	1844-1906
		1858-1877	3940-3958		

Description and Succession Books		Service Ret'ns No. 1	MMG's Cas. Index	Index to Cas. Ret'ns	Casualty Returns		Soldiers' Documents	
Years	WO 25/ (uos)	WO 25/	WO 25/	WO 25/	Years	WO 25/	1760-1854 WO 97/	1855-1872 WO 97/
1814-1830	334-336	930	1235	2502 2503	1809-1830 1811-1817 (1825-1830	1574-1578 1579 1580:Dep.)	332-340	1424-1427
		931	1236	2504 2505	1809-1845	1581-1590	341-348	1428-1431
1791-1812 1805-1818	337-338 339	932 933	1237	2506 2507	1810-1831 1809-1817	1591-1596 1597	349-360	1432-1435
1813-1816 (1818-1823	340 341	934 (Depot)			1813-1816	1598		
		934 935	1238 1239	2508 2509	1809-1830 1809-1816 (1827-1830	1599-1602 1603 1604:Dep.)	361-367	1436-1439
		936	1240	2510 2511	1809-1840 (1825-1828	1605-1611 1612:Dep.)	368-376	1440-1443
Depot: 1830-1887	WO 67/ 8-11	937	1241 1242	2512 2513	1810-1847	1613-1617	377-384	1444-1446
1806-1851	342-343	938 939	1243	2514 2515	1810-1845 1809-1814 (1825-1830	1618-1620 1621 1622:Dep.)	385-392	1447-1450
		940	1244	2516 2517	1809-1830 (1826-1830	1623-1626 1627:Dep.)	393-400	1451-1455
1809-1831 Depot: 1823-1881	344-346 WO 67/ 12-13	941	1245 1246	2518 2519	1809-1836	1628-1632	401-408	1460-1463
		942 943	1247	2520 2521	1809-1848 1809-1816 (1825-1828	1633-1637 1638 1639:Dep.)	409-417	1464-1467
		944	1248	2522 2523	1809-1855 (1826-1830	1640-1644 1645:Dep.)	418-425	1464-1467

REGIMENTS OF INFANTRY Best known pre-1914 titles given with dates of original formation and renaming		Muster Books and Pay Lists		Regimental Registers	
Foot	Battalion	Years	WO 12/	Marriages Years	Births/Bapt Years
23 (1689)	1	1760-1877	3959-4035	1808-1908	1805-1908
Royal Welch Fusiliers (1727)	2	1805-1814	4036-4039		
(Welsh 1881, Welch 1920)		1858-1877	4040-4058		
24 (1689)	1	1760-1877	4059-4132	1803-1908	1804-1908
2nd Warwickshire (1782)	2	1804-1814	4133-4138	1871-1906	1871-1906
South Wales Borderers (1881)		1858-1877	4139-4157		
25 (1689)	1	1760-1877	4158-4225	1823-1908	1827-1908
King's Own Borderers (1805)	2	1804-1816	4226-4232	1877-1907	1877-1907
King's Own Scottish Borderers (1887)		1859-1877	4233-4249		
26 (1689)	1	1766-1877	4250-4319	1792-1908	1793-1908
Cameronians (1786)	2	1803-1814	4320-4327		
(Scottish Rifles 1881 - See 90th)	Dep				
27 (1689)	1	1759-1857	4328-4398	1857-1908	1862-1908
Inniskilling	2	1800-1817	4399-4408		
Royal Inniskilling Fusiliers (1881)	3	1805-1816	4409-4415		
See 108th	Mil			1880-1917	1880-1917
28 (1694)	1	1795-1877	4416-4484	1823-1906	1823-1906
North Gloucestershire (1782)	2	1803-1814	4485-4492		
Gloucestershire (1881)	Dep				
See 61st	Dep				
29 (1694)	1	1765-1877	4493-4560	1826-1907	1836-1907
Worcestershire (1782) See 36th	2	1784-1797	4494		
30 (1702), 1st Cambridgeshire (1782)	1	1760-1877	4561-4639	1791-1908	1803-1908
East Lancashire (1881) See 59th	2	1803-1817	4640-4647		
31 (1702), Huntingdonshire (1782)	1	1760-1877	4648-4719	1841-1909	1852-1909
East Surrey (1881) See 70th	2	1805-1814	4720-4724		
32 (1702), Cornwall (1782)	1	1760-1877	4725-4796	1846-1908	1853-1908
Duke of Cornwall's Light Infantry (1881)	2	1804-1814	4797-4801		
See 46th	Dep	1857-1858	4700		
33 (1702)	1	1760-1877	4802-4865	1803-1913	1810-1913
1st Yorkshire West Riding (1782)	2				
Duke of Wellington's (1853) See 76th	Dep				
34 (1702)	1	1760-1877	4866-4942	1838-1914	1845-1914
Cumberland (1782)	2	1805-1817	4943-4948		
Border (1881) See 55th	Dep				
35 (1701)	1	1759-1877	4949-5015	1854-1908	1857-1908
Dorsetshire (1782)		1770	6710		
Sussex (1805)	2	1799-1817	5016-5024		
Royal Sussex (1832) See 107th	Dep				
36 (1701)	1	1760-1877	5025-5095	1799-1909	1801-1909
Herefordshire (1782)	2	1804-1814	5096-5099		
2nd Bn Worcestershire (1881)	Dep				

Description and Succession Books		Service Ret'ns No. 1	MMG's Cas. Index	Index to Cas. Ret'ns	Casualty Returns		Soldiers' Documents	
Years	WO 25/ (uos)	WO 25/	WO 25/	WO 25/	Years	WO 25/	1760-1854 WO 97/	1855-1872 WO 97/
1814-1830	347-349	945	1249	2524	1809-1830	1646-1649	426-433	1468-1471
1809-1817	350	946		2525	1809-1814	1650		
					(1825-1830	1651:Dep.)		
		947	1250	2526	1809-1830	1652-1656	434-441	1472-1475
Depot:	WO 67/	948		2527	1808-1814	1657		
1881-1897	30-31				(1829-1830	1658:Dep.)		
1810-1818	351	949	1251	2528	1809-1842	1659-1661	442-450	1476-1479
1809-1818	352	950		2529	1809-1816	1662		
					(1825-1830	1663:Dep.)		
1803-1843	353-354	951	1252	2530	1809-1843	1664-1669	451-458	1480-1483
		952		2531	1809-1815	1670		
1850-1858	355							
1816-1829	356	953	1253	2532	1810-1830	1671-1673	459-468	1484-1485
		954	1254	2533	1809-1817	1674		
			1254	2534	1809-1816	1675		
					(1825-1830	1676:Dep.)		
1795-1806	357	955	1255	2535	1809-1847	1677-1681	469-476	1486-1487
1803-1830	358-362	956		2536	1809-1814	1682		
1806	363				1825-1830	1683		
(1792-1866	WO 67/	24-27)						
1826-1831	364	957	1256	2537	1809-1830	1684-1687	477-483	1488-1489
				2538	(1826-1830	1688: Dep.)		
		958	1257	2539	1809-1830	1689-1694	484-493	1490-1492
		959		2540	1809-1817	1695		
1814-1818	365	960	1258	2541	1809-1846	1696-1704	494-503	1493-1494
				2542	1809-1814	1705		
1815-1829	366-367	961	1259	2543	1809-1830	1706-1708	504-509	1495-1496
1808-1816	368	962		2544	1809-1814	1709		
					1825-1830	1710		
1813-1825	369	963	1260	2545	1809-1830	1711-1715	510-515	1497-1499
				2546				
					1825-1830	1716		
		964	1261	2547	1809-1830	1717-1721	516-520	1500-1502
	WO 67/	965		2548	1809-1817	1722		
1803-1873	14				1829-1830	1723		
1811-1823	370-372	966	1262-3	2549	1809-1830	1724-1728	521-528	1503-1504
		967		2550	1809-1817	1729		
1817-1832	373				1825-1830	1730		
1804-1838	374-375	968	1264	2551	1809-1830	1731-1734	529-535	1505-1506
		969		2552	1809-1814	1735		
1840-1857	376				1825-1830	1736		

REGIMENTS OF INFANTRY Best known pre-1914 titles given with dates of original formation and renaming		Muster Books and Pay Lists		Regimental Registers	
Foot	Battalion	Years	WO 12/	Marriages Years	Births/Bapt Years
37 (1702)	1	1760-1877	5100-5168	1824-1906	1811-1906
North Hampshire (1782)	2	1813-1817	5169-5170		
Hampshire (1881) See 67th	Dep				
38 (1705)	1	1760-1877	5171-5240	1819-1909	1830-1909
1st Staffordshire (1782)					
South Staffordshire (1881) See 80th	2	1805-1814	5241-5245		
39 (1702)	1	1769-1877	5246-5309	1834-1908	1844-1908
East Middlesex (1782)	2	1803-1815	5310-5316		
Dorsetshire (1807/1881) See 54th	Dep				
40 (1717), 2nd Somersetshire (1782)	1	1759-1877	5317-5396	1799-1913	1804-1913
Prince of Wales's Volunteers (South	2	1799-1815	5397-5403		
Lancashire) (1881) See 82nd	Dep				
41 (1719), The Welsh (1831)	1	1760-1877	5405-5476	1810-1908	1816-1908
The Welch (1881) See 69th	2	1812-1813	5477		
42 (1738)	1	1759-1877	5478-5552	1825-1880	1832-1880
Royal Highland (1758)	2	1759-1783	5553		
The Black Watch (1861)		1803-1814	5554-5560		
(Royal Highlanders 1881) See 73rd	Dep				
43 (1739), Monmouthshire (1782)	1	1759-1877	5561-5630	1811-1908	1814-1908
Oxfordshire Light Infantry (1881)	2	1804-1817	5631-5636	1796-1849	1803-1849
(and Bucks 1908) See 52nd	Dep/3				
44 (1739), East Essex (1782)	1	1759-1877	5637-5710	1852-1913	1854-1913
Essex (1881) See 56th	2	1803-1816	5711-5717		
45 (1739), Nottinghamshire (1779)	1	1759-1877	5718-5791	1876-1909	1876-1909
Sherwood Foresters/Derbys. (1881)		1804-1814	5792-5795		
See 95th	2				
46 (1739), South Devonshire (1782)	1	1761-1877	5796-5867	1815-1906	1821-1906
2nd Bn Duke of Cornwall's Light	2/Dep	1800-1802	5868-5870		
Infantry (1881)	Mil			1825-1906	1834-1905
47 (1739), Lancashire (1782)	1	1759-1877	5871-5948	1798-1913	1804-1913
Loyal North Lancashire (1881)	2	1803-1816	5949-5956		
See 81st					
48 (1739)	1	1759-1877	5957-6024	1868-1914	1868-1914
Northamptonshire	2	1803-1804	6025-6031		
(1782/1881) See 58th	Mil/3			1822-1909	1835-1909
49 (1739), Hertfordshire (1782)	1	1774-1877	6032-6100	1826-1908	1818-1908
Princess Charlotte of Wales's (1816)	2	1813-1814	6101		
Berkshire (1881) See 66th	Dep			1785-1843	1803-1843
50 (1739), West Kent (1782)	1	1760-1877	6102-6170	1844-1908	1839-1908
Queen's Own (1831), Queen's Own	2	1804-1814	6171-6175		
(Royal West Kent) (1881) See 97th	Dep				
51 (1739), 2nd Yorkshire West	1	1756-1877	6176-6239	1848-1914	1854-1914
Riding (1782), King's Own Yorkshire	2				
Light Infantry (1887) See 105th	Dep				

Description and Succession Books		Service Ret'ns No. 1	MMG's Cas. Index	Index to Cas. Ret'ns	Casualty Returns		Soldiers' Documents	
Years	WO 25/ (uos)	WO 25/	WO 25/	WO 25/	Years	WO 25/	1760-1854 WO 97/	1855-1872 WO 97/
		970	1265	2553 2554	1809-1830 1813-1817 1825-1830	1737-1739 1740 1741	536-542	1507-1508
1790-1831 1848-1868	377 378	971 972	1266	2555 2556	1809-1836 1809-1814	1742-1749 1750	543-549	1509-1511
1857-1892	WO 67/ 15-16	973 974	1267	2557 2558	1809-1847 1809-1816 1827-1828	1751-1757 1758 1759	550-558	1512-1513
1824-1865	WO 67/ 17	975	1268 1269	2559 2560	1809-1845 1809-1815 1827	1760-1765 1766 1767	559-567	1514-1515
		976	1270	2561 2562	1810-1843 1813	1768-1776 1777	568-575	1516-1518
1795-1816 1803-1805 1825-1830	379-383 384 385	977 978	1271	2563 2564	1809-1830 1809-1814 1825-1830	1778-1780 1781 1782	576-582	1519-1521
1818-1838	386-388	979 980	1272 1272 1273	2565 2566	1809-1830 1809-1816 (1825-1830	1783-1785 1786 1787:Dep.)	583-590	1522-1524
		981 982	1274	2567 2568	1809-1842 1809-1816	1788-1794 1795	591-596	1525-1527
1815-1832 1826-32:Dep	389-392 393	983 984	1275	2569 2570	1809-1837 1809-1814	1796-1806 1807	597-602	1528-1531
1810-1856 1813-1864	394-398 399-402	985	1276	2571 2572	1809-1833	1808-1816	603-610	1532-1534
		986 987	1277	2573 2574	1809-1830 1809-1816	1817-1821 1822	611-621	1535-1537
1812-1825	403-404	988	1278	2575 2576	1809-1834 1809-1814	1823-1827 1828	622-628	1538-1540
		989	1279	2577 2578	1810-1843 1813-1814 1825-1828	1829-1834 1835 1836	629-635	1541-1543
		990 991	1280	2579 2580	1809-1848 1810-1814 1825-1827	1837-1840 1841 1842	636-644	1544-1546
		992	1281	2581 2582	1809-1854 1825-1830	1843-1848 1849	645-652	1547-1549

REGIMENTS OF INFANTRY Best known pre-1914 titles given with dates of original formation and renaming		Muster Books and Pay Lists		Regimental Registers	
Foot	Battalion	Years	WO 12/	Marriages Years	Births/Bapt Years
52 (1739), Oxfordshire (1782)	1	1765-1877	6240-6306	1798-1907	1802-1907
2nd Bn Oxfords Light Infantry (1881)	2	1799-1816	6307-6315		
(and Buckinghamshire - 1908) Dep/Mil/3				1839-1908	1842-1908
53 (1739), Shropshire (1782)	1	1760-1877	6316-6388	1803-1908	1804-1908
The King's (Shropshire Light	2	1803-1817	6389-6397		
Infantry) (1882 See 85th Dep/Mil				1836-1883	1850-1883
54 (1741)	1	1760-1861	6398-6450	1794-1907	1812-1907
West Norfolk (1782)		1861-1862	6526		
2nd Bn Dorsetshire (1881)		1862-1877	6452-6468		
	2	1800-1802	6469		
55 (1741)	1	1759-1861	6470-6525	1797-1908	1799-1908
Westmorland (1782)		1861-1862	6451		
2nd Bn Border (1881)		1862-1877	6527-6542		
	2				
56 (1741)	1	1760-1877	6543-6619	1856-1914	1858-1914
West Essex (1782)	2	1804-1817	6620-6630		
2nd Bn Essex (1881)	Mil/3	1813-1814	6631	1829-1907	1840-1906
	Mil/4			1833-1913	1840-1913
57 (1741)	1	1760-1877	6632-6704	1799-1921	1802-1921
West Middlesex (1782)	2	1803-1815	6705-6709		
Duke of Cambridge's Own	Dep/&c				
(Middlesex) (1881) See 77th	Dep				
58 (1741)	1	1759-1877	6710-6779	1878-1916	1878-1916
Rutlandshire (1782)	2	1804-1815	6780-6785		
2nd Bn Northamptonshire (1881)	Dep				
	Res				
59 (1741), 2nd Nottinghamshire	1	1765-1877	6786-6864	1795-1905	1804-1905
(1782), 2nd Bn East Lancashire (1881)	2	1805-1816	6865-6870		
60 (1741)	1	1763-1877	6871-6934	1832-1913	1833-1913
Royal American Regiment (1756)	2	1764-1877	6935-6997	1812-1891	1810-1892
Duke of York's Rifle Corps (1824)	3	1757-1819	6998-7009		
The King"s Royal Rifle Corps		1855-1877	7010-7032		
Regiment of Foot (1830)	4	1757-1819	7033-7044		
The King's Royal Rifle Corps (1881)		1857-1877	7045-7064		
	5	1798-1818	7065-7076		
	6	1799-1818	7077-7087		
	7	1813-1818	7088-7089		
	Mil/8	1814-1816	7090	1835-1901	1840-1902
	Mil/9			1830-1907	1840-1907
61 (1739)	1	1760-1877	7091-7157	1802-1907	1808-1907
South Gloucestershire (1782)	2	1803-1814	7158-7163		
2nd Bn Gloucestershire (1881)	Mil/3			1829-1885	1842-1885
	Mil/4			1834-1908	1837-1908

Description and Succession Books		Service Ret'ns No. 1	MMG's Cas. Index	Index to Cas. Ret'ns	Casualty Returns		Soldiers' Documents	
Years	WO 25/ (uos)	WO 25/	WO 25/	WO 25/	Years	WO 25/	1760-1854 WO 97/	1855-1872 WO 97/
1783-1829 1807-1821 1824-1830	405-407 408-410 411	993 994	1282	2583 2584	1809-1856 1809-1816 1825-1830	1850-1854 1855 1856	653-661	1550-1551
1795-1825 1803-1818 1807-1859	412-414 415-416 417-419	995	1283	2585 2586	1817-1855 1809-1817 1829-1830	1857-1865 1866 1867	662-668	1552-1553
1801-1812	420	996	1284 1285	2587 2588	1809-1840	1868-1875	669-677	1554-1556
1814-1832	421-423	997	1286	2589 2590	1809-1843 (1825-1830	1876-1883 1884:Dep.)	678-687	1557-1559
		998 999	1287	2591 2592	1810-1830 1810-1817 1814 (1825-1826	1885-1889 1890 1891 1892:Dep.)	688-695	1560-1561
1820-1840 1803-1821 1806-1877 1854-1866	424-425 426-428 429-433 434	1000 1001	1288	2593 2594	1809-1846 1809-1815 1825-1827	1893-1897 1898 1899	696-704	1562-1564
1756-1830 1806-1815 1816-1825 1818-1831	435-442 443-444 445 446	1002 1003	1289	2595 2596	1809-1830 1809-1815 1827-1830	1900-1903 1904 1905	705-712	1565-1566
		1004	1290	2597 2598	1809-1830 1809-1816	1906-1910 1911	713-723	1567-1568
1854	447	1005 1006	1291 1292 1293	2599 2600 2601	1809-1830 1809-1830 1809-1819	1912-1914 1915-1917 1918-1919	724-745	1569-1575
		1007	1294	2602	1809-1819	1920-1921		
		1008 1009	1295 1296 1296 1296	2603	1809-1817 1810-1817 1813-1817 1810-1817 (Dep 1826-1830	1922 1923 1924 1925 1926-27)		
		1010 1011	1297	2604 2605 (Dep	1809-1850 1809-1814 1827-1830	1928-1932 1933 1934)	746-752	1576-1578

REGIMENTS OF INFANTRY Best known pre-1914 titles given with dates of original formation and renaming		Muster Books and Pay Lists		Regimental Registers	
Foot	Battalion	Years	WO 12/	Marriages Years	Births/Bapt Years
62 (1742), Wiltshire (1782)	1	1772-1877	7164-7232	1867-1908	1867-1908
Duke of Edinburgh's (1881) See 99th	2	1799-1817	7233-7240		
63 (1743)	1	1771-1877	7241-7307	1833-1912	1839-1912
West Suffolk (1782)	2	1804-1814	7308-7311	1892-1907	1892-1907
Manchester (1881) See 96th	Mil/3			1887-1906	1887-1906
	Mil/4			1887-1906	1887-1906
64 (1745), 2nd Staffordshire (1782),	1	1760-1877	7312-7376	1843-1908	1847-1908
Prince of Wales's (North					
Staffordshire) (1881) See 98th	Dep				
65 (1745)	1	1768-1877	7377-7457	1858-1914	1807-1914
2nd Yorkshire (North Riding) (1782)					
York and Lancaster (1881) See 84th	Dep				
66 (1745), Berkshire (1782)	1	1759-1877	7458-7527	1839-1909	1845-1909
2nd Bn Princess Charlotte of Wales's	2		7528-7535		
(Royal Berkshire) (1885)	Mil/3			1841-1909	1850-1909
67 (1745)	1	1760-1877	7536-7615	1831-1881	1832-1881
South Hampshire (1782)	2	1804-1817	7616-7621		
2nd Bn Hampshire (1881)	3			1830-1906	1837-1907
68 (1745)	1	1760-1877	7622-7689	1852-1914	1853-1914
Durham (1782) See 106th	2	1800-1802	7690-7692		
Durham Light Infantry (1808/1881)	Dep				
69 (1745)	1	1760-1877	7693-7772	1800-1907	1807-1907
South Lincolnshire (1782)	2	1795	7695		
2nd Bn The Welch (1881)		1803-1816	7773-7779		
70 (1745), Surrey (1782), Glasgow	1	1774-1877	7780-7846	1810-1908	1811-1908
Lowland (1813), Surrey (1825),	Mil/3			1865-1907	1865-1907
2nd Bn East Surrey (1881)	Mil/4			1865-1908	1865-1908
71 (1745), Highland (1786)	1	1764-1877	7847-7918	1798-1908	1798-1908
Glasgow Highland (1808) See 74th	2	1776-1783	7847		
Highland Light Infantry (ca 1810)		1805-1816	7919-7923		
72 (1745), Highland (1786) See 78th	1	1764-1877	7924-7991	1808-1908	1806-1908
Duke of Albany's Own Highlanders	2	1804-1816	7992-7996		
(1823), Seaforth Highlanders (1881) Dep					
73 (1745), Highland (1786)	1	1764-1877	7997-8058	1792-1873	1799-1874
Perthshire (1862), 2nd Bn Black Watch	2	1779-1817	8059-8062		
(Royal Highlanders) (1881)	Res/Dep				
74 (1745), Highland (1787), Assaye	1	1763-1877	8063-8128	1797-1907	1810-1907
(1803), 2nd Bn Highland Light Infantry					
(1881)	Mil/3			1856-1908	1851-1908
75 (1745), Abercromby's Highlanders	1	1763-1877	8129-8190	1839-1909	1844-1909
(1787), Stirlingshire (1862) See 92nd					
Gordon Highlanders (1881)	Res				

Description and Succession Books		Service Ret'ns No. 1	MMG's Cas. Index	Index to Cas. Ret'ns	Casualty Returns		Soldiers' Documents	
Years	WO 25/ (uos)	WO 25/	WO 25/	WO 25/	Years	WO 25/	1760-1854 WO 97/	1855-1872 WO 97/
		1012	1298	2606	1809-1847	1935-1941	753-760	1579-1580
		1013	1299	2607	1809-1817	1942		
		1014	1300	2608	1809-1817	1943-1948	761-771	1581-1582
		1015		2609	1809-1814	1949		
				(Dep	1826-1828	1950)		
1797-1800	448	1016	1301	2610	1809-1854	1951-1954	772-781	1583-1585
1814-1816	449			2611				
					1826-1827	1955		
		1017	1302	2612	1809-1830	1956-1960	782-788	1586-1587
	WO 67/			2613				
1826-1873	18				1829-1830	1961		
1825-1865	450-452	1018	1303	2614	1803-1830	1962-1966	789-797	1588-1590
		1019		2615	1809-1817	1967		
					1827-1830	1968		
1806-1817	453	1020	1304	2616	1809-1830	1969-1974	798-806	1591-1593
				2617	1809-1817	1975		
				(Dep	1825-1826	1976)		
		1021	1305	2618	1809-1830	1977-1979	807-815	1594-1596
	WO 67/		1306	2619				
1873-1901	21-23				1825-1829	1980		
1826-1830	454-455	1022	1307	2620	1809-1830	1981-1985	816-823	1597-1598
and 1855				2621	1809-1817	1986		
				(Dep	1825-1826	1987)		
		1023	1308	2622	1809-1854	1988-1992	824-829	1599-1600
				2623				
				(Dep	1825-1827	1993)		
1809-1818	456-457	1024	1309	2624	1809-1830	1994-1997	830-838	1601-1602
1810-1822	458-460	1025		2625	1809-1815	1998		
				(Dep	1825-1830	1999)		
1801-1808)	(Only	1026	1310	2626	1809-1831	2000-2002	839-846	1603-1604
1812-1822)	(Bn 1	1027		2627	1809-1815	2003		
	(461-462				1827-1830	2004		
1786-1867)	Bn 1 463	1028	1311	2628	1809-1830	2005-2008	847-857	1605-1606
1809-1872)	(465-466			2629	1809-1817	2009		
(1809-1841	464	Res/Dep)		(Dep	1827-1830	2010)		
1810-1830	467-470	1029	1312	2630	1810-1830	2011-2014	858-864	1607-1609
	WO 67/			2631				
1853-1868	19			(Dep	1825-1830	2015)		
1778-1783	471-472	1030	1313	2632	1809-1831	2016-2019	865-871	1610-1612
				2633				
					1830	2020		

REGIMENTS OF INFANTRY Best known pre-1914 titles given with dates of original formation and renaming		Muster Books and Pay Lists		Regimental Registers	
Foot	Battalion	Years	WO 12/	Marriages Years	Births/Bapt Years
76 (1745), Hindoostan (to 1812) 2nd Bn Duke of Wellington's (West Riding Regiment) (1881)	1 Dep	1778-1877	8191-8253	1853-1914	1863-1914
77 (1745) East Middlesex (1807) 2nd Bn Duke of Cambridge's Own (Middlesex Regiment)	1 Mil/3 Mil/4 Mil/5	1778-1877	8254-8313	1830-1908 1831-1919 1838-1908 1831-1908	1863-1914 1848-1919 1862-1908 1848-1908
78 (1745), Highland (1793) Ross-shire Buffs (1794/6) 2nd Bn Seaforth Highlanders (Ross-shire Buffs, The Duke of Albany's) (1881)	1 2 Mil/3	1778-1785 1793-1802 1806-1877 1804-1816	8314 8314 8315-8373 8374-8379	1793-1908 1832-1907	1806-1908 1837-1908
79 (1745) Cameron Highlanders (1804) Queen's Own Cameron Highlanders (1873)	1 2 Res/Dep	1780 1794-1877 1804-1815	8380 8380-8448 8449-8453	1794-1909	1795-1909
80 (1758) Staffordshire Volunteers (1793) 2nd Bn South Staffordshire Regiment (1881)	1 Dep	1778-1784 1793-1797 1808-1877	8454 8455 8456-8518	1854-1908	1853-1908
81 (1758) Loyal Lincolnshire Volunteers (1793) 2nd Bn Loyal North Lancashire Regiment (1881)	1 2 Mil3/4	1760-1763 1778-1783 1794-1877 1803-1816	8519 8520-8521 8522-8588 8589-8596	1816-1906 1834-1906	1802-1906 1849-1906
82 (1758) Prince of Wales's Volunteers (1793) 2nd Bn Prince of Wales's Volunteers (South Lancashire) (1881)	1 2	1760-1763 1778-1784 1793-1877 1794-1795 1804-1815	8597 8597 8597-8665 8666 8667-8670	1805-1907	1815-1907
83 (1758), Fitch's Grenadiers (1793) County of Dublin (1859) 2nd Bn Royal Irish Rifles (1881)	1 2 Dep	1778-1877 1804-1817	8671-8734 8735-8740	1876-1914	1876-1914
84 (1758) York and Lancaster (1809) 2nd Bn York and Lancaster (1881)	1 2 Dep	1780-1877 1778-1796 1808-1817	8741-8805 8806 8807-8811	1820-1914	1822-1914
85 (1759), Bucks Volunteers (1793) King's Light Infantry (1821), 2nd Bn The King's (Shropshire Light Infantry) (1882)	1 2	1780-1783 1794-1877 1800-1802	8812 8812-8881 8882-8883	1829-1906	1844-1906

Description and Succession Books		Service Ret'ns No. 1	MMG's Cas. Index	Index to Cas. Ret'ns	Casualty Returns		Soldiers' Documents	
Years	WO 25/ (uos)	WO 25/	WO 25/	WO 25/	Years	WO 25/	1760-1854 WO 97/	1855-1872 WO 97/
		1031	1314	2634 2635 (Dep	1809-1830 1825-1829	2021-2023 2024)	872-877	1613-1615
1811-1833		1032	1315	2636 2637	1809-1831	2025-2028	878-884	1616-1618
		1033 1034	1316	2638 2639 (Dep	1809-1850 1809-1816 1826-1830	2029-2037 2038 2039)	885-890	1619-1621
1809-1842 1809-1842 1809-1850	477,479 478,479 480(Res)	1035 1036	1317	2640 2641 (Dep	1809-1830 1809-1815 1825-1830	2040-2043 2044 2045)	891-897	1622-1623
1804-1881 Des.Book is held at RHQ	Staffs Regt at Lichfield	1037	1318	2642 2643	1810-1854 1825-1830	2046-2054 2055	898-904	1624-1625
1801-1863 (1839-1863	481-487 488	1038	1319	2644 2645 Dep	1809-1830 1809-1816 1825-1830	2056-2058 2059 2060)	905-913	1626-1628
1799-1831 1804-1817	489-492 493-494	1039 1040	1320	2646 2647 (Dep	1809-1830 1809-1815 1825-1830	2061-2063 2064 2065)	914-922	1629-1630
1812-1868	495-497	1041 1042	1321	2648 2649	1809-1830 1809-1817 1825-1830	2066-2070 2071 2072	923-932	1631-1633
1793-1831 1807-1824 1855-1859 (1826-1866	498-503 504-505 (506 1 & WO 67/	1043 2 Bn) 20	1322	2650 2651 Dep	1809-1830 1809-1817 1826-1830	2073-2075 2076 2077)	933-941	1634-1636
1811-1833	507-510	1044	1323 1324	2652 2653 (Dep	1809-1830 1825-1830	2078-2081 2082)	942-949	1637-1639

REGIMENTS OF INFANTRY Best known pre-1914 titles given with dates of original formation and renaming		Muster Books and Pay Lists		Regimental Registers	
Foot	Battalion	Years	WO 12/	Marriages Years	Births/Bapt Years
86 (1759) Shropshire Volunteers (1793) Leinster (1809) Royal County Down (1812) 2nd Bn Royal Irish Rifles (1881)	1 2 Dep	1781-1783 1793-1799 1806-1877 1814-1815	8884 8885 8886-8947 8948	1854-1907	1854-1907
87 (1759), Prince of Wales's Irish (1793) Royal Irish Fusiliers (1827) Princess Victoria's (RIF) (1881)	1 2	1782-1877 1805-1818	8949-9016 9017-9022	1792-1907 (see also	1802-1907 89th)
88 (1759) Connaught Rangers (1881) see 94th	1 2 Dep	1780 1794-1877 1804-1816	9023 9023-9085 9086-9090	1847-1917	1860-1917
89 (1759), Princess Victoria's (1866) 2nd Bn Princess Victoria's (Royal Irish Fusiliers) (1881)	1 2	1780-1783 1793-1877 1804-1816	9091 9091-9164 9165-9169	1792-1907	1802-1907
90 (1759) Perthshire Volunteers (1793) 2nd Bn Cameronians (Scottish Rifles) (1881)	1 2	1779-1783 1794-1877 1794-1795 1804-1816	9170 9170-9237 9238 9239-9243	1807-1907	1809-1907
91 (1760) Argyllshire Highlanders (1794) Princess Louise's (Sutherland and Argyll Highlanders) (1881)	1 2 Dep	1779-83,93- 95, 98-1877 1804-1815	9244 9245-9315 9316-9319	1797-1908 (see also	1801-1908 93rd)
92 (1760) Gordon Highlanders (1794) 2nd Bn Gordon Highlanders (1881)	1 2 Dep	1780,93-5 1798-1877 1803-1814	9320 9321-9386 9387-9392	1816-1914	1816-1914
93 (1760) Highland (1799) 2nd Bn Princess Louise's (Sutherland and Argyll Highlanders) (1881)	1 2 Dep	1780-3,93-5 1800-1877 1813-1816	9393 9394-9456 9457	1835-1902	1836-1891
94 (1760), Scotch Brigade (1802-1816) 2nd Bn Connaught Rangers (1881)	1	1794-5, 98 1803-1877	9458 9458-9514	1826-1915	1843-1907
95 (1760) Rifle Brigade (1803-1815) Derbyshire (1825) 2nd Bn Sherwood Foresters (1881) (Nottinghamshire and Derbyshire)	1 2 3 Dep	1780-3,93-6 1800-1817 1805-1815 1809-1815	9515 9516-9576 9577-9585 9586-9590	1839-1909	1839-1909
96 (1761) Queen's Own (1798-1818) 2nd Bn Manchester Regiment (1881)	1 2 Dep	1780,94-6 1803-1877 1804-1814	9591 9592-9650 9651-9654	1798-1818	1801-1818

260

Description and Succession Books		Service Ret'ns No. 1	MMG's Cas. Index	Index to Cas. Ret'ns	Casualty Returns		Soldiers' Documents	
Years	WO 25/ (uos)	WO 25/	WO 25/	WO 25/	Years	WO 25/	1760-1854 WO 97/	1855-1872 WO 97/
1806-1832	511-515	1045	1325	2654 2655	1809-1830	2083-2085	950-957	1640-1642
					1814	2086		
					1826-1830	2087		
		1046	1326	2656	1807-1830	2088-2092	958-966	1643-1645
					1856	2093		
		1047			1809-1817	2094		
1814-1816	516	1048	1327	2657	1809-1830	2095-2097	967-977	1646-1649
1823-1830	517			2658				
1811-1828	518-519	1049			1809-1815	2098		
1828-1830	520				1825-1830	2099		
		1050	1328	2659 2660	1809-1830	2100-2104	978-985	1650-1652
		1051			1810-1816	2105		
1804-1841	521-522	1052	1329	2661 2662	1809-1830	2106-2109	986-996	1653-1655
1812-1831	523-524	1053			1810-1815	2110		
				(Dep	1825-1830	2111)		
1815-1831	525-526	1054	1330	2663 2664	1809-1830	2112-2116	997-1005	1656-1657
1814-1826	527	1055			1809-1815	2117		
1822-1831	528				1825-1830	2118		
1818-1843	529-532	1056	1331	2665 2666	1809-1830	2119-2123	1006-1014	1658-1659
		1057			1809-1814	2124		
					1825-1828	2125		
		1058	1332	2667 2668	1809-1830	2126-2130	1015-1021	1660-1661
					1814-1815	2131		
					1825-1830	2132		
1815-1830	533-535	1059	1333	2669 2670	1809-1854	2133-2137	1022-1029	1662-1663
					1825-1830	(2138	Dep)	
1816-1819	536	1060	1334 1335	2671 2672	1809-1831	2139-2142	1030-1037	1664-1666
					1809-1817	2143		
		1061			1809-1816	2144		
		1062			1825-1830	2145		
1779-1783	537	1063	1336	2673 2674	1809-1831	2146-2148	1038-1043	1667-1668
1800-1818	538-539				1849-1854	2149		
		1064			1809-1814	2150		
					1825-1830	2151		

REGIMENTS OF INFANTRY Best known pre-1914 titles given with dates of original formation and renaming		Muster Books and Pay Lists		Regimental Registers	
Foot	Battalion	Years	WO 12/	Marriages Years	Births/Bapt Years
97 (1761), Earl of Ulster's (1824)	1	1780-3,94-5	9655	1798-1908	1810-1908
2nd Bn Queen's Own (Royal West		1799-1877	9656-9724		
Kent) (1881)	Dep				
98 (1761), Prince of Wales's (1876)	1	'94-'98,1804	9725	1878-1908	1879-1908
2nd Bn Prince of Wales's (North		1805-1877	9726-9783		
Staffordshire) (1881)	Dep				
99 (1761), Lanarkshire (1824), Duke of	1	1782-3,94-5	9784	1802-1908	1817-1908
Edinburgh's (1874), 2nd Bn Duke of		1805-1877	9785-9846		
Edinburgh's (Wiltshire) (1881)	Dep				
100 (1761), Prince of Wales's Leinster	1	1794-1797	9847	1812-1908	1812-1908
(1858), (Royal Canadians) see 109th		1805-1877	9848-9875		
101 (1761)	1	1794-1795	9876	1846-1908	1849-1908
Royal Bengal Fusiliers (1861)		1806-1877	9877-9897		
Royal Munster Fusiliers (1881)	Dep	(gap from	1818-61)		
102 (1761), New South Wales Corps	1	1793-1795	9898	1851-1906	1861-1906
(1798-1812), Royal Madras Fusiliers		1798-1818	9899-9907		
(1861), Royal Dublin Fusiliers (1881)		1862-1877	9908-9922		
103 (1761)	1	1782-4,94-5	9923	1796-1914	1805-1914
Royal Bombay Fusiliers (1861)		1808-1818	9924-9928		
2nd Bn Royal Dublin Fusiliers (1881)		1862-1877	9929-9944		
104 (1761)	1	1782-3,94-5	9945	1889-1908	1889-1908
Bengal Fusiliers (1861)		1803-1817	9946-9950		
2nd Bn Royal Munster Fusiliers (1881)		1862-1877	9951-9966		
105 (1761), 2nd Madras LI (1839-61)	1	1782-4,94-5	9967	1836-1913	1834-1913
2nd Bn King's Own (Yorkshire LI) (1887)		1862-1877	9968-9984		
106 (1761), 2nd Bombay LI (1826-61)	1	1794-1795	9985, 86-	1844-1914	1858-1914
2nd Bn Durham Light Infantry (1881)		1862-1877	10001		
107 (1761), 3rd Bengal Infantry		1794	10002	1829-1907	1836-1907
(1854-62)	1				
2nd Bn Royal Sussex (1881)		1862-1877	10003-18		
108 (1761), 3rd Madras Infantry		1795	10019		
(1854-62)	1				
2nd Bn Royal Inniskilling Fusiliers (1881)		1862-1877	10020-35		
109 (1761), Bombay Infantry		1794	10036	1854-1905	1854-1908
(1853-61)	1				
2nd Bn Prince of Wales's Leinster (1881)		1862-1877	10037-52		
110-135		1794-1795	10053		
Rifle Brigade	1	1816-1877	10054-109	Rifle	
Rifle Corps (1800)	2	1816-1877	10110-167	Brigade has	
95th (1803-1815)	3	1816-1819	10168	several	
Rifle Brigade (1816)		1855-1877	10169-191	registers	
Prince Consort's Own (1862)	4	1857-1877	10192-211	ca	
	Dep	1873-1877	10212-215	1800-1914	

Description and Succession Books		Service Ret'ns No. 1	MMG's Cas. Index	Index to Cas. Ret'ns	Casualty Returns		Soldiers' Documents	
Years	WO 25/ (uos)	WO 25/	WO 25/	WO 25/	Years	WO 25/	1760-1854 WO 97/	1855-1872 WO 97/
1810-1865	540-546	1065	1337	2675 2676	1810-1831	2152-2155	1044-1051	1669-1671
1838-1855	547				1825-1830	2156		
1812-1818	548-549	1066	1338	2677 2678	1809-1831 1842-1855 1825-1830	2157-2160 2161 2162	1052-1059	1672-1673
1816-1833	550-552	1067	1339	2679 2680	1810-1830 1825-1830	2163-2164 2165	1060-1068	1674-1676
		1068	1340	2681	1810-1818	2166-2168	1069	1677
1810-1815	553-554	1069	1341	2682	1809-1817	2169	1069	1678-1679
1810-1815	555-556							
1814-1817	557	1070	1342	2683	1810-1817	2170	1069	1680
1815-1817	558		1343	2684	1809-1817	2171	1070	1681-1682
		1071	1344	2685	1810-1817	2172	1071	1683
							1072	1684
							1072	1685-1686
							1072	1687
							1072	1688
							1072	1689
							1072	
1800-1867	559-564			2686 2687 2688	1817-1830 1817-1830 1816-1818	2173-2175 2177-2179 2181-2182	1073-1090	1690-1697
1856-1865	565				1825-1830	2176&2180		

APPENDIX THREE
War Office Department

The records of the *War Office Department* at the National Archives, Kew, comprise the major holding of material about the British Army. Formerly called a letter-code, the prefix WO soon becomes familiar to all researchers.

It is useful to have a ready-reference to all the series in the War Office Department. One of the most commonly used series is WO 97, Soldiers' Documents. ('Series' used to be termed 'class'.)

This appendix lists all four hundred and ten series now in the War Office Department. For each series, there follows:

> *the covering dates*
> *the title*
> *number of pieces*

Using WO 25 as an example, the covering dates are given as 1660 to 1938, and its ponderous title is

War Office and predecessors: Secretary at War, Secretary of State for War, and Related Bodies, Registers.

The series WO 25 contains 4001 'pieces'. As may be seen from Appendix Two, many of these pieces are registers listing soldiers and are therefore of primary interest to the family historian.

It should be noted that the covering dates quoted would refer to the earliest and latest dates for a 'series' (eg WO 25) and not for every piece in that series.

series	covering date	title	piece
WO 1	1732-1868	'War Office and predecessors: Secretary-at-War, Secretary of State for War, and Commander-in-Chief, In-letters and Miscellaneous Papers'	1138
WO 2	1759-1858	War Office and predecessors: Indexes to Out-letters	107
WO 3	1765-1868	Office of the Commander-in-Chief: Out-letters	619
WO 4	1684-1861	'War Office: Secretary-at-War, Out-letters'	1054
WO 5	1683-1852	Secretary-at-War: Marching and Militia Orders	123
WO 6	1793-1859	'War Department and successors: Secretary of State for War and Secretary of State for War and the Colonies, Out-letters'	214
WO 7	1715-1862	War Office and predecessors: Various Departmental Out-letters	130
WO 8	1710-1823	Muster Master General of Ireland: Out-letters	12
WO 9	1679-1915	'Secretary-at-War and War Office: Militia, Yeomanry, and other miscellaneous accounts'	49
WO 10	1708-1878	Commissary General of Musters Office and successors: Artillery Muster Books and Pay Lists	2877
WO 11	1816-1878	War Office and predecessors: Engineers Muster Books and Pay Lists	432
WO 12	1732-1878	Commissary General of Musters Office and successors: General Muster Books and Pay Lists	13307
WO 13	1778-1878	War Office and predecessors: Militia and Volunteers Muster Books and Pay Lists	4675
WO 14	1854-1856	War Office: Scutari Depot Muster Books and Pay Lists	130
WO 15	1854-1856	'War Office: Foreign Legions Muster Books, Pay Lists and Courts Martial Register'	102
WO 16	1877-1898	War Office: Muster Books and Pay Lists	3049
WO 17	1754-1866	Office of the Commander in Chief: Monthly Returns to the Adjutant General	2815
WO 18	1770-1820	'Ordnance Office: Vouchers for Agents' Disbursements, Artillery'	214
WO 19	1901-1906	War Office: Royal Garrison Regiment: Records of Service	9
WO 22	1842-1883	Royal Hospital Chelsea: Returns of Payment of Army and Other Pensions	300
WO 23	1702-1933	'Royal Hospital Chelsea: Admission Books, Registers and Papers'	181
WO 24	1661-1966	War Office: Papers concerning Establishments	1182

WO 25	1660-1938	'War Office and predecessors: Secretary-at-War, Secretary of State for War, and Related Bodies, Registers'	4001
WO 26	1670-1817	'War Office: Entry Books of Warrants, Regulations and Precedents'	42
WO 27	1750-1914	Office of the Commander-in-Chief and War Office: Adjutant General and Army Council: Inspection Returns	511
WO 28	1746-1926	War Office: Records of Military Headquarters	390
WO 29	1879	War Office: Prince Imperial Verification Deed	1
WO 30	1684-1951	'War Office, predecessors and associated departments: Miscellaneous Papers'	147
WO 31	1793-1870	Office of the Commander-in-Chief: Memoranda and Papers	1565
WO 32	1845-1985	War Office and successors: Registered Files (General Series)	21862
WO 33	1853-1969	'War Office: Reports, Memoranda and Papers (O and A Series)'	3218
WO 34	1712-1786	'War Office: Baron Jeffrey Amherst, Commander in Chief: Papers'	260
WO 35	1775-1923	War Office: Army of Ireland: Administrative and Easter Rising Records	215
WO 36	1773-1799	'War Office: Military Headquarters, North America: Entry Books, American Revolution'	5
WO 37	1762-1922	'War Office: General Sir George Scovell, Intelligence Branch of Quartermaster General in Spain, later Chief Cipher Officer: Papers'	13
WO 38			
WO 39			
WO 40	1753-1815	'War Office: Secretary-at-War, In-letters and Reports'	32
WO 41	1810-1828	Secretary-at-War: Office of Army Accounts: In-letters relating to Accounts ('A' Papers)	98
WO 42	1755-1908	'War Office: Officers' Birth Certificates, Wills and Personal Papers'	73
WO 43	1809-1857	'War Office: Secretary-at-War, Correspondence, Very Old Series (VOS) and Old Series (OS)'	1059
WO 44	1682-1873	Ordnance Office and War Office: Correspondence	732
WO 45	1783-1870	Ordnance Office and Office of the Commander in Chief: Reference Books to Correspondence	298

WO 46	1660-1861	Ordnance Office: Out-letters	169
WO 47	1644-1856	Ordnance Office: Board of Ordnance: Minutes	2897
WO 48	1660-1847	Ordnance Office: Ledgers	357
WO 49	1592-1858	Ordnance Office: Various Accounts	294
WO 50	1677-1778	Ordnance Office: Bill Books (Series I)	21
WO 51	1630-1806	Ordnance Office: Bill Books (Series II)	313
WO 52	1782-1859	Ordnance Office: Bill Books (Series III) 782	
WO 53	1660-1822	Ordnance Office: Bill Books (Series IV) 534	
WO 54	1594-1871	Ordnance Office and War Office: Entry Books and Registers	948
WO 55	1568-1923	Ordnance Office and War Office: Miscellaneous Entry Books and Papers	3071
WO 57	1806-1826	Office of the Commander-in-Chief: Commissariat Department: In-letters	58
WO 58	1793-1888	War Office and predecessors: Commissariat Department: Out-letters	178
WO 59	1816-1854	Treasury: Commissariat Department: Minutes	76
WO 60	1774-1858	War Office and predecessors: Commissariat Department: Accounts	112
WO 61	1791-1889	War Office and predecessors: Commissariat Department: Registers	135
WO 62	1798-1885	War Office and predecessors: Commissariat Department: Miscellaneous Letter Books and Papers	53
WO 63	1789-1852	'Office of the Commander-in-Chief and Treasury: Commissariat Department, Ireland: Records'	161
WO 64	1702-1823	War Office: Manuscript Army Lists	18
WO 65	1754-1879	War Office: Printed Annual Army Lists	168
WO 66	1879-1900	War Office: Printed Quarterly Army Lists	86
WO 67	1768-1913	War Office: Depot Description Books	36
WO 68	1759-1925	War Office and predecessors: Records of Militia Regiments	568
WO 69	1755-1917	'Ordnance Office, Military Branch, and War Office: Royal Artillery Records of Service and Papers'	905
WO 70	1860-1964	'War Office: London and Middlesex Volunteer Regiment, Muster Rolls and Battalion Order Books, and Territorial Army Precedent Books'	58
WO 71	1668-1993	Judge Advocate General's Office: Courts Martial Proceedings and Board of General Officers' Minutes	1586

WO 72	1696-1850	Judge Advocate General's Office: Courts Martial Correspondence and Papers	103
WO 73	1859-1950	Office of the Commander in Chief and War Office: Distribution of the Army Monthly Returns	183
WO 74	1758-1908	War Office: Army Purchase Commission: Records	194
WO 75			
WO 76	1764-1961	War Office: Records of Officers' Services	554
WO 77	1814-1838	'Treasury: Thomas Archer, Principal Clerk of Treasury Commissariat Department: Entry Books'	7
WO 78	1627-1953	War Office and predecessors: Maps and Plans	6015
WO 79	1709-1965	War Office: Papers of Various Private Collections	106
WO 80	1804-1859	'War Office: Sir George Murray, Master General of the Ordnance: Papers'	13
WO 81	1715-1962	Judge Advocate General's Office: Letter Books	197
WO 82	1817-1951	Judge Advocate General's Office: Daily Registers of Letters (Day Books)	49
WO 83	1871-1953	Judge Advocate General's Office: Minute Books	103
WO 84	1857-1948	Judge Advocate General's Office: Courts Martial Charge Books	92
WO 85	1751-1910	Judge Advocate General's Office: Deputation Books	9
WO 86	1829-1979	'Judge Advocate General's Office: District Courts Martial Registers, Home and Abroad'	124
WO 87	1865-1875	'Judge Advocate General's Office: District Courts Martial Registers, London'	1
WO 88	1878-1945	'Judge Advocate General's Office: District Courts Martial Registers, India'	7
WO 89	1666-1829	Judge Advocate General's Office: General Courts Martial Entry Books and Registers	5
WO 90	1779-1960	'Judge Advocate General's Office: General Courts Martial Registers, Abroad'	9
WO 91	1806-1904	'Judge Advocate General's Office: General Courts Martial Reports, Confirmed at Home'	51
WO 92	1666-1960	'Judge Advocate General's Office: General Courts Martial Registers, Confirmed at Home'	10
WO 93	c1650-1969	Judge Advocate General's Office: Miscellaneous Correspondence and Papers	68
WO 94	1610-1941	Tower of London: Constable's Office: Records	110
WO 95	1914-1923	War Office: First World War and Army of Occupation War Diaries	5500

WO 96	1806-1915	War Office: Militia Attestation Papers	1522
WO 97	1760-1913	Royal Hospital Chelsea: Soldiers Service Documents	6383
WO 98	1856-1977	War Office: Correspondence and Papers Concerning the Victoria Cross	11
WO 99			
WO 100	1793-1949	War Office: Campaign Medal and Award Rolls (General Series)	493
WO 101	1846-1919	'War Office: Meritorious Service Awards, Registers'	10
WO 102	1831-1953	'War Office: Long Service and Good Conduct Awards, Registers'	24
WO 103	1803-1965	War Office and Associated Departments: Submissions for Royal Approval	91
WO 104	1894-1949	'War Office: Order of the Bath, Returns'	15
WO 105	1835-1913	'War Office: Lord Frederick Roberts, Commander in Chief (South Africa and England) and President of National Service League: Papers'	48
WO 106	1837-1962	'War Office: Directorate of Military Operations and Military Intelligence, and predecessors: Correspondence and Papers'	6369
WO 107	1763-1946	Office of the Commander in Chief and War Office: Quartermaster General's Department: Correspondence and Papers	297
WO 108	1896-1913	'War Office: Correspondence and Papers, South African War'	415
WO 109	1714-1749	'Paymaster General of the Guards and Garrisons and Paymaster General of the Forces: Accounts, Estimates and Warrants'	107
WO 110	1881-1888	'War Office: William H Smith, Secretary of State for War: Papers'	10
WO 111	1901-1967	War Office: Army Ordnance Corps: Orders and Papers	14
WO 112	1876-1960	War Office: Army Estimates	43
WO 113	1855-1963	War Office: Finance Department and predecessors: Precedent Books	37
WO 114	1890-1921	War Office: Adjutant General's Department: Strength Returns of the Army	115
WO 115	1902-1938	'War Office: Directorate of Army Medical Services: Reports, Returns and Summaries'	98

WO 116	1715-1913	'Royal Hospital, Chelsea: Disability and Royal Artillery Out-Pensions, Admission Books'	252
WO 117	1823-1920	'Royal Hospital Chelsea: Length of Service Pensions, Admission Books'	77
WO 118	1704-1922	'Royal Hospital, Kilmainham: Pension Admission Books'	48
WO 119	1783-1822	'Royal Hospital, Kilmainham: Pensioners' Discharge Documents (Certificates of Service)'	70
WO 120	c1715-1857	'Royal Hospital, Chelsea: Regimental Registers of Pensioners'	70
WO 121	1760-1887	'Royal Hospital, Chelsea: Discharge Documents of Pensioners'	258
WO 122	1816-1817	'Royal Hospital, Chelsea: Discharge Documents of Pensioners, Foreigners' Regiments'	14
WO 123	1711-1992	'Ministry of Defence and predecessors: Army Circulars, Memoranda, Orders and Regulations'	492
WO 124	c1720-1777	'Secretary of State, Southern Department, and Ordnance Office, Military Branch: Papers Concerning Demolition of Fortifications at Dunkirk'	22
WO 126	1899-1902	'War Office: Local Armed Forces, Enrolment Forms, South African War'	167
WO 127	1899-1902	'War Office: Local Armed Forces, Nominal Rolls, South African War'	23
WO 128	1899-1902	'War Office: Imperial Yeomanry, Soldiers' Documents, South African War'	165
WO 129	1899-1902	'War Office: Imperial Yeomanry, Registers and Casualty Books, South African War'	13
WO 130			
WO 131	1838-1896	'Royal Hospital, Chelsea: Documents of Soldiers Awarded Deferred Pensions'	44
WO 132	1872-1901	'War Office: Papers of Sir Redvers H Buller, General Commanding, Natal Army, South African War and Commander in Chief, Aldershot Division'	26
WO 133	1792-1820	'War Office: General Sir Robert Brownrigg, Military Secretary to Commander in Chief, Quartermaster General and Governor of Ceylon (Sri Lanka): Papers'	17
WO 134	1808-1814	'War Office: General Sir W Marmaduke Peacocke, Commander at Lisbon: Papers'	6

WO 135	1805-1851	'War Office: Lieutenant General Sir Harry G W Smith, Adjutant General in India and Governor of Cape Colony: Papers'	3
WO 136	1900-1902	War Office: Brigadier-General Richard Beale Colvin Papers	9
WO 137	1921-1923	'War Office: Edward, 17th Earl of Derby, Secretary of State for War: Private Office Papers'	12
WO 138	1830-1963	War Office: Personal Files	78
WO 139	1826-1901	War Office: Correspondence Subject Indexes	13
WO 140	1853-1928	'War Office: School of Musketry, Hythe: Records of Experiments and Trials'	15
WO 141	1912-1946	War Office: Registered Papers (Special Series)	107
WO 142	1905-1967	'Ministry of Munitions, Trench Warfare and Chemical Warfare Departments, and War Office, Chemical Warfare Research Department and Chemical Defence Experimental Stations (later Establishments), Porton: Reports and Papers'	341
WO 143	1801-1980	'Royal Military Asylum for Children of Soldiers of the Regular Army, later Duke of York's Royal Military School, and Royal Hibernian Military School: Records'	85
WO 144	1918-1920	'War Office: Inter-Allied Armistice Commission: War Diary, and Despatches of Chief of British Delegation'	35
WO 145	1883-1994	War Office: Registers of Recipients of the Royal Red Cross	3
WO 146	1855-1909	'War Office: Distinguished Conduct Medal, Submissions to Sovereign'	1
WO 147	1860-1889	'War Office: Field Marshal Viscount Garnet Joseph Wolseley, Adjutant General of Army: Papers'	64
WO 148	1900-1905	'War Office and Colonial Office: Civilian Claims to Military Compensation Boards, South African War'	48
WO 149	1790-1939	War Office and predecessors: Royal Military Academy Woolwich: Registers of Cadets	10
WO 150	1787-1895	War Office and predecessors: Royal Military Academy Woolwich: Correspondence and Letter Books	138

WO 151	1806-1946	War Office and predecessors: Royal Military College Sandhurst: Registers of Cadets	20
WO 152			
WO 153	1880-1929	War Office: War of 1914-1918: Maps and Plans	1354
WO 154	1914-1920	'War Office: War Diaries (Supplementary), First World War'	342
WO 155	1919-1927	War Office: Allied Military Committee of Versailles and its commissions: Papers	65
WO 156	1808-2004	'War Office: UK and overseas garrisons: Registers of Baptisms, Confirmations, Deaths/Burials, and Marriage'	633
WO 157	1914-1923	'War Office: Intelligence Summaries, First World War'	1310
WO 158	1909-1929	'War Office: Military Headquarters: Correspondence and Papers, First World War'	995
WO 159	1914-1916	'War Office: Field Marshal Lord Kitchener, Secretary of State for War: Private Office Papers'	23
WO 160	1916-1923	War Office: Military Intelligence Papers (Special Series) First World War	24
WO 161	1914-1944	'War Office: Miscellaneous Unregistered Papers, First World War'	117
WO 162	1715-1971	Commander-in-Chief and War Office: Adjutant General's Department: Papers	372
WO 163	1806-1973	'War Office and Ministry of Defence and predecessors: War Office Council, later War Office Consultative Council, Army Council, Army Board and their various committees: Minutes and Papers'	750
WO 164	1720-1899	Royal Hospital Chelsea: Prize Records	663
WO 165	1938-1947	'War Office: Directorates (Various): War Diaries, Second World War'	145
WO 166	1930-1946	'War Office: Home Forces: War Diaries, Second World War'	17955
WO 167	1939-1950	'War Office: British Expeditionary Force, France: War Diaries, Second World War'	1447
WO 168	1939-1940	'War Office: British North West Expeditionary Force, Norway: War Diaries, Second World War'	110
WO 169	1939-1956	'War Office: British Forces, Middle East: War Diaries, Second World War'	24939
WO 170	1942-1946	'War Office: Central Mediterranean Forces, (British Element): War Diaries, Second World War'	9162

WO 171	1943-1946	'War Office: Allied Expeditionary Force, North West Europe (British Element): War Diaries, Second World War'	11101
WO 172	1939-1946	'War Office: British and Allied Land Forces, South East Asia: War Diaries, Second World War'	11401
WO 173	1939-1948	'War Office: West African Command: War Diaries, Second World War'	1332
WO 174	1942	'War Office: British Forces, Madagascar: War Diaries, Second World War'	49
WO 175	1941-1943	'War Office: Allied Forces, North Africa (British Element): War Diaries, Second World War'	1349
WO 176	1938-1947	'War Office: British Forces, Various Smaller Theatres: War Diaries, Second World War'	396
WO 177	1939-1946	'War Office: Army Medical Services: War Diaries, Second World War'	2980
WO 178	1939-1946	'War Office: British Military Missions: War Diaries, Second World War'	92
WO 179	1939-1946	'War Office: Canadian, South African, New Zealand and Indian (United Kingdom) Forces (Dominion Forces): War Diaries, Second World War'	5930
WO 180	1800-1915	'Royal Hospital, Chelsea: Invaliding Board: Minutes and Papers'	78
WO 181	1887-1985	War Office: Directorate of Military Survey and predecessors: Papers	388
WO 182			
WO 183			
WO 184			
WO 185	1930-1968	Ministry of Supply: Registered Files	388
WO 186	1852-1993	War Office and successors: Proof and Experimental Establishments: Reports	298
WO 187	1919-1938	'War Office: Royal Engineer Board, later Royal Engineer and Signals Board: Extracts of Proceedings'	32
WO 188	1916-1995	'War Office, Ministry of Supply, Ministry of Defence: Chemical Defence Research Department and Chemical Defence Experimental Establishment, later Chemical and Biological Defence Establishment, Porton: Correspondence and Papers'	2192

WO 189	1920-1983	'War Office, Ministry of Supply, Ministry of Defence : Chemical Defence Experimental Establishment, later Chemical and Biological Defence Establishment, Porton: Reports and Technical Papers'	4492
WO 190	1922-1941	War Office: Directorate of Military Operations and Intelligence: German and adjacent Countries Military Situation Reports (Appreciation Files)	893
WO 191	1927-1948	'War Office: Peacetime Operations Abroad, War Diaries and Headquarters Records'	90
WO 192	1892-1957	Commander-in-Chief and War Office: Fort Record Books	324
WO 193	1934-1958	'War Office: Directorate of Military Operations and Plans, later Directorate of Military Operations: Files concerning Military Planning, Intelligence and Statistics (Collation Files)'	1008
WO 194	1921-1984	'Ministry of Defence and predecessors: Military Vehicles and Engineering Establishment and predecessors: Reports, Minutes and Papers'	2759
WO 195	1939-1969	'Ministry of Defence and predecessors: Advisory Council of Scientific Research and Technical Development, later Scientific Advisory Council: Reports and Papers'	16894
WO 196	1892-1969	'War Office: Director of Artillery, later Director of Royal Artillery: Reports and Appreciations'	93
WO 197	1939-1941	'War Office: British Expeditionary Force, France: Military Headquarters Papers, Second World War'	138
WO 198	1940	'War Office: North West Expeditionary Force, Norway: Military Headquarters Papers, Second World War'	17
WO 199	1914-1956	'War Office: Home Forces: Military Headquarters Papers, Second World War'	3392
WO 201	1936-1946	'War Office: Middle East Forces; Military Headquarters Papers, Second World War'	2889
WO 202	1938-1952	'War Office: British Military Missions in Liaison with Allied Forces; Military Headquarters Papers, Second World War'	1019
WO 203	1932-1949	'War Office: South East Asia Command: Military Headquarters Papers, Second World War'	6469

WO 204	1941-1948	'War Office: Allied Forces, Mediterranean Theatre: Military Headquarters Papers, Second World War'	13050
WO 205	1942-1947	'War Office: 21 Army Group: Military Headquarters Papers, Second World War'	1251
WO 206	1919-1954	'War Office: Directorate of Army Medical Service, Army Pathology Advisory Committee: Minutes'	8
WO 207	1931-1933	War Office: India Defence Expenditure Tribunal: Circulated Papers and Notes for Counsel	14
WO 208	1917-1974	'War Office: Directorate of Military Operations and Intelligence, and Directorate of Military Intelligence; Ministry of Defence, Defence Intelligence Staff : Files'	5635
WO 209	1880-1938	Judge Advocate General's Office: Original Submissions	126
WO 210			
WO 211	1838-1884	War Office: Lieutenant General Henry George Hart: Correspondence and Copies of Hart's Army List	153
WO 212	1939-1949	'War Office: Orders of Battle and Organisation Tables, Second World War'	692
WO 213	1909-1963	'Judge Advocate General's Office: Field General Courts Martial and Military Courts, Registers'	72
WO 214	1941-1946	'War Office: Earl Alexander of Tunis, Supreme Allied Commander Mediterranean Theatre: Papers'	71
WO 215	1939-1946	'War Office: General Headquarters Liaison Regiment: War Diaries and Papers, Second World War'	63
WO 216	1935-1964	War Office: Office of the Chief of the Imperial General Staff: Papers	971
WO 217	1939-1951	'War Office: Private War Diaries of Various Army Personnel, Second World War'	37
WO 218	1940-1952	'War Office: Special Services War Diaries, Second World War'	252
WO 219	1939-1947	'War Office: Supreme Headquarters Allied Expeditionary Force: Military Headquarters Papers, Second World War'	5335
WO 220	1940-1949	'War Office: Directorate of Civil Affairs: Files, Reports and Handbooks'	686
WO 221	1920-1963	'Contracts Co-ordinating Committee and Sub-committees: Minutes, Papers and Reports'	44

WO 222	1914-1949	War Office: Medical Historians' Papers: First and Second World Wars	2152
WO 223	1947	'War Office: Staff College Camberley, 1947 Course Notes on D-Day Landings and Ensuing Campaigns'	161
WO 224	1941-1947	War Office: International Red Cross and Protecting Powers (Geneva): Reports concerning Prisoner of War Camps in Europe and the Far East	230
WO 225	1938-1940	'Army and Air Force Court Martial Committee (Oliver Committee): Memoranda, Minutes and Reports'	16
WO 226	1912-1943	'Committee on Detention Barracks (Oliver Committee): Memoranda, Minutes and Report'	12
WO 227	1939-1981	War Office: Office of the Engineer-in-Chief: Papers	142
WO 228	1943-1946	'War Office: Allied Forces, Mediterranean Theatre: Military Headquarters Papers, Second World War'	27
WO 229	1943-1945	War Office: Supreme Headquarters Allied Expeditionary Force and 21 Army Group: Microfilms	101
WO 230	1939-1951	War Office: British Military Administration of African Territories: Papers	325
WO 231	1940-1978	'War Office: Directorate of Military Training, later Directorate of Army Training: Papers'	129
WO 232	1939-1950	War Office: Directorate of Tactical Investigation: Papers	98
WO 233	1941-1948	War Office: Directorate of Air: Papers	61
WO 234	1939-1943	'War Office: North African and Mediterranean Theatres; Military Headquarters Maps, Second World War'	112
WO 235	1940-1967	'Judge Advocate General's Office: War Crimes Case Files, Second World War'	1124
WO 236	1936-1959	War Office: General Sir George Erskine: Papers	26
WO 237	1900-1947	War Office: Committee Lists and Recommendations' Abstracts	30
WO 238	1949	Judge Advocate General's Office: Trial of Field Marshal von Manstein: Sound Recordings and Log Book	20
WO 239			
WO 240	No date	War Office: Mulberry Harbour: Photographs	2
WO 241	1944-1945	War Office: Directorate of Army Psychiatry: Reports	6
WO 242	1906-1913	'War Office: Directors' Meetings, Minutes'	8

WO 243	1898-1914	War Office: Advisory Board for Army Medical Services: Minutes and Reports	28
WO 244	1936-1950	War Office: Directorate of Signals: Papers	165
WO 245	1702-1947	Royal Hospital Chelsea: Accounts and Finance Papers	134
WO 246	1715-1962	Royal Hospital Chelsea: Letter books	139
WO 247	1715-1913	Royal Hospital Chelsea: Miscellaneous Administrative Papers	79
WO 248	1703-1866	Royal Hospital Chelsea: Warrants	36
WO 250	1703-1953	Royal Hospital Chelsea: Board Minutes and Papers	484
WO 251	1806-1920	Royal Hospital Chelsea: Correspondence	7
WO 252	1913-1968 '	Admiralty, Inter-service Topographical Department, and Ministry of Defence, Joint Intelligence Bureau Library: Surveys, Maps and Reports'	1486
WO 253	1939-1945	War Office: Directorate of Labour: Papers	12
WO 254	1900-1963	War Office and Ministry of Supply: Contracts Precedent Books	6
WO 255	1939-1944	'War Office: Brigadier Thomas Denis Daly, Area Commander, North Caribbean: Papers'	7
WO 256	1914-1918	'War Office: Field Marshal Sir Douglas Haig, Commander in Chief of British Forces, Western Front: Diaries'	38
WO 257	1942-1945	'War Office: Ship Signal Sections: War Diaries, Second World War'	12
WO 258	1936-1962	War Office: Department of the Permanent Under Secretary of State: Private Office Papers	142
WO 259	1937-1953	War Office: Department of the Secretary of State for War: Private Office Papers	88
WO 260	1939-1946	War Office: Directorate of Staff Duties: Papers	51
WO 261	1946-1950	War Office: Middle East Land Forces: Quarterly Historical Reports	788
WO 262	1946-1949	War Office: Central Mediterranean Forces: Quarterly Historical Reports	96
WO 263	1946-1950	War Office: British Troops in Austria: Quarterly Historical Reports	137
WO 264	1946-1950	War Office: British Element Trieste Force: Quarterly Historical Reports	30
WO 265	1946-1950	War Office: British Troops in Malta: Quarterly Historical Reports	88

WO 266	1946-1950	War Office: Gibraltar Forces: Quarterly Historical Reports	57
WO 267	1946-1967	War Office: British Army of the Rhine: Quarterly Historical Reports	637
WO 268	1946-1950	War Office: Far East Land Forces: Quarterly Historical Reports	801
WO 269	1940-1950	War Office: East and West Africa Forces: Quarterly Historical Reports	239
WO 270	1946-1950	War Office: Caribbean Forces: Quarterly Historical Reports	22
WO 271	1945-1950	War Office: Home Forces: Quarterly Historical Reports	163
WO 272	1942-1971	War Office: Directorate of Supplies and Transport: Papers	30
WO 273	1884-1891	War Office: Intelligence Branch: Narrative of British Operations in China (1840-1842) by Major J S Rothwell	2
WO 274			
WO 275	1940-1948	'War Office: Sixth Airborne Division, Palestine: Papers and Reports'	121
WO 276	1902-1964	War Office: East Africa Command: Papers	545
WO 277	1948-1961	'War Office: Department of the Permanent Under Secretary of State, C.3. Branch: Historical Monographs'	37
WO 278	1923-1970	War Office and successors: Chemical Inspection Department: Reports and Papers	90
WO 279	1876-1990	War Office and Ministry of Defence: Confidential Print	794
WO 280	1843-1976	War Office and predecessor and successor: Registers of Deputy Lieutenants' Appointments	12
WO 281	1950-1957	'War Office: British Commonwealth Division of United Nations Force: War Diaries, Korean War'	1320
WO 282	1936-1941	War Office: Field Marshal Sir John Greer Dill: Papers	7
WO 283	1940-1945	'War Cabinet: Joint Intelligence Committee, Inter-Services Security Board: Minutes'	14
WO 284	1720-1982	War Office: Gibraltar Garrison: Orders	201
WO 285	1944-1969	War Office: General Miles Christopher Dempsey: Papers	29

WO 286	1946-1978	Ministry of Supply and successors: Branch Registry Files	86
WO 287	1904-1949	War Office: Confidential Printed Papers (B Papers)	281
WO 288	1956-1958	War Office: Suez Campaign Headquarters: Papers and War Diaries	167
WO 290	1920-1964	War Office: War Department Industrial Council: Minutes	4
WO 291	1941-1982	'Ministry of Supply and War Office: Military Operational Research Unit, successors and related bodies: Reports and Papers'	2688
WO 292	1803-1805	Ordnance Office: Royal Engineers; Sheerness: Letter Book	1
WO 293	1914-1964	War Office: Army Council: Instructions	54
WO 294	1949-1956	War Office: Headquarters West Africa Command and Allied Joint Staff: Papers	45
WO 295	1957-1977	War Office: Army Air Corps: War Diaries and Operations Record Books	51
WO 296	1904-1978	'War Office and Ministry of Defence: Central Department C2 Branch, later C2 (AD) Army Department: Policy and Precedents Notes'	143
WO 297	1909-1919	War Office: Geographical Section General Staff: War of 1914-1918: Western Front: Maps	6649
WO 298	1897-1925	War Office: Geographical Section General Staff: War of 1914-1918: Salonika Campaign: Maps	835
WO 299	1915-1974	War Office and Ministry of Defence: Lands Branch and Directorate of Lands: Precedent Books	1
WO 300	1875-1938	'War Office: Geographical Section General Staff: War of 1914-1918: West, South-West and East Africa Campaign: Maps'	441
WO 301	1905-1929	'War Office: Geographical Section General Staff: War of 1914-1918: Gallipoli Campaign, Dardanelles Commission and Post-War Maps of Turkey'	667
WO 302	1902-1936	War Office: Geographical Section General Staff: War of 1914-1918: Mesopotamia Campaign and post-War Maps	826
WO 303	1880-1984	War Office: Geographical Section General Staff and Historical Section: War of 1914-1918: Palestine Campaign: Maps	514

WO 304	1947	'War Office: Roll of Honour, Second World War'	41
WO 305	1705-1981	War Office and Ministry of Defence: Army Unit Historical Records and Reports	4334
WO 306	1940-1971	Claims Commission: Minutes	8
WO 307	1939-1946	'Prisoners of War Information Bureau: Correspondence and Papers, Second World War'	3
WO 308	1946-1957	'War Office: British and Commonwealth Forces: Historical Records and Reports, Korean War'	102
WO 309	1943-1986	'War Office: Judge Advocate General's Office, British Army of the Rhine War Crimes Group (North West Europe) and predecessors: Registered Files (BAOR and other series)'	2247
WO 310	1943-1948	'War Office: Judge Advocate General's Office, War Crimes Group (South East Europe) and predecessors: Case Files (SEE and other series)'	259
WO 311	1939-1953	'Judge Advocate General's Office, Military Deputy's Department, and War Office, Directorates of Army Legal Services and Personal Services: War Crimes Files (MO/JAG/FS and other series)'	753
WO 312			
WO 313	1920-1940	War Office: Committee on Awards to Inventors: Minutes and Papers	5
WO 314	1918	'War Office and predecessors: Royal Military Academy, Woolwich: Miscellaneous Books and Records'	1
WO 315	1932-1959	War Office: Army Records Centre (Polish Section): Records concerning Polish Forces and Polish Resettlement Corps	71
WO 316	1914-1918	War Office: War of 1914-1918: Western Front: Photographs	58
WO 317	1915-1919	War Office: War of 1914-1918: Gallipoli Campaign: Photographs	14
WO 318			
WO 319	1916-1918	War Office: War of 1914-1918: Palestine Campaign: Photographs	6
WO 320	1950-1966	'War Office: Directorate of Weapons and Development: British Atomic Trials, Maralinga, Australia, Photographs'	13

WO 321	1932-1974	Ministry of Supply and War Office: Military Engineering Experimental Establishment and predecessors: Registered Files	107
WO 322	1944-1960	War Office and Air Ministry: Directorate of Military Survey: Suez Campaign: Maps	528
WO 323	1916-1918	War Office: War of 1914-1918: Italian Campaign: Photographs	12
WO 324	1923-1981	Royal Hospital Chelsea: Personal Files of Deceased Pensioners	269
WO 325	1941-1949	'War Office: General Headquarters, Allied Land Forces, (South East Asia) War Crimes Group: Investigation Files'	171
WO 326	1930-1948	'War Office: Gallantry Medal and Award Rolls, Military Medal'	1
WO 327			
WO 328	1945	'War Office: Allied Forces Headquarters (Central Mediterranean): Statements by Former Political Prisoners, Second World War'	43
WO 329	1917-1926	'War Office and Air Ministry: Service Medal and Award Rolls, First World War'	3272
WO 330	1892-1935	'War Office: Service Medal and Award Rolls, Volunteer Officers' Decoration and King George V's Coronation Medal'	4
WO 331	1944-1946	'War Office: Headquarters Allied Land Forces Norway, War Crimes Investigation Branch: Registered Files (A/G1/WCI Series)'	64
WO 332	1646-1971	War Office: Lands Branch: Miscellaneous Registers and Papers	61
WO 333	1939-1946	'War Office: Southern Rhodesian Forces: War Diaries, Second World War'	2
WO 334	1817-1892	War Office: Army Medical Department: Returns and Reports	175
WO 335	1914-1974	War Office: Selected Civilian Personal Files	9
WO 336	1948-1962	War Office: Headquarters British Forces Caribbean Area: Files	37
WO 337	1957-1971	War Office: Headquarters British Forces Gulf Area: Files	18
WO 338	1870-1922	'War Office: Officers' Services, First World War, Index to Long Number Papers'	23

WO 339	1914-1939	'War Office: Officers' Services, First World War, Long Number Papers (numerical)'	139908
WO 340	1870-1958	War Office: Officers Services (including Civilian Dependants and Civilian and Military Staff Appointments): Registers	13
WO 341	1947-1980	War Office and Ministry of Defence: Royal Armoured Corps: Correspondence and Reports	208
WO 342	1951-1964	War Office: Army Operational Research Group later Army Operational Research Establishment: Registered Files	4
WO 343	1942-1945	'War Office: South East Asia Command British Army Aid Group, China: Microfiche Copies'	1
WO 344	1945-1946	War Office: Directorate of Military Intelligence: Liberated Prisoner of War Interrogation Questionnaires	410
WO 345	1942-1945	'War Office: Japanese Index Cards of Allied Prisoners of War and Internees, Second World War'	58
WO 346			
WO 347	1942-1947	'War Office: Allied Prisoners of War Hospitals, Thailand and Burma, Registers and Papers, Second World War'	13
WO 348	1945-1975	'Military Personnel Research Committee and Sub-committees, later Army Personnel Research Committee: Minutes and Papers'	118
WO 349			
WO 350	1947-1964	War Office: Department of the Permanent Under-Secretary of State: Reports	13
WO 351	1950-1976	War Office and Ministry of Defence: Headquarters British Army of the Rhine: Technical Reports	75
WO 352	1950-1962	Ministry of Supply and War Office: Clothing and Equipment Physiological Research Establishment and Clothing and Stores Experimental Establishment: Reports and Technical Memoranda	109
WO 353	1944-1948	'War Office: Judge Advocate General's Office, Military Deputy's Department: War Crimes, Europe, Card Indexes, Second World War'	24
WO 354	1942-1948	'War Office: Judge Advocate General's Office, Military Deputy's Department: War Crimes, Europe, Card Indexes of Perpetrators, Witnesses and Accused, Second World War'	57

WO 355	1940-1957	'War Office: War Crimes, Europe, Card Index of Persons Passed to or Wanted by Various Allied Authorities, Second World War'	2
WO 356	1940-1957	'War Office: Judge Advocate General's Office, Military Deputy's Department: War Crimes, South East Asia, Card Indexes, Second World War'	24
WO 357	1945-1948	'War Office: South East Asia Command, War Crimes Branch: Record Cards'	5
WO 358	1964-1975	War Office: Directorate of Mechanical Engineering: Reports	5
WO 359	1858-1939	War Office: Army Clothing Department: Register of Changes	21
WO 360	1950-1973	War Office and Ministry of Defence: Inspectorate of Armaments: Reports	18
WO 361			
WO 362	1960-1983	War Office and Ministry of Defence: Inspectorate of Fighting Vehicles and Mechanical Equipment: Reports	64
WO 363	1914-1920	'War Office: Soldiers' Documents, First World War 'Burnt Documents' (Microfilm Copies)'	29889
WO 364	1914-1920	'War Office: Soldiers' Documents from Pension Claims, First World War (Microfilm Copies)'	5804
WO 365	1937-1957	'War Office: Department of the Adjutant General, Statistics Branch: Published Statistical Reports (S Prefix)'	224
WO 366	1944-1963	'War Office: Department of the Permanent Under Secretary of State, C3 Branch: Memoranda on Historical Monographs'	54
WO 367	1942-1945	'War Office: Japanese Registers of Allied Prisoners of War and Civilian Internees held in Camps in Singapore, Second World War'	3
WO 368	1961	War Office: Directorate of Equipment Policy: Reports	2
WO 369	1890-1990	War Office: Geographical Section General Staff and Historical Section: War of 1914-1918: Italian Campaign: Maps	836
WO 370	1837-1960	Ordnance Office and War Office: Warrants of Royal Approval	47

WO 371	1906-1921	War Office: Boy Messenger Friendly Society and War Office School: Records	3
WO 372	c1914-1922	'War Office: Service Medal and Award Rolls Index, First World War'	24
WO 373	1935-1990	War Office and Ministry of Defence: Military Secretary's Department: Recommendations for Honours and Awards for Gallant and Distinguished Service (Army)	191
WO 374	1898-1922	'War Office: Officers' Services, First World War, personal files (alphabetical)'	77829
WO 375			
WO 376	1814-1974	War Office and Ministry of Defence: Gibraltar Garrison: Miscellaneous Minutes and Papers	20
WO 377	1801-1995	Ministry of Defence and predecessors: Defence Clothing and Textiles Agency and predecessors: Papers	73
WO 378	1958-1964	War Office and Ministry of Defence: Lands Branch: Registered Files (DLS Series)	1
WO 379	1737-1967	'Office of the Commander-in-Chief and War Office: Adjutant General's Office: Disposition and Movement of Regiment, Returns and Papers (Regimental Records)'	129
WO 380	1803-1991	'Office of the Commander-in-Chief and War Office: Adjutant General's Office: Designation, Establishments and Stations of Regiments, Returns and Papers (Regimental Records Series I-IV)'	24
WO 381	1733-1964	Ordnance Office and War Office: Personnel and Office Management Records	43
WO 382	1946	'War Office: Headquarters British Troops Egypt: Alexandria and Cairo Riots, Court of Inquiry, Papers'	4
WO 383	1956-1973	'War Office and Ministry of Defence: Sovereign Base Areas Administration, Cyprus: Registered Files (SBA Series)'	19
WO 384	1950-1976	'War Office and Ministry of Defence: Army Statistical Organisation, later Defence Statistical Organisation: Abstracts of Army Statistics'	108
WO 385	1783-1983	'Board of Ordnance Office and successors: Royal Gunpowder Factory and successors, Waltham Abbey: Maps and Plans'	86

WO 386	1954-1974	War Office and Ministry of Defence: Headquarters Middle East and successors: Records	28
WO 387	1920-1949	War Office: Military Secretary's Honours and Awards Branch: Order of the British Empire Register	2
WO 388	1914-1928	War Office: Military Secretary's Honours and Awards Branch: Exchange of Army Decorations between Britain and the Allies Registers	16
WO 389	1911-1982	War Office and Ministry of Defence: Military Secretary's Department: Distinguished Service Order and Military Cross Registers	26
WO 390	1886-1945	War Office: Military Secretary's Honours and Awards Branch: Distinguished Service Order Register	13
WO 391	1854-1920	War Office: Military Secretary's Honours and Awards Branch: Distinguished Conduct Medal Register	7A
WO 392	1944-1945	'War Office: Directorate of Prisoners of War: Prisoners of War Lists, Second World War'	26
WO 393			
WO 394	1916-1920	'War Office: Department of the Secretary, C5 Statistics Branch: Statistical Abstracts'	20
WO 395	1878-1938	War Office: Directorate of Army Contracts and predecessors: Annual Reports	6
WO 396	1830-1902	War Office: Fortifications Branch and successors: Unregistered Records	110
WO 397			
WO 398	1917-1920	'War Office: Women's (later Queen Mary's) Army Auxiliary Corps: Service Records, First World War (Microfilm Copies)'	240
WO 399	c1902-c1922	'War Office: Directorate of Army Medical Services and Territorial Force: Nursing Service Records, First World War'	15789
WO 400	1799-1920	Soldiers' Documents: The Household Cavalry	301
WO 401	1908-1996	War Office and Ministry of Defence: Survey Services: Directorate of Military Survey and Survey Units: Map and Chart Catalogues	158

WO 402	1891-1993	'War Office and Ministry of Defence: Survey Services: Directorate of Military Survey and Survey Units: reports and conferences, 1940-1993'	422
WO 403			
WO 404	1965-1994	Reports of the Army Personnel Research Establishment	104
WO 405	1916-1919	War Office: The Macedonian Mule Corps in World War I	1
WO 406			
WO 407			
WO 408	1859-1990	'War Office and Ministry of Defence: Survey Services: Directorate of Military Survey and Survey Units: Geographical Section, General Staff Allocation Books and Receipt Books (Registers)'	48
WO 410			
WO 900	1798-1959	War Office: Specimens of Series of Documents Destroyed	51

APPENDIX FOUR
TNA Research Guides

The National Archives at Kew has always provided very useful guides to research in particular specialised fields, and these have been especially helpful to the growing 'army' of genealogists and family historians over the past thirty years.

In its former existence as the Public Record Office, such guides were categorised and numbered.

For example, the records for Gallantry Medals awarded to the Armed Services were described on Military Records Information (Sheet) 77.

Nowadays, the corresponding and up-to-date information would be found in the relevant 'TNA Research Guide'.

This is listed as: Medals: British Armed Services, Gallantry. There is also a supplement entitled Medals: British Armed Services, Gallantry, Further Information.

TNA Research Guides are listed alphabetically in this Appendix.

Any guide may be downloaded from the website of TNA - www.nationalarchives.gov.uk

Admiralty Correspondence, How to use the Admiralty Indexes and Digests, ADM 12
Admiralty Maps and Charts
Admiralty, High Court of
Agricultural Statistics
America and the West Indies, Transportation to, 1615-1776
America and West Indies: Calendars of State Papers Colonial, 1574-1739

America and West Indies: Colonies before 1782
American Revolution
Apprenticeship Records as Sources for Genealogy
Archaeology
Architectural Drawings in The National Archives
Architectural History, Sources for
Armed Forces, Sources for the History of
Armed Forces, Tudor and Stuart Militia Muster Rolls
Armed Forces: Medieval and Early Modern Soldiers
Armed Forces: Militia, 1757-1914
Art, Sources for the History of Fine Art and Artists
Arts, Broadcasting and Film: An Overview
Assizes: Criminal Trials, 1559-1971
Assizes: English, 1656-1971, Key to Series for Civil Trials
Assizes: English, Key to Criminal Trials, 1559-1971
Assizes: Welsh, 1831-1971, Key to Classes for Criminal and Civil Trials
Australia, Transportation to, 1787-1868
Bankruptcy Records After 1869
Bankrupts and Insolvent Debtors, 1710-1869
Births, Marriages and Deaths at Sea
Boundaries, International: Maps and other documents
British Army Lists
British Army: Auxiliary Forces (Volunteers, Yeomanry, Territorials and Home Guard),
    1769-1945
British Army: Campaign Records, 1660-1714
British Army: Campaign Records, 1714-1815
British Army: Campaign Records, 1816-1913
British Army: Campaign Records, 1914-1918, First World War
British Army: Campaign Records, 1939-1945, Second World War
British Army: Campaign Records, 1945-
British Army: Courts Martial, 17th-20th Centuries
British Army: Courts Martial: First World War, 1914-1918
British Army: Muster Rolls and Pay Lists, c1730-1898
British Army: Officers' Commissions
British Army: Officers' Records, 1660-1913
British Army: Officers' Records, 1914-1918, First World War
British Army: Soldiers' Discharge Papers, 1760-1913
British Army: Soldiers' Papers, 1914-1918, First World War
British Army: Soldiers' Pensions, 1702-1913
British Army: Useful Sources for Tracing Soldiers

Royal Naval Research and Development
Royal Naval Reserve
Royal Naval Volunteer Reserve
Royal Navy: Commissioned Officers' Pay and Pension Records
Royal Navy: Log Books and Reports of Proceedings
Royal Navy: Officers' Service Records
Royal Navy: Officers' Service records, First World War, 1914-1918, and Confidential
    Reports, 1893-1943
Royal Navy: Operational Records, 1660-1914
Royal Navy: Operational Records, First World War, 1914-1918
Royal Navy: Operational Records, Second World War, 1939-1945
Royal Navy: Operations and Policy after 1945
Royal Navy: Ratings Service Records, 1667-1923
Royal Navy: Ratings' Pension Records
Royal Navy: Warrant Officers' Pension Records
Royal Warrant Holders and Household Servants
Royal Warrant Holders and Suppliers of Goods From 1600
Seals
Second World War: Home Front, 1939-1945
Second World War: The War Cabinet, 1939-1945
Second World War: War Crimes, 1939-1945
Ships Wrecked or Sunk
Slave Trade, British Transatlantic: Abolition - NEW
Slave Trade, British Transatlantic: Acts of Parliament - NEW
Slave Trade, British Transatlantic: Britain and the Trade - NEW
Slave Trade, British Transatlantic: Emancipation - NEW
Slave Trade, British Transatlantic: Introduction - NEW
Slave Trade, British Transatlantic: Slavery - NEW
State Papers Domestic: Charles II - Anne, 1660-1714
State Papers Domestic: Commonwealth, 1642-1660
State Papers Domestic: Edward VI - Charles I, 1547 - 1649
State Papers Domestic: George I to George III, 1714-1782
State Papers Domestic: Miscellaneous Classes
State Papers: Foreign
State Papers: Ireland, 1509-1782
State Papers: Letters and Papers of Henry VIII
Supreme Court: Appeal Cases After 1875
Supreme Court: Chancery Division Cases After 1875
Taxation Records Before 1689
Titanic
Tithe Records

INDEX

New Zealand 58, 95, 129, 130, 131, 138, 139, 187, 188, 211, 225-7, 232, 233, 237

Newspapers 50, 79, 94, 95, 137, 141, 173, 174, 177, 294

Officers Died (in the Great War) 112, 161, 220,

Ordnance (Corps) 2, 21, 25, 27, 73, 90, 100-2, 104, 131, 266-271, 280, 284, 285, 294

Pay Lists - see Muster Books and Pay Lists

Pension (Returns) 21, 26, 27, 33, 40, 42, 44, 51, 55-61, 63, 64, 69, 71, 72, 83, 85, 86, 88-92, 100, 101, 109, 130, 132, 138, 139, 142, 143, 148, 177, 211, 217, 225, 227, 230, 266, 271, 282, 284, 290, 296

Pensions to (Wounded) Officers 7, 21, 23, 25-7

Police Gazette 94, 95, 131

Prisoners of War vii, 26, 80, 85, 94, 133-8, 155, 171-3, 175, 179, 190, 191, 210, 224, 230, 277, 281-4, 286, 291, 295

Prize Records 93, 94, 273

Regimental Number 76, 80, 81, 117, 152, 161,

Regimental Registers 32-37, 40, 44, 60, 85, 89, 115, 121, 239 and on, 271, 285

Roll of Honour viii, ix, 115, 145, 160, 179, 182, 193, 208, 211

Royal Flying Corps 101, 157, 162

Royal Wagon Train 103, 104

Sandhurst 2, 26, 27, 103, 273

Sappers 83, 101,

Scotland 1, 5, 30, 38, 47, 49, 55, 58, 127, 214, 230, 231

Scutari Depot 73, 80, 266

Service Corps 79, 102-4, 158, 194, 195

Service Papers/Records - see Army Service Records

Service Returns No 1 vii, 44, 51, 52, 54, 241 and on

Service Returns No 3 51, 52,

Signals 2, 101, 102, 274, 278

Society for Army Historical Research 143, 144, 239

Society of Genealogists 129, 145, 213, 226

Soldiers Died (in the Great War) 147, 161, 193, 208, 220, 229, 231

Soldiers' Documents vii, 29, 30, 33, 36, 40, 41, 44, 48, 51, 55, 60, 63, 64, 66, 72, 73, 85, 91, 100, 101, 104, 115, 228, 239, 241 and on, 265, 270, 284, 286

South Africa 64, 69, 108, 109, 113, 126, 139, 140, 184, 187, 188, 189, 218, 220, 232, 236-8, 270-2, 274

Transport 102-4, 137, 158, 279

USA 132, 140

Veterans 42, 55, 112, 119, 145, 177, 185, 194, 209,

Veterans Agency 177, 209

Veterinary Corps 2, 102, 103, 142

Volunteers 2-4, 6, 15, 21, 27, 47, 63, 73, 80, 100, 104, 105-9, 117, 140, 141, 165, 169, 177, 200, 210, 219, 252, 258, 260, 266, 268, 282, 290

Wagon Train 103, 104

Wales 1, 30, 34, 47, 55, 56, 120, 126, 160, 230, 291, 292, 294

War, Boer 108, 112, 115, 127, 131, 139, 168, 187, 218, 232, 238

War, Crimean 48, 55, 80, 103, 112, 113, 118, 128, 141, 168, 218, 232, 237